Dramaturgas Chilenas

For inquiries about the translations for *Medusa* by Ximena Carrera, *The City of Fruit* by Leyla Selman, *Hilda Peña* by Isidora Stevenson Bordeu, and *Sentiments* by Carla Zúñiga M., please contact the playwrights directly or contact the editors at agarci21@nd.edu.

For inquiries about the translation of *School for Girls* by Nona Fernández, please contact Beth Blickers, Michael Moore Agency, 450 West 24th Street, Suite 1C, New York, NY 10011, Office: (212) 221-0400 Email: beth@michaelmooreagency.com.

Dramaturgas Chilenas

Plays by Chilean Female Writers in the Early 21st Century

Medusa by Ximena Carrera
Hilda Peña by Isidora Stevenson Bordeu
School for Girls by Nona Fernández
The City of Fruit by Leyla Selman
Sentiments by Carla Zúñiga M.

Edited by
COCA DUARTE, ANNE GARCÍA-ROMERO AND INÉS STRANGER

methuen | drama
LONDON • NEW YORK • OXFORD • NEW DELHI • SYDNEY

METHUEN DRAMA
Bloomsbury Publishing Plc, 50 Bedford Square, London, WC1B 3DP, UK
Bloomsbury Publishing Inc, 1359 Broadway, New York, NY 10018, USA
Bloomsbury Publishing Ireland, 29 Earlsfort Terrace, Dublin 2, D02 AY28, Ireland

BLOOMSBURY, METHUEN DRAMA and the Methuen Drama logo are trademarks of Bloomsbury Publishing Plc

First published in Great Britain 2026

Copyright © Anne García-Romero, Inés Stranger, Verónica Duarte and Contributors, 2026
Medusa © Ximena Carrera, 2013
Medusa translation © Ximena Carrera, 2026
Hilda Peña © Isidora Stevenson Bordeu, 2018, 2024
Hilda Peña translation © Constanza Brieba, 2026
School for Girls © Nona Fernández, 2016
School for Girls translation © Andrea Thome, 2026
The City of Fruit © Leyla Selman, 2024
The City of Fruit translation © Leyla Selman, 2026
Sentiments © Carla Zúñiga M., 2019
Sentiments translation © Carla Zúñiga M., 2026

Thea authors have asserted their right under the Copyright, Designs and Patents Act, 1988, to be identified as authors of this work.

For legal purposes the Acknowledgements on p. ix constitute an extension of this copyright page.

Cover Design and Illustration by Megan Wilson

All rights reserved. No part of this publication may be: i) reproduced or transmitted in any form, electronic or mechanical, including photocopying, recording or by means of any information storage or retrieval system without prior permission in writing from the publishers; or ii) used or reproduced in any way for the training, development or operation of artificial intelligence (AI) technologies, including generative AI technologies. The rights holders expressly reserve this publication from the text and data mining exception as per Article 4(3) of the Digital Single Market Directive (EU) 2019/790.

Bloomsbury Publishing Plc does not have any control over, or responsibility for, any third-party websites referred to or in this book. All internet addresses given in this book were correct at the time of going to press. The author and publisher regret any inconvenience caused if addresses have changed or sites have ceased to exist, but can accept no responsibility for any such changes.

A catalogue record for this book is available from the British Library.

Library of Congress Cataloging-in-Publication Data

Names: Duarte Loveluck, María Verónica editor | García-Romero, Anne editor | Stranger, Inés Margarita editor
Title: Dramaturgas chilenas : plays by Chilean female writers in the early 21st century : Medusa ; Hilda Peña ; School for girls ; The city of fruit ; Sentiments / edited by Coca Duarte, Anne García-Romero and Inés Stranger.
Description: London ; New York : Methuen Drama, 2026. | Series: Methuen drama play collections | Includes bibliographical references and index. | Summary: "How do female Chilean playwrights address historical trauma, gender critique and collective memory in post-dictatorship, democratic Chile? Dramaturgas Chilenas features five, new, English translations of plays by Chile's leading female playwrights, exploring and decoding their lived experience. This collection enables English-speakers to engage with this contemporary canon for the very first time. From the shocking true story of women being coerced into serving as government spies, and heart-breaking accounts of the killings as the country returned to democracy, to examinations of young women protesting and demanding justice, this collection provides a wealth of insight into the contemporary, female Chilean experience"—Provided by publisher.
Identifiers: LCCN 2025030879 | ISBN 9781350549302 hardback | ISBN 9781350549296 paperback | ISBN 9781350549319 pdf | ISBN 9781350549326 epub
Subjects: LCSH: Chilean drama—Women authors—Translations into English | Chilean drama—21st century—Translations into English | Chile—Drama | LCGFT: Drama
Classification: LCC PQ8071.E5 D73 2026
LC record available at https://lccn.loc.gov/2025030879

ISBN: HB: 978-1-3505-4930-2
PB: 978-1-3505-4929-6
ePDF: 978-1-3505-4931-9
eBook: 978-1-3505-4932-6

Series: Methuen Drama Play Collections

Typeset by RefineCatch Limited, Bungay, Suffolk
Printed and bound in Great Britain

For product safety related questions contact productsafety@bloomsbury.com.

To find out more about our authors and books visit www.bloomsbury.com and sign up for our newsletters.

Contents

List of Figures vi
List of Contributors vii
Acknowledgements ix

Introduction 1

Medusa: Testimony, Torture, and Betrayal Inés Stranger, translation by Christine Ann Hills 15

Medusa Ximena Carrera, translation by the author 21

Hilda Peña: Unconventional Motherhood, Grief, and Subjectivity
Coca Duarte, translation by Constanza Brieba 57

Hilda Peña Isidora Stevenson Bordeu, translation by Constanza Brieba 63

School for Girls: Student Protests, Political Victims, and Temporal Paradox
Inés Stranger, translation by Christine Ann Hills 91

School for Girls Nona Fernández, translation by Andrea Thome 97

The City of Fruit: Sexual Violence, Witness, and Transformation
Coca Duarte, translation by Constanza Brieba 153

The City of Fruit Leyla Selman, translation by Alexandra Ripp 161

Sentiments: Gendered Cruelty, Dark Comedy, and the Ethics of Spectatorship
Anne García-Romero 193

Sentiments Carla Zúñiga M., translation by Susan E. Bowen and Yael Prizant 201

Appendix of Works by Chilean female playwrights 237
Works Cited 239

Figures

1. Nina (Ximena Carrera) contemplates her disguise as Berta in *Medusa* by Ximena Carrera, directed by Sebastián Vila, Sala Lastarria 90, Santiago, Chile, 2010. (Photo: © Elio Frugone Piña www.fototeatro.cl)   18
2. Hilda Peña (Paula Zúñiga) grieves for her deceased son in *Hilda Peña* by Isidora Stevenson Bordeu, directed by Aliocha de la Sotta, Centro Cultural Matucana 100, Santiago, Chile, 2014. (Photo: © Diego Carrasco)   60
3. Riquelme (Roxana Naranjo), Fuenzalida (Nona Fernández), and Maldonado (Carmina Riego) defy the Teacher (Francisco Medina) in *School for Girls* by Nona Fernández, directed by Marcelo Leonart, Teatro de la Universidad Católica de Chile, 2015. (Photo: © Maglio Pérez)   93
4. Her (Catalina Saavedra) attempts to confront Maradona (Guillermo Ugalde), Grandpa (Francisco Ossa), and Pillow (Jaime Leiva), in *The City of Fruit* by Leyla Selman, directed by Rodrigo Pérez, Teatro de la Memoria, Santiago, Chile, 2019. (Photo: © Paula Campos)   155
5. Miss Francisca (Coca Miranda) lectures Antofagasta (Carla Gaete) and her mother Nelly María (Viviana Basoalto) in *Sentiments* by Carla Zúñiga, directed by Javier Casanga, Teatro Sidarte, 2017. (Photo: © Nicolás Calderón)   196

Contributors

Playwrights

XIMENA CARRERA is a Chilean actor, playwright, producer, screenwriter, and teacher. In 1997, she founded the theatre company, La Trompeta, with actor and director Sebastián Vila. Her works include *Por encargo del olvido*, *Naturaleza Muerta*, *Medusa*, and *Ningún pájaro canta por cantar*. She's the 2010 winner for Best Play from the Chile Drama Critics Circle.

NONA FERNÁNDEZ is a Chilean actor, playwright, and novelist. Her plays include *El Taller*, winner of the 2012 Altazor y Nuez Martín prizes, *Liceo de niñas*, and *Paren la Música*, winner of the 2021 Best Play from the Chile Drama Critics Circle. Her award-winning novels include *Twilight Zone*, *Space Invaders*, and *Voyager*.

LEYLA SELMAN is a Chilean actor, poet, and playwright. She is a member of the Colectivo Frío, a collective focusing on art, theatre, and film. Her plays include *El mejor truco de magia jamás visto*, *Ifigenia, Otra Muerta Anunciada*, *La Ciudad de la Fruta*, and *Los Ojos de Lena*. She's the 2024 winner for Best Play from the Chile Drama Critics Circle.

ISIDORA STEVENSON BORDEU is a Chilean playwright, director, and teacher. Her works include *Campo*, *Hilda Peña*, *Réplica*, *Guerra*, *Bernarda*, *El nudo*, *Informe de una mujer que arde*, *Soledad Escobar*, *Niebla*, *Mi corazón es un ancla*, *Fin*, and *Amanda Labarca*. She's the 2014 winner of the Chile National Theater Festival.

CARLA ZÚÑIGA M. is a Chilean actor, playwright, and teacher. In 2012, she founded the company, La Niña Horrible, with Javier Casanga. Her works include *Sentimientos*, *La trágica agonía de un pájaro azul*, and *El amarillo sol de tus cabellos largos*. She's the 2020 winner for Best Play from the Chile Drama Critics Circle.

Translators

SUSAN E. BOWEN is a director, translator, and deviser. She has served as Artist in Residence at the Pritzker Pucker Studio Lab at Northwestern University and as the Workshop Coordinator for the Physical Theater Festival Chicago. Susan has trained with Adam Versényi, Wynn Handman, and SITI Company. She holds an M.F.A. in Directing from Northwestern University, and a B.A. in Spanish from the University of North Carolina at Chapel Hill.

CONSTANZA BRIEBA is a Chilean director, actor, translator, and arts administrator. She studied at the London Academy of Music and Dramatic Arts. She has served as a theatrical translator in Chile for the British Council, the North American Institute of Culture, and the French Institute of Culture. Her theatrical translations have been produced in Chile, England, and Switzerland.

CHRISTINE ANN HILLS is a native English teacher and translator who has lived in Santiago, Chile, for the past twenty-five years. She holds a Master of Arts with honors

(MA; Hons) in Hispanic Studies from the University of Glasgow, Scotland. She has translated academic articles and cultural texts from Spanish to English.

YAEL PRIZANT is an adapter, translator, deviser, and dramaturg. She holds a Ph.D. in Theatre, an M.F.A. in Dramaturgy, and has taught at UCLA, the University of Notre Dame, and Johns Hopkins SAIS. Her book, *Cuba Inside Out: Revolution and Contemporary Theatre* (2013), investigates the effects of politics and globalization on the stage. She has translated works of Cuban playwrights and is the dramaturg and translator for *Confessionário—Relatos de Casa* in Porto Alegre, Brazil.

ALEXANDRA RIPP is a dramaturg, translator, and arts administrator. She has worked at the International Festival of Arts and Ideas, Carolina Performing Arts, Five College Dance, and most recently with movement-based artist nora chipaumire. She served as co-editor of *Imagined Theatres 06: Chile*. She holds an MFA and DFA from the David Geffen School of Drama at Yale University.

ANDREA THOME is a Chilean/Costa Rican-American playwright and translator. Recent plays: *Fandango for Butterflies (and Coyotes)*, *Cymbeline* (modern verse translation), *A Dozen Dreams* (installation), and *Pinkolandia* (multiple U.S. productions; translated into Russian). Spanish-English translations include Guillermo Calderón's *Neva* (Public Theater, CTG) and Rodrigo García's *You Should Have Stayed Home, Morons* (Radar LA). She studied at New York University (MFA) and Harvard (BA), and teaches Theatre and Performance at SUNY Purchase.

Editors

COCA DUARTE is an Associate Professor and Associate Director of the Pontificia Universidad Católica de Chile School of Theatre. She's the author of *Writing the Scene, Tracing the Present: Dramaturgical Strategies of the Chilean Theater 2007-2017* (2023). Her plays include *Juana de Arco*, *Mala Leche*, *Mal*, and *Plaga*.

ANNE GARCÍA-ROMERO is Professor of Film, Television, and Theatre at the University of Notre Dame. She's the author of *The Fornés Frame: Contemporary Latina Playwrights and the Legacy of María Irene Fornés* (2016). In 2018, she received a Luksic Foundation grant to teach in Chile. Her plays include *Paloma*, *Juanita's Statue*, *Earthquake Chica*, and *Santa Concepcíon*.

INÉS STRANGER is Professor of Theatre at the Pontificia Universidad Católica de Chile School of Theatre. She's the author of *Playwriting Notebook: Theory, Technique and Exercises* (2011). Her plays include *Cariño*, *Malo*, *Malinche*, and *Tálamo*. She received the Fondo del Libro award from Chile's Council on Art and Culture.

Acknowledgements

This volume would not be possible without the collaboration of our five playwrights: Ximena Carrera, Nona Fernández, Leyla Selman, Isidora Stevenson Bordeu, and Carla Zúñiga M. Their generosity in sharing their work and their reflections with us provide the foundation for this bridge we are building between Chilean theatre and the English-speaking world. We are also grateful for our wonderful translators Susan E. Bowen, Constanza Brieba, Christine Ann Hills, Yael Prizant, Alexandra Ripp, and Andrea Thome, and their bilingual, theatrical expertise.

We must thank our university partners for their support that makes this volume possible. At the Pontificia Universidad Católica de Chile, we thank Mario Costa, Director, School of Theatre; Alexei Vergara, Dean, College of the Arts; and Maureen Boys, Administrator, College of the Arts and the Vicerrectoría de Asuntos Internacionales. At the University of Notre Dame, we thank the Department of Film, Television and Theatre (James Collins and Pam Wojcik, Chairs, Jo Ann Norris, Administrator, Professor Anton Juan, and Macy Mateer, Research Assistant), College of Arts and Letters (Peter Holland and Michael Schreffler, Associate Deans for the Arts), Notre Dame Global (Michael Pippenger, Vice President and Associate Provost for Internationalization, Geraldine Meehan, Senior Director for Faculty Engagement and Global Research, and Juan Esteban Montes, Director in Santiago, Chile), the Kellogg Institute for International Studies (Aníbal Perez Linan, Director, and Mauricio Benítez Iturbe, Executive Director, Holly Rivers, Associate Director; and Ashley Avalos, Kimberly Martinez, Jill McEntee, and María Del Rosario Villalaz, research assistants), the Franco Family Institute for Liberal Arts and the Public Good (Kate Marshall, Director), and the Notre Dame Law School (Beth Ferrettie, Office Coordinator, Kathleen Brothers, Facilities Administrator, Dan Manier, Director, Law School Technology). We also thank the Luksic Foundation for their generous support of this project at the Pontificia Universidad Católica de Chile and the University of Notre Dame.

We offer special thanks to director and translator Susan E. Bowen for her marvelous casting and direction of the readings with professional actors in Chicago that provided an essential developmental process for these new play translations. We are also grateful to the Chicago actors who contributed their considerable talents and insights: Charín Álvarez, Liam Bouza Díaz, Jazmín Corona, Alice da Cunha, Sandra Delgado, Ricardo Gamboa, Meighan Gerachis, Roy Gonzalez, John Judd, Macy Mateer, Aysette Muñoz, Laura Murillo Hart, Aurora Real De Asua, Alix Rhode, Jonathan Shaboo, Raquel Torre, and Ivan Vega.

Thanks are also due to Methuen Drama. We are grateful to have worked with Mark Jones, Sam Nicholls, Dom O'Hanlon, and Sarah Skinner throughout this process. Thanks to Andrew Ascherl for his keen eye in copy-editing the manuscript.

Finally, we wish to acknowledge each other. This collection likely would not have happened without the bicultural and bilingual compatibility of our respective strengths in service of this collection and our shared commitment to documenting and advocating for these remarkable plays by Chilean female writers.

Introduction
Anne García-Romero

Dramaturgas Chilenas: Plays by Chilean Female Writers in the Early 21st Century provides compelling, female perspectives on contemporary Chilean society through this collection of new, English language translations of plays by five award-winning, Chilean playwrights: Ximena Carrera, Nona Fernández, Leyla Selman, Isidora Stevenson Bordeu, and Carla Zúñiga M. These playwrights present fascinating female protagonists including captive spies, a grieving mother, student activists, a sexual abuse survivor and a rebellious teenager, who all seek new levels of personal and political freedom. These plays, produced between 2010 and 2019, have been published in Chile but have never been published in English until now. Since the early 2000s, a generation of female playwrights, trained in the Chilean university system as actors and writers, emerged as a significant force in Chilean theatre. Their works have been produced on prominent stages in Chile and have received prestigious awards. While there are certainly additional important contemporary female playwrights in Chile (as noted in the volume's appendix), these five women represent a generation of female playwrights who have created their own theatre companies in the early twenty-first century, where they developed many of the plays in this volume. Their works have been widely produced and have generated considerable theatre scholarship. These playwrights have also served as each other's collaborators, acting in each other's plays, directing each other's works, and serving as each other's consultants and advocates, thus forming part of a close community of Chilean female playwrights.

These play translations, by leading Chilean and U.S. translators including Susan E. Bowen, Constanza Brieba, Yael Prizant, Alexandra Ripp, and Andrea Thome, in collaboration with the authors and co-editors, have not yet been staged. However, in 2025, each play translation was developed through a series of private readings with professional theatre artists in Chicago, cast and directed by Bowen. Each developmental process began with a brief rehearsal, followed by a reading viewed by the Chilean and U.S. translators via Zoom, concluding with a conversation between the U.S. and Chilean theatre artists. These developmental readings served as a key tool to ensure that these English translations are well-positioned for future production. In this collection, each translation is preceded by a substantive biography of the playwright and a production history of the play. Each translation also begins with a character/setting page that lists the characters, their ages, a few descriptors, and the time and place of the play's action. This character/setting page practice is not always followed in Chilean playwriting. However, we felt it would be useful to incorporate this English-language tradition to facilitate the reading and production of these works. The translations also contain some annotations to illuminate the plays' cultural, political, and historical contexts.

The collection's essays by the co-editors aim to contextualize these Chilean works for an English-language audience. Each essay analyzes the dramatic texts and provides political, social, and cultural context for each play. This introduction also includes excerpts from interviews with the playwrights conducted in Santiago, Chile, in 2023 and 2025, in which each playwright discusses her creative process, artistic formation, play development, production process, political and artistic aesthetics, and how her work connects to the contemporary Chilean theatre community. Lastly, the volume concludes with an appendix that lists numerous Chilean female playwrights and their representative works, as well as a bibliography of primary and secondary sources. Our aim with this collection is to facilitate greater English-language access for the research and production of this remarkable canon of plays by Chilean female writers in the early twenty-first century.

Theatre artists in Chile, both during and after dictatorship, have addressed issues of political repression and social injustice. During the dictatorship years, through frequent censorship and limited opportunities, Chilean theatre artists often addressed human rights violations, including torture and disappearance. As Chile shifted into the democratic era, Chilean theatre artists have addressed the consequences of dictatorship and ongoing systemic violence. Contemporary Chilean plays in the early twenty-first century often examine present circumstances that are linked to past realities. Theatre scholar Maria de la Luz Hurtado recounts that Chilean plays written since 2000

> [go] beyond the schematic before/after of the military dictatorship and its binary axes of good/evil ... the post-dictatorship projects axes of continuity in terms of the manipulation of bodies and ideologies, delving into the critique of fraud and cultural and factual violence, with its other/same betrayals and abuses of the weakest (ethnic, social, generational, gender).[1]

The works in this volume adhere to Hurtado's reflection and all ask the question: How do female Chilean playwrights address historical trauma, gender critique, and collective memory? Each playwright here engages with the controversies that arise from responses to this question. Their plays employ themes including female resilience in the wake of heteronormative physical and sexual violence, female resistance to dictatorship, reframing patriarchal memory, unconventional motherhood, and trauma recovery. These playwrights' dynamic, aesthetically diverse works offer important, new perspectives on understanding democratic, post-dictatorship Chile.[2]

Medusa by Ximena Carrera

Set in 1970s Santiago, Chile, *Medusa* (2010) by Ximena Carrera, translated by the author, considers three women, Mariana, Carmen, and Nina, who struggle to survive while serving as informants during the military dictatorship. As Inés Stranger writes in her essay, "Based on real events, [*Medusa*] features three female characters who were collaborators of Pinochet's secret services: Marcia Alejandra Merino, Luz Arce Sandoval, and María Alicia Uribe. The three women were former militants of the Socialist Party and the Movimiento de Izquierda Revolucionaria (MIR, Revolutionary Left Movement) who were broken and subdued through torture."[3] While Carrera interviewed an anthropologist for an earlier play, she first heard an anecdote about Merino, whose nickname was La Flaca Alejandra (The Skinny Alejandra). Carrera recounts:

> And [the anthropologist] tells me this anecdote that when she was twelve years old, she was in a store in downtown Santiago, she was with her older sister, and suddenly she feels her sister grab her hand, and it's like her [sister's] hand is made of stone ... and she pulls her into those coat racks. And she, a little girl,

twelve years old, not understanding anything, stays quiet. And a few seconds later, the sister grabs her and takes her away. She says the sister looked pale, and well, then she tells her, she says, "It happened that I saw La Flaca Alejandra." And La Flaca Alejandra, this woman, knew the sister. The sister then said, "Well, if she sees me, I disappear." And that anecdote … stayed bouncing around in my head, and I didn't know how to get it into [that earlier play], but it felt like that thing that happens to you with those obsessions that you bring to the writing, that you don't know why they settle in your imagination, but they settle in very strongly.[4]

Carrera first began to develop the play while studying playwriting in Buenos Aires, Argentina, with the acclaimed Argentine playwright Ricardo Monti, through an Iberescena fellowship. As she began researching these women, she learned they had been stationed in an apartment in the San Borja towers in downtown Santiago. She reflects:

when I was a girl I used to go to those towers because I had an uncle who lived there. So, the crazy thing was that on one of those Sunday afternoons when I was having family tea time, five floors up or down, these three gorgons were living, making a life, and it's that dichotomy of wanting to make a normal life out of the horror that seemed super attractive to me. I imagined very everyday situations. I wondered, what is the daily life of these women like? Will they come to an agreement? They didn't like each other at all.[5]

In her play, Carrera explores how these three characters, Mariana, Carmen, and Nina, exhibit resilience in the wake of the physical and sexual violence they experienced at Villa Grimaldi, a torture site during the dictatorship. Carrera also explores unconventional motherhood as Carmen is a mother who tries to protect her young son, who is being cared for by her sister. Each of the women is in the process of trying to recover from the trauma of detention, torture, and imprisonment. In creating these roles based on these controversial women, she aimed to avoid any judgment. Carrera states:

I think what perhaps allowed me not to judge these characters is that, of course, they also went through torture, and I think any human being who goes through that horror from then on, I don't feel capable of judging what they do. I think it's the horror, I think it's the unhinging … obviously after an experience of that nature. So, these three women who are constantly playing the power game, being victims and at the same time victimizers, allowed me to create the structure and elements of the narrative, but also allowed me not to judge them.[6]

As Carrera developed her play with her company, La Trompeta (The Trumpet), she also played the role of Nina, which gave her a unique, embodied experience of her play. The cast also included Carmina Riego and Nona Fernández, another writer in this collection. Carrera speaks to the unique perspective of being an actor in her own play:

I sort of encountered for the first time this very strange phenomenon: if I act in something I've written, what the playwright knows isn't necessarily what the actor knows. And I was always asking myself questions, "Hey, why don't I know?" And I really don't know. I felt like there was something the scene needed that had to be found on stage, and that it was nice that each female actor put her body and her being into the acting, and that I didn't tell them, "No, look, the character is doing this when you do that." No, I didn't want to, because what was appearing was very beautiful. The intentions were very different, perhaps, from what I had thought, but it was the acting choices, let's say, of Carmina, of Nona, and certainly mine, that were at play.[7]

Medusa was produced by Carrera's theatre company, directed by Sebastián Vila, and premiered in 2010 at the Sala Lastarria 90. After its world premiere, *Medusa* transferred to Sidarte Theatre, then to Mori Bellavista Theatre. The play received a fourth production at the Santiago A Mil International Theater Festival (2011) and a fifth production at GAM (Gabriela Mistral Cultural Center, 2013). It has also been produced in Argentina, Brazil, and Mexico. The play was named the winner of "The Best National Play 2010" by the Chilean Press Circle Awards. It also received an Honorable Mention from the "Casa de las Américas" Awards, Cuba, 2012, and finally won the "2012 Best Play" award given every year by the Council of the City of Santiago, Chile. Carrera's play was published by Ceibo Ediciones in 2013.

Hilda Peña by Isidora Stevenson Bordeu

Hilda Peña (2014) by Isidora Stevenson Bordeu, translated by Constanza Brieba, is set in 1990 in Santiago, Chile, and considers a grieving mother who mourns the death of her adopted son killed in the early days of Chile's return to democracy. As Coca Duarte states in her essay, this play explores a middle-aged woman, Hilda Peña, who is struggling with the "loss of her son during a police shooting in response to a 1993 bank robbery by the Lautauro, an armed militant group."[8] While based on a true event, Stevenson Bordeu creates a fictional work that examines a mother's grief. Stevenson Bordeu began developing this play while taking a playwriting workshop led by director Marcelo Leonart and fellow playwrights Ximena Carrera and Nona Fernández. Each playwright was asked to begin with an image that they could question. Stevenson Bordeu recounts:

> And I started walking around downtown Santiago … and on San Antonio and Santo Domingo, there are some galleries, some hair salons, photocopy shops, and I'm walking and I see a woman smoking in front of a hair salon. I used to smoke at the time, too, and I asked her for a light, and her nails were really bitten, and when I was little, I used to bite my nails, so I know how much those fingers hurt when they're like that. Then I saw her and I said, "Oh." I found the landscape, the context, her tone of voice, and the hair salon interesting. I spent the whole afternoon there talking to her. Then at seven, I went to the studio, and my image was the hairdresser from downtown Santiago with her nails bitten off. That's how the project began.[9]

As she continued to question that image, she reflected on what would cause a woman to bite her nails so intensely and she decided the self-harm was a response to the intense pain of death. Then, as she considered what her character might have suffered, she recalled the incident of the Lautaro bank robbery, which occurred during her youth:

> absurd deaths are something that have always caught my attention. Like those inexplicable deaths that don't make any sense. And I thought about that shooting at the O'Higgins Bank, which is like a story I have inside me. My dad worked at the O'Higgins Bank [in another branch] at the time. So, I listened to the radio . . . at home, the radio was always on with the news around lunchtime. I went to school in the afternoon. So, I heard: "shooting, O'Higgins Bank, Apoquindo Lighthouse." I went to the Apoquindo Lighthouse to have ice cream when I was a kid ... so that memory stayed with me. And that's where I started weaving those landscapes.[10]

Stevenson Bordeu then began to write her play about a mother who had lost her son in the bank robbery. However, she explores unconventional motherhood in that the child is an unofficially adopted son, a homeless boy who had been living in a local plaza, whom her protagonist befriended and decided to invite into her home. In the play, Hilda Peña recounts her relationship with the boy as he grows and becomes a man. As a single mother, the loss she feels is a trauma that she tries to recover from through daily visits to the cemetery, where she bribes the cemetery guards with sex in order to view the decomposing body of her son. In a country where bodies were systematically disappeared during the dictatorship, this mother's commitment to her son's body is particularly compelling.

Stevenson Bordeu's play was selected for the 2014 16th National Chilean Playwriting Festival with an unusual approach: three productions of her play with different directors and actors. Director Aliocha de la Sotta directed actor Paula Zúñiga in a solo performance. An audio-visual version by director Rocío Hernández featured actor Amparo Noguera. Another production by Los Contadores Auditores (the Auditory Accountants, directed by Felipe Riveros and Juan Andrés Rivera) presented the work with three actors: Ximena Rivas, Marcela Salinas, and Francisca Muñoz. Stevenson Bordeu was thrilled by this opportunity for *Hilda Peña*, her second produced play. However, as a young playwright, she allowed changes to be made to her work, most notably the removal of the original ending, which she later restored and published. In the original ending, Stevenson Bordeu reveals that her protagonist has been speaking to a healer, who has the purported ability to resurrect dead bodies. At the festival, one of the productions cut this ending with the reason that it made the protagonist seem less intelligent. Stevenson Bordeu reveals:

> I was so amazed at being in the festival, that it was put on by people I admired so much, that I didn't care. But now I think about it in retrospect and I say, "How could we not understand who Hilda Peña is talking to?" Like, "How could we not finally understand who's listening to her?" And of course, there was speculation at that time that it was like a judge, a lawyer, a doctor, a therapist, whatever, but in reality it has to do with something else, which is precisely the space I come from in Los Ángeles, in the countryside, which has to do with beliefs that are suddenly assumed to be ignorant . . .[11]

Additionally, Stevenson Bordeu was interested in the notion of the incorruptible bodies of saints. She reflects, "And between the incorrupt saints and dislocation, I find there's a universe of hallucinatory imaginaries. Like dislocation, like bleeding statues, like all those things fascinate me. The mysteries, the strange things."[12] Her play is therefore grounded in a connection to the supernatural as the mother pleads with the healer to resurrect her son. The play received its world premiere at Matucana 100, Santiago, Chile, at the 16th National Playwriting Festival in 2014, where Stevenson Bordeu won the Emerging Writer Award. *Hilda Peña* also won the City of Santiago's 2015 Playwriting Prize. Subsequently, the play received numerous productions throughout Chile, including Sala Los Andes, Concepción (2015), Corporación Municipal de Los Ángeles (2015), Sala de artes escénicas de Valparaíso (2015), Teatro de Coyhaique (2015), Quilicura Teatro (2016), Cine Artes de Viña del Mar (2016), Cámara Chilena de la Construcción, Antofagasta y Ovalle (2016), Teatro UC (2017), Centro GAM, Fitam, (2018), Teatro Ictus (2018), Centro GAM (2015-2018), FEDAM región del Maule (2019), and Festival Cielos del Infinito (2019). In Latin America, the play was presented at the Festival de Artes Escénicas FAE, Lima, Perú (2016), Teatro Cervantes, Buenos Aires, Argentina (2016), and Feria de Artes Escénicas, Uruguay (2018). Stevenson Bordeu's play was published in 2024 by Oxímoron, one of Chile's leading theatre publishers.

School for Girls by Nona Fernández

School for Girls (*Liceo de Niñas*, 2015) by Nona Fernández, translated by Andrea Thome, is set in 2015 Santiago, Chile, and delves into the lives of three high school girls who protested during the dictatorship, went into hiding at their public school, and reappear many years later to protest again. As Inés Stranger recounts in her essay, Fernández's play was inspired by the "2006 student protests, known as the Pingüina revolution, which marked the first protests carried out by students after the return to democracy in Chile in 1990. The play also addresses subsequent protests, as students have mobilized almost every year since 2006" and places those protests in conversation with the 1980s protests during the dictatorship in which "high school students opposed the Pinochet regime and faced severe repression for doing so."[13] Fernández, who was a student during the 1980s, noticed the similarities between the protests during and after the dictatorship. She remarked:

> So, this idea of encapsulated time appeared there, that time did not pass, that again the young people were there in the street, who were already other bodies, but they were circulating part of the same ideas and an image appeared, which is the image that summons this play, which is the image that for me was Carmina Riego, she was always the actor [for this play], who came out of a pipe in one of the basements, let's say from this one high school, and it was a woman, but in a school uniform. And that was the image. I had nothing but that image and the great desire I had to talk about this.[14]

Fernández began her play with that image, which led to a consideration of observing the history of student activism from other spaces, including outer space. The seed of this fascination with outer space also arose from her childhood in Chile during the dictatorship, when her family would watch the U.S. television series *Cosmos*, with host astronomer Carl Sagan. The notion of being able to travel to the outer reaches of the universe while living in an enclosed dictatorship was very moving to Fernández, as she recalls:

> And for me, one of the moments of greatest pleasure as a teenager was when I watched Carl Sagan's *Cosmos* ... he appeared on the screen with wonderful dubbing by a Mexican [actor] and we had the possibility of that journey in a world as tiny as Chile was in the 80s and 70s, which was all very small, very enclosed. If we think about it from the perspective of what it is now, everything was super enclosed, sometimes with a curfew, no channels, no internet. Yes, it was craziness. I mean, I didn't experience it as the claustrophobia I see it as now, but for me it was a very important point of escape. And I always thought, well, what we're experiencing can be observed from above. There's another plane that's above my neighborhood, my city, my school, my country, probably my continent, and probably the world. And I think that idea still kind of haunts me.[15]

Additionally, Fernández frequently incorporates the archive in her works. In this case, she began investigating the history of specific student activists in the 1980s who were martyrs of the movement, including the Vergara-Toledo brothers, Eduardo (1965-1985) and Rafael (1967-1985), as well as Marco Ariel Antonioletti (1969-1990). As Fernández continued to develop her play, she explored how these three high school girls were resisting dictatorship in the 1980s. Then, after a cosmic time warp of thirty years, they emerge from hiding, and the memory of the past is reframed in 2015. Some aspects of life have changed dramatically, like their bodies are now middle-aged bodies, yet other aspects continue to be the same, such as the ongoing student protests. Additionally, with a character called the Aged Youth, Fernández explores, in a documentary-theatre style, the narratives of the movement's martyrs.

Fernández developed this play with her theatre company, La Pieza Oscura (The Dark Room), directed by Marcelo Leonart. In the world premiere production at Teatro de la Universidad Católica de Chile in 2015, Fernández performed the role of Fuenzalida, the student activist who remains mute for much of the play. She mainly communicates through written notes. Playing this role reflected Fernández's philosophy of playwriting and acting: "One of the reasons I write plays is because I want to act out those characters and those stories. I also want to embody them and experience them from a space that isn't just that of the idea."[16] However, Fernández recounts the challenge of being an actor in her own play:

> It's not that I knew what I was going to do. As a playwright, I never know what I'm going to do on the stage ... And that's another reason ... why I tried to end the playwriting process well before, because when I become an actor, I don't know anything about the text. I forget the text. In fact, the actors start asking you questions, and the director too. I mean, I don't know, I don't know if the woman who wrote this play is offstage. I really don't know. And if you need answers, wait a week and the woman will lock herself back inside, but I don't know how to make them coexist. It's very difficult for me, or it was very difficult for me at that time.[17]

And yet Fernández gained new insight into her character, who becomes a witness to not only the atrocities she has experienced but to the action unfolding in the play. Additionally, the character of Fuenzalida is a playwright who writes a play about the death of one of her fellow activists. Thus, Fernández also creates a metatextuality as the playwright playing the character who is a playwright. After its world premiere, *School for Girls* was published by Oxímoron in 2016, then produced in 2018 at the Teatro Nacional Chileno by La Pieza Oscura, directed by Leonart. In 2022, the play was produced in Germany at Teatro de Dormut, directed by Anna Tanti.

The City of Fruit by Leyla Selman

The City of Fruit (*La Ciudad de la Fruta,* 2019) by Leyla Selman, translated by Alexandra Ripp, set in 2010s Chile, considers a woman attempting to heal from the trauma of sexual abuse. As Coca Duarte writes in her essay, the play "explores the sexual abuse the playwright suffered as a child at the hands of her grandfather and three of her uncles."[18] Selman creates multiple levels in her non-linear, poetic, and powerful play: a character called Her, as well as her therapist who confronts the abuse, and a grandfather and his three sons who attempt to address the abuse. Duarte observes, "As the play unfolds, it reveals a structure that interweaves all these dimensions through a single dramatic motor: Her's potential healing through narration and confrontation."[19] Selman began writing her autobiographical play inspired by a conversation with Chilean poet Omar Lara (1941-2021). Selman recounts:

> One day I asked [Lara], "What did it mean? What was it like to write about one's life?" And he told me it was difficult because . . . "Why?," I asked him. He said it was difficult to do it well. So I, who have always been, I don't know if ambitious, or both curious and ambitious ... I mean, I was interested in doing it well. So that's when I wrote *The City of Fruit*, trying to do it well.[20]

Selman's playwriting career developed in Concepción, the second largest city in Chile, where she lives, approximately five hundred kilometers south of Santiago, the nation's capital. She briefly produced an earlier, shorter version of the play there. However, her work has continued to be developed and produced in Santiago, primarily through her long-time collaboration with director Rodrígo Pérez and his company Teatro la Provincia. Selman developed the full-length version of *The City of Fruit* with Pérez, who served as director and dramaturg, guiding her to amplify her play to include the therapist character, among other aspects. After developing prior works with Pérez, the playwright and director developed a deep, collaborative bond, based on a close listening to each other. Selman explains:

> I feel like I have the ability to listen really well to Rodrigo, or I try. I also make a lot of effort, like in reality, in general, what I do well is listen, because I don't read as much as I ought to . . . So, now, when I teach classes, I say, well, what's interesting is also listening to the story. So, I feel like I can listen to Rodrigo very well, and we've caught on to that dynamic to the point that, even today, when I write my texts without Rodrigo, I always feel the need for Rodrigo to visit them and give me some comment. He's a very important person, with

whom I've also learned a lot about writing better, and at some point we arrived at *The City of Fruit*, and it happened in a way that was super therapeutic … because, also, since Rodrigo is a psychologist and Rodrigo is fascinating, he's truly a super extraordinary person. So he would tell me things, ask me for others, and that's how we still continue like this.[21]

In her play, through Her's journey to confront her perpetrators, Selman stages female resilience in the wake of heteronormative physical and sexual violence. She also examines the parallels between her abuse and the crimes perpetrated by the dictatorship. She reflects:

And I began to write *The City of Fruit*, drawing this parallel between my story, and [the dictatorship] and little by little I discovered or tried to answer, deep down, why do I feel so responsible? And it's because, of course … while the crime was happening to our people, to our community, it was also happening to me in another way … I experienced the same crime as a kind of mirror from another perspective. Did I begin to gather my thoughts so that, through this text, I could understand why? And not feel so ashamed of feeling so sensitive about something I didn't experience, but that I also experienced from another perspective. Perhaps that explains why? Because *The City of Fruit* ultimately explains my relationship with the crimes that occurred during the dictatorship.[22]

However, in her play, especially with the male characters, Selman also weaves in dark humor, to show the absurd humanity of these perpetrators. Somehow being able to laugh at these men creates a level of empathy for the protagonist as well as the antagonists. Selman reveals:

but what I did was use humor as much as possible and make it so that one could laugh with [the men]. Like technically, that one could at least empathize with them. The stakes on stage are more difficult. It's more difficult, according to me in the text it's easier or maybe not, but I do it with that intention of building these people, as I really do it with a lot of love, like technically, with a lot of love like without hate, I don't write with hate. I don't write as if I'm trying to portray it as something so dark, but rather I try to make them truly idiotic, like each one in their own stupidity …[23]

Selman highlights the men's comic impotence as they argue with each other and never know how exactly to address Her's accusations. However, the play served as a catharsis for Selman as she exposed family secrets through her theatrical work. She reflects on this important role that theatre can play in unearthing secrets to stop future abuse:

Of course, deep down, I … always reaffirm that what matters to me is that it doesn't keep happening … but this thing, the family secret, is super strong. So you have to dismantle it a little. This family secret thing isn't necessary. It's super cultural … if you mobilize it a little, it can tend to dilute over time.[24]

For Selman, writing and producing her play served to be a transformative experience. As Coca Duarte writes, "Selman affirms that bringing *The City of Fruit* to the stage healed her."[25] Her work resonated powerfully with audiences as well. After Pérez's production of *The City of Fruit* was presented at the Teatro de la Memoria in Santiago, Chile,

Selman's play was subsequently produced as part of the 2019 Santiago A Mil International Theater Festival, at Teatro de la Memoria, and published by Oxímoron in 2024.

Sentiments by Carla Zúñiga M.

Sentiments (Sentimientos, 2013) by Carla Zúñiga M., translated by Susan E. Bowen and Yael Prizant, examines the plight of a teenage, Chilean girl, Antofagasta, a student at a private, parochial high school in 2013, who challenges heteronormative, patriarchal society as she tries to navigate her relationship with her girlfriend and a group of boys at her school. Zúñiga explores the dire consequences that arise as Antofagasta attempts to be resilient yet experiences diminished agency when confronted by the female adults in her life, as well as online bullying that crescendos to in-person violence. At the play's conclusion, the protagonist tragically chooses to end her life. In my essay, I mention that Zúñiga's "play is inspired by a local news story about one of Chile's first viral videos, but departs from the actual events to delve into a broader consideration of the ethics of spectatorship in the internet age."[26] Zúñiga reflects:

> Well, this play is based on a true story. And it was one of the first viral videos seen here in Chile. I was young when this happened, but it was something that really angered me. This happened at a private school … and something that really angered me was the school principal. When this happened, the first thing [the principal] did was call the parents and show them the video. And that seemed really violent to me, like the way the school handled it. And those parents, could have also chosen, "I don't want to see that video" or for the girl to ultimately lose any kind of privacy. It really angers me that the first thing he wanted to do was call the girl's parents … and show them the video, which was a video of their daughter with highly sexual content.[27]

Zúñiga trained as an actor at Universidad Arcis with director Javier Casanga, where they were mentored by celebrated Chilean playwright and director Ramón Griffero (born 1954). During their studies, Griffero instilled in them an intense theatricality that emphasized physical theatre, politics, and themes of gender and sexuality. In 2012, after graduation, they formed their own theatre company, The Horrible Girl (La Niña Horrible), and *Sentiments* was their inaugural production. As Zúñiga began to write her play for the new company, her work was influenced by her mentorship with Griffero as well as her childhood reaction to the viral video. Zúñiga recounts:

> So, we started from a place that emphasized the grotesque and politics, the only thing we knew was that we wanted to create a play that was an explosion of the feminine. We wanted to create a play with all female characters. And that they all address women's themes. We wanted to see menstruation, lesbianism, menopause, infidelity, hypersexual women, repressed women … I wanted to make a collage of purely feminine themes. That was our first desire. And for that, I started thinking about stories that would fit that. And I remembered the [viral video] news story and I said, like, there was something there that I found interesting, how what had happened to [that girl] made me really angry.[28]

Zúñiga created a fictional work about a teenage girl, her single, widowed mother, her teenage girlfriend, her lustful, female neighbor, her domineering female teacher, and a door-to-door cosmetics sales lady. In her play, Zúñiga's exploration of unconventional motherhood, gendered cruelty, and women's tragic inability to recover from patriarchal and misogynist trauma is infused with an absurdist, dark humor. The playwright reflects, "Almost all the characters suffer from being a woman in some way, and the creation of the characters is based on that female wound. Yes. And that's where that wound is, that's also where the humor is."[29] Zúñiga and Casanga found success in their first collaboration, with a heightened theatricality that fueled their absurd, grotesque, and tragic critique of traditional gender roles. Their collaboration grew from this intersection of dark comedy and tragic circumstances, as Zúñiga describes:

> It's something we found. I don't know if we were really looking for it. Yes, I think it had to do with us, with how I see the world, with our humor—Javier and I both have a very dark sense of humor—so that's how we created that production. The only thing I remember is that we rehearsed and laughed. We laughed like with feeling, like let's go there ... Whenever we rehearsed, when we weren't laughing, it was like, let's see what's going on. As I revised, we found that interesting, like getting away from that binary of sad or funny, and that it can be both at the same time. And that's going to make it sadder and funnier ... and more terrible overall.[30]

Zúñiga and Casanga developed their singular aesthetic strategy with this production that combined comic, tragic, grotesque, and absurd elements. In my essay, I describe the production aesthetic embracing an

> absurdist acting style [that] included an elongated vocal delivery, a complex physical gestural vocabulary, and a balletic physicality that generated a pervasively dark comedic tone throughout. Elizabeth Pérez's design included characters wearing brightly colored wigs ... as well as her monochromatic, aqua blue colored one room set, with a large, asymmetrical, antique-style black sofa centerstage."[31]

This absurdist mixture of uproarious laughter and stunned silence began with this production and became a hallmark of their company, which continued with five additional productions until they concluded in 2020. Their aesthetic, which grew with each subsequent production, remained rooted in the values instilled in them by Griffero: theatricality, physicality, politics, and sexuality. *Sentiments* received its world premiere by La Niña Horrible, Teatro El Ladrón de Bicicletas, Santiago, Chile, in 2013, directed by Casanga. After its world premiere, *Sentiments* was produced at the 2014 Santiago A Mil International Theatre Festival, Teatro del Puente (2014), and Teatro Sidarte (2017). Zúñiga's play was published by Oxímoron in 2019, with additional productions at Matucana 100 (2023) and Centro Cultural Ceina (2024).

Volume Editors

Each volume editor is a professional playwright, a theatre scholar, and a university professor. Our shared artist-scholar practice provides us with in-depth access and insight into the playwriting process. Additionally, my co-editors Inés Stranger and Coca Duarte have been very influential in Chilean theatre, and I could not have edited this collection without them. In the recent volumes, *Evidencias: Las otras dramaturgias* (*Evidences: The other playwriting*, Oxímoron, 2020 and 2024), two play collections featuring works by Chilean female playwrights, edited by Lorena Saavedra González, Patricia Artés Ibáñez, and Martiza Farías Cerpa, Dr. Stranger and Dr. Duarte are among the twenty-two female playwrights featured. Dr. Stranger's playwriting work made an important impact on 1990s Chilean theatre. The production of her play *Cariño Malo* (*Bad Affection*, 1990) "was significant for the national theatre scene in that it was made solely by women (director, playwright, and actors) and centered on the theme of love from a gendered perspective that questioned roles assigned to women …"[32] Dr. Duarte formed part of an important new generation of female playwrights at the turn of the twenty-first century. Her play, *Juana de Arco: El Misterio de la Luz* (*Joan of Arc, The Mystery of Light*, 2000) explores the fifteenth-century figure through a fragmentary lens to highlight how "the woman is alienated and judged by involving herself in areas that have been considered solely for the masculine gender: … the diverse conflicts of war."[33] Both have served as theatre journal editors and have published widely on Chilean theatre. Dr. Stranger trained both Dr. Duarte and Ximena Carrera. Thus, our work also benefits from this ongoing lineage of Chilean female playwright training. Together, we have collaborated to build bridges between Chilean and U.S. theatre communities through our shared research and passion for these remarkable plays by Chilean female writers.

Notes

1. Hurtado, María de la Luz, "Teatro chileno: historicidad y autorreflexión" *Revista Nuestra América* no. 7, Aug.-Dec. 2009, p. 154.
2. For an in-depth consideration of contemporary Chilean theatre, please see Boyle, Bulman, Cornejo, Grass, Hurtado, Opazo, Thompson and Villegas.
3. Stranger, Inés. "*Medusa*: Testimony, Torture and Betrayal," *Dramaturgas Chilenas: Plays by Chilean Female Writers in the Early 21st Century*, edited by Coca Duarte, Anne García-Romero and Inés Stranger, Methuen Drama, 2025, p. 15.
4. Carrera, Ximena. Personal Interview.19 Oct. 2023.
5. Ibid.
6. Ibid.
7. Ibid.
8. Duarte, Coca. "*Hilda Peña*: Unconventional Motherhood, Grief and Subjectivity," *Dramaturgas Chilenas: Plays by Chilean Female Writers in the Early 21st Century*, edited by Coca Duarte, Anne García-Romero and Inés Stranger, Methuen Drama, 2025, p. 57.
9. Stevenson Bordeu, Isidora. Personal interview.19 Oct. 2023.
10. Ibid.
11. Ibid.
12. Ibid.
13. Stranger, Inés. "*School for Girls*: Student Protests, Political Victims and Temporal Paradox," *Dramaturgas Chilenas: Plays by Chilean Female Writers in the Early 21st Century*, edited by Coca Duarte, Anne García-Romero and Inés Stranger, Methuen Drama, 2025, p. 91.

14 Fernández, Nona. Personal interview. 18 Oct. 2023.
15 Ibid.
16 Ibid.
17 Ibid.
18 Duarte, Coca. "*The City of Fruit*: Sexual Violence, Witness and Transformation," *Dramaturgas Chilenas: Plays by Chilean Female Writers in the Early 21st Century*, edited by Coca Duarte, Anne García-Romero and Inés Stranger, Methuen Drama, 2025, p. 153.
19 Ibid.
20 Selman, Leyla. Personal interview. 16 Oct. 2023.
21 Ibid.
22 Ibid.
23 Ibid.
24 Ibid.
25 Duarte, Coca. *The City of Fruit*, p. 159.
26 García-Romero, Anne. "*Sentiments*: Gendered Cruelty, Dark Comedy, and the Ethics of Spectatorship," *Dramaturgas Chilenas: Plays by Chilean Female Writers in the Early 21st Century*, edited by Coca Duarte, Anne García-Romero and Inés Stranger, Methuen Drama, 2025, p. 197.
27 Zúñiga, Carla. Personal interview. 7 May 2025.
28 Ibid.
29 Ibid.
30 Ibid.
31 García-Romero, Anne. *Sentiments*, p. 195.
32 Núcleo de investigación y creación escénica (Chile). *Evidencias: Las Otras Dramaturgias: Un Siglo de Escrituras de Mujeres Chilenas*. Edited by Lorena Saavedra González et al., Ediciones Oximoron, 2020 pp. 24-25.
33 Artés Ibáñez, Patricia, et al., editors. *Evidencias 2: Las Otras Dramaturgias: Un Siglo de Escrituras de Mujeres Chilenas*. Oxímoron: NCE, Núcleo de Investigación y Creación Escénica, 2024, p. 21.

Medusa:

Testimony, Torture, and Betrayal

Inés Stranger

English translation
Christine Ann Hills

Medusa by Ximena Carrera deals with memory, politics, torture, and a particular relationship based on hate and need that formed between three women. The play premiered in 2010 and remained on stage until 2013, when it formed part of the commemoration of the 40th anniversary of the 1973 coup d'état in Chile. Based on real events, this play features three female characters who were collaborators of Pinochet's secret services: Marcia Alejandra Merino, Luz Arce Sandoval, and María Alicia Uribe. The three women were former militants of the Socialist Party and the Movimiento de Izquierda Revolucionaria (MIR, Revolutionary Left Movement) who were broken and subdued through torture.[1] These women were forced to live together in 1975. By that time, the National Intelligence Directorate (DINA) was already established as a structured organization with resources and stable collaborators. The job of these three female collaborators was to denounce militants—their former comrades—who were still operating clandestinely. In practice, it was a horribly simple operation. If the secret police agents knew that a meeting was going to take place, in other words, contact was going to be made between two activists, then they would pick the women up so they could identify the people involved. It was straightforward snitching. While it is true that the women had agreed to collaborate with the dictatorship's agents in order to save their lives, they were still prisoners and under very tight control. The slightest mistake could cost them their privileges and result in them being sent back to a torture center. They were both victims and victimizers.

According to Ximena Carrera, the writing process for this play took several years. It began when a former female MIR activist told her about the fear that bumping into one of these informers in the street could invoke for them during the early years of the dictatorship. That prompted Carrera to begin digging for information and study the many documents that human rights organizations had been collecting. Later, she read the books *El Infierno* (*The Inferno*) by Luz Arce, and *Mi verdad: más allá del horror yo acuso* (*My Truth: Beyond the horror, I accuse*) by Marcia Alejandra Merino. Carrera realized from the outset that the subject was controversial. The situation of these three women, forced to live together to carry out the dirty work of informing, was interesting and charged with drama. However, by writing about them, she ran the risk of humanizing women who were ultimately responsible for abject crimes. Carrera had to find the proper distance and rely on information that the members of the audience would already have regarding historical facts. With this, she constructed a series of reflections and dislocations that allowed the development of fictional characters with whom it was morally possible to empathize. At the same time, she was able to refer to these real-life people who provoked rejection. This interplay of reflections between fiction and reality is one of the great strengths of *Medusa*.

In the stage production, the characters Carmen, Mariana, and Nina were played by the actors Carmina Riego, Nona Fernández, and Ximena Carrera herself. They managed to embody these characters with theatrical authenticity while also quoting the real-life people with the background provided by the text itself. Mariana's nervousness, her remorse, and her fragility fully reflect the perception viewers form when watching the documentary *La flaca Alejandra* by Carmen Castillo or reading her autobiographical book *Mi verdad: más allá del terror, yo acuso*. Carmen's authority, her concern for her son, and the relationship she had with the camp's officer resonate with the autobiographical elements expressed in *El infierno* by Luz Arce. However, when constructing Nina's character, Carrera based her work on the combined memories of her two companions, as María Alicia Uribe never published her memoirs, nor has she ever publicly acknowledged her role as an informer. In fact, she remained in the armed forces until she retired.

The setting for the action is an apartment in the San Borja towers, found in the historic center of Santiago where Alameda Avenue meets Portugal Avenue. They were, at that time, an example of the new social architecture. Today, the buildings are poorly maintained and have significantly deteriorated; all common infrastructure and shared areas have been eliminated. What was the Diego Portales building is found on the other side of Alameda Avenue; Pinochet and the Military Junta operated from within its sinister offices. Today, Santiago's most important cultural center, the Gabriela Mistral Center, GAM, is housed there. The proximity to the offices of Pinochet's government put a lot of pressure on the lives of the play's characters. Secret police agents were aware of everything the women did and could come looking for them in five minutes. The characters live in this place, but they have not turned it into a home. In this apartment, there is a cat abandoned by its former owners (because they are exiled, prisoners or disappeared). It is an unstable and suicidal cat that Nina looks after. Inside, the space is illuminated by a bare light bulb that hangs from the ceiling. There are a few pieces of furniture: an armchair, a couple of chairs, and a door, which is kept permanently locked; Carmen guards the key closely. The action takes place over five scenes, probably over a few days, no more than ten days.

The play begins with Carmen talking to her young son on the phone. It is an anxious conversation because the boy is not very enthusiastically engaged and wants to go back to playing with the toy car he has been given. Carmen is alarmed by this and tries to find out who gave the toy to him. She asks to speak to her sister, who she reproaches for allowing a stranger to approach her son. She hangs up and calls Adolfo to plead with him to allow her to bring her son to live with her. Adolfo Schiller is based on Rolf Wenderoth, the commander of the political prisoner camp Villa Grimaldi,[2] who was Luz Arce's partner and who recently died in Chile's high-security prison.

Scene two opens in darkness. We hear an exchange between the three women who are outside, trying to open the door. They manage to get inside, and the light comes on. Nina is in a good mood; she has had a few drinks and is humming a song. Mariana, who we see is the most upset out of the three, hits Nina's cat, whose name is Che—a clear reference to Che Guevara. Mariana leaves. Nina says that the agent assigned to them, the one they call Huaso, has given her some earrings. Carmen observes that they are stained with blood, and Nina realizes that these earrings probably belonged to a woman who has been tortured. Carmen continues to interrogate her. Nina admits that a stranger approached her in a café, and she gave him her telephone number. They argue about this reckless behavior. Carmen's authority is established based on her relationship with Adolfo Schiller.

There is a strange physical closeness between the women. They are damaged bodies that recognize each other in their precariousness. Mariana, who has been sleeping, enters the room dressed in a slip. She is overwhelmed, she has wet herself, and her slip is stained. This seems neither strange nor embarrassing. Mariana says the light bothers her. She says she was invited to a café where she saw some girls studying. This scene represents an important ideological advance. The girls, who were studying philosophy, did not understand that language marks the limit between humans and animals. Mariana wanted to explain this to them. She implies that she reported them because they laughed at her, but she does not confirm it. She tries to fix the light by hanging a dress over it like a shade. She does not manage to do it. This is the light we deserve, she says.

In scene three, a couple of days later, Carmen and Nina are correcting some tests, and we understand that they give classes on Marxism to the security guards. They comment on the answers and the guards' poor spelling, that it seems that one of them copied and so should be punished. Carmen suggests to Nina that she should report it. "They're not going to send you to 'the chicken coop'[3] for reporting it, not for that."[4] Meanwhile, Mariana is sleeping. Carmen is worried because she thinks that Mariana's actions—reporting the girls from the café and taking a whole bottle of tranquilizers—will have consequences. Mariana comes in to get some water. Carmen asks her why she did it, but Mariana is evasive, saying only that she overstepped a little. Mariana denies having handed over the girls, saying she never got around to it. However, she confesses something worse, that she saw "her Alejandro," and she got nervous, and maybe they (the secret police) saw him too, as people end up dead because of her and her roommates. This dialogue clearly describes what snitching entails: how they have to walk the streets and identify their former colleagues. "I can't take this anymore," says Mariana, "every person I see ends up dead."[5] Nina silences her by invoking their agreement not to talk about work at home. The phone rings. Nina answers and says it is a wrong number. There is a knock at the door, and they are told to get ready to go out and identify some bodies.

Scene four opens in the dark. As in scene two, the women's voices can be heard speaking outside as they open the door. They are exhausted. It is not clear where they have come from, but we know they took a helicopter. Nina is drinking from a bottle Huaso stole. They went to identify a body that turned out to be Alejandro, the same man Mariana was talking about. Mariana blames herself; it is her fault that Huaso and Tito took him prisoner. Carmen gives her a tranquilizer. Mariana threatens to take all the pills. Carmen warns her that even if she does, they will not let her die; they will call the doctor again. The phone rings.

Mariana confronts Nina and accuses her of stealing the apartment keys so she can go and meet Ignacio, a guy she met a few days ago. Carmen finds out. She threatens to ask Schiller to arrest the man before he comes up. Mariana proposes to the others that they make an escape. Tomorrow, as they do not have a guard, they could take advantage and get away. Carmen replies that she cannot leave her son and tells the others that she is going to bring him to live with them. Both of them object. Nina downs the whole bottle in one go. Night falls.

1 Nina (Ximena Carrera) contemplates her disguise as Berta in *Medusa* by Ximena Carrera, directed by Sebastián Vila, Sala Lastarria 90, Santiago, Chile, 2010. (Photo: © Elio Frugone Piña www.fototeatro.cl)

The fifth scene takes place the next day. Nina is looking for the missing cat. Carmen asks to speak to her. Nina tells her she has nothing against her son, but that she does not like children. They realize that Mariana is missing. Just at that moment, Commander Schiller calls to say he will pick them up in fifteen minutes. This distresses Carmen as a change of plan indicates they know something. She thinks they are going to be sent to 'the chicken coop.' She decides to call him back and tell him that Mariana has disappeared, but Mariana turns up. Mariana explains that she went to the Vicaria de la Solidaridad (Vicariate of Solidarity),[6] and that Father Graciano is going to help them get political asylum; all they need to do is testify, the three of them together, in front of some lawyers. They discuss the pros and cons. The play ends when they open the door. Their decision is left hanging in suspense.

Carrera's text follows classic dramatic structure: it presents the characters in a situation, they interact in the present, a conflict develops, the action progresses with threats to Carmen's son, Nina's encounter with Ignacio, the involuntary betrayal of Alejandro, Mariana's suicide attempt, Nina's love fantasies, and, finally, the offer to take them to safety from Father Graciano from the Vicaria de la Solidaridad. The innovative twist in this classic plot structure is that when the dramatic tension reaches its peak, the situation is left unresolved. The play ends right at the moment when the characters must decide whether or not to change their destiny, whether or not to go and testify, or whether or not to stay trapped in their current life. Despite the narrative frustration it creates, this interruption of the action is the most fundamental and provocative feature of *Medusa*. The play does not take responsibility for the characters' decision: we can find the answer to that question in reality itself. We know that the three women who collaborated with DINA did not go to any Father Graciano from any Vicariate and that they did not testify before the justice system until 1990. It was after the plebiscite[7] and the return to democracy when Luz Arce and Marcia Merino testified before the Truth and Justice Commission set up by President Patricio Aylwin.

However, what is more serious is that the action cannot be resolved either in reality or in the context of this play. The characters were deprived of any possibility of making a decision individually. By making the characters confront this decision, the playwright leads them to a terminal paradox. These three women are not individuals but a collective entity, a three-headed monster, whose will is split. Even Father Graciano, who should or could help them, insists they act as a block. (In her autobiographical book, Luz Arce says they were called "the package").[8]

The three women are prisoners of an impossible situation; they are blocked on all fronts. They are obviously watched, controlled, and manipulated by outside forces, but at the same time, and this is more complex, they also control and watch each other. They are not friends. They do not trust each other. They have no empathy or solidarity with each other. They are not together to help or understand each other. Their relationship is one of functional dependence. They tolerate each other, but only the minimum necessary for survival.

None of the three women can exercise their free will. Carmen wants to live with her son, but Nina is opposed to this, saying she does not like children, while Mariana thinks it is inappropriate. Mariana tries to commit suicide, but Carmen and Nina prevent her, not because they care if she dies, but because they think her death could put them in danger. Nina wants to go on a date, but neither Mariana nor Carmen is willing to risk giving her a moment of happiness; Carmen even threatens to have the man arrested to prevent them from meeting up.

The impossible action manifested in this play may express an unconscious reflection about the collective narrative Chileans have constructed for themselves about the dictatorship: the coup d´état was an enormous, imminent, and excessive force that paralyzed everyone's free will.

The French language has the verb *méduser*; it refers to the stupefaction that consumes free will. The secret police agents knew the strategies of fear; they knew how to exploit them to turn one against another, how to feed insecurity, and how to destabilize the women. The terror system not only consisted of killing and torturing, but it was also about dominating and seducing: it was about capriciously exercising power and authority to prevent trust.

Therefore, *Medusa*'s open ending may express not only the characters' inability to make a decision, but also the imminent, overwhelming, and immobilizing force of fear. The door opens, and fear petrifies them. This is how the play is resolved; it is perpetuated in the myth of Medusa.

In 2013, at least twenty-one plays were premiered in Santiago to commemorate the 40th anniversary of the coup d'état. Two female playwrights, Nona Fernández with *El Taller* and Ximena Carrera with *Medusa*, broadened the perspective by staging abject characters who do not correspond to traditional victims. Is this a distinctive feature of the female perspective, perhaps a greater capacity for empathy? It is a hypothesis to be tested.

In Chile, theatre artists have taken on the task of elaborating trauma and keeping memory alive, which are undoubtedly very important tasks. However, in studying this play and its references, especially the book *El Infierno* written by Luz Arce, I have come to understand that this self-imposed task is beyond the realm of theatre. Elaborating a shared narrative has to be a task taken on by society as a whole.

Notes

1. The events are based on the lives of Marcia Alejandra Merino, Luz Arce Sandoval, and María Alicia Uribe. The experiences of these collaborators are recorded in the books *El Infierno* (*The Inferno*) written by Luz Arce, published in April 1991, and *Mi verdad: más allá del horror yo acuso* (*My Truth: Beyond the horror, I accuse*) by Marcia Alejandra Merino, published in 1993.
2. Villa Grimaldi was an important site used by DINA during Pinochet's dictatorship for the detention, torture, and execution of political prisoners. It is now a memory site.
3. 'El gallinero' (the chicken coop) is a euphemism for a clandestine torture center used during Pinochet's dictatorship.
4. Carrera, Ximena. *Medusa, Dramaturgas Chilenas: Plays by Chilean Female Writers in the Early 21st Century*, edited by Coca Duarte, Anne García-Romero and Inés Stranger, Methuen Drama, 2025, p. 33.
5. Carrera, p. 38.
6. The Vicaria de la Solidaridad (Vicariate of Solidarity) was a human rights organization created by the Catholic Church to help those affected by Pinochet's dictatorship.
7. The 1988 plebiscite asked Chileans whether General Pinochet who had led the military dictatorship should become President for a further eight years under civilian rule. The "No" side won with 56% of the vote and put an end to Pinochet's rule.
8. It is interesting that at this point, the vicariate is transformed into a new enemy for the characters, on a par with the agents, guarding them. Through the characters, we see an inverted reality, where the Vicariate of Solidarity represents new dangers.

Further Reading

Arce, Luz. *The Inferno: A Story of Terror and Survival in Chile*. University of Wisconsin Press, 2004.

Baboun G., Isabel. "Matar con los ojos: delación y emancipación en Medusa." *Apuntes De Teatro*, 137, 2013, pp. 127-33. https://revistaapuntes.uc.cl/index.php/RAT/article/view/32237

Frankel, Emily E. "When Surviving Is Not Enough: From Militancy to Collaboration: On the Ethical Implications of Researching the Political Transformations of Marcia Alejandra Merino Vega, Luz Arce Sandoval, and María Alicia Uribe Gómez." *Chasqui*, vol. 50, no. 2, 2021, pp. 305–28.

Gómez-Barris, Macarena, et al. "The Female Perpetrator." In *A Companion to Contemporary Documentary Film*, John Wiley & Sons, Inc., 2015, pp. 524-35, https://doi.org/10.1002/9781118884584.ch24.

Grass Kleiner, Milena. "Medusa y El Taller: cuando el teatro pone en escena la zona gris" *Revista Arte Escena*, 2016, no. 1, pp. 2-13.

Lazzara, Michael J., and Luz Arce. *Luz Arce and Pinochet's Chile: Testimony in the Aftermath of State Violence*. First edition., Palgrave Macmillan, 2011.

Merino Vega, Marcia Alejandra. *Mi verdad: "más allá del horror, yo acuso . . ."* M. Merino Vega, 1993.

Medusa

Ximena Carrera

English translation by the author

Ximena Carrera Venegas, actor, playwright, producer, screenwriter, and educator, was born in 1971 in Santiago, Chile. She received a degree in acting from the Pontificia Universidad Católica de Chile School of Theatre in 1994. From 2005 to 2009, she studied theatre arts (acting and playwriting) in Buenos Aires, Argentina. In 1997, she created La Trompeta (The Trumpet), a theatre company, with actor and director Sebastián Vila. Her plays have been developed in her company as well as other national theatre companies and institutions such as the Municipal Theater of Santiago. Her works include *Café* (*Coffee*, 2000, First Prize winner in the Gabriela Mistral Literary Competition), *Por encargo del olvido* (*On behalf of oblivion*, 2000), *DFL2* (2004, selected for the 2nd Festival Off of the National Playwriting Festival), *Naturaleza Muerta* (*Nature Death*, 2003), *Medusa* (2010), *Jemmy Button* (2010), *Ningún pájaro canta por cantar* (*No Bird sings to sing*, 2014), *La noche fuera del tiempo* (*The night outside of time*, 2014), *Lucía* (2015), *Greta* (2019), *Desgracia* (*Disgrace*, 2020), *Arrau, el otoño del emperador* (*Arrau, the autumn of the emperor*, 2021), *Una historia de abejas* (*A history of bees*, 2021), *La Felicidad de las Tórtolas* (*Happiness of Turtledoves*, 2022), and *Callas, la hija del destino* (*Callas, the daughter of destiny*, 2023). Her performance in *Grita* (*Uproar*, 2004), written and directed by Marcelo Leonart, earned her a nomination for best female performance in 2004 in the ranking of the Chilean newspaper *El Mercurio*. She has also worked as a screenwriter for television series *16* (2003), *17* (2005), *Los treinta* (*The thirty*, 2005), *Disparejas* (*Disparates*, 2006), *40 y tantos* (*40 and more*, 2010-2011), *El laberinto de Alicia* (*Alicia's labyrinth*, 2011), *Dulce amargo* (*Sweet bitter*, 2012), and *Secretos en el jardín* (*Secrets in the garden*, 2014). Currently, she is a professor of playwriting at the Universidad Diego Portales, as well as offering workshops in Colombia and Mexico. In 2007, she received the Iberescena Playwriting Fellowship. Her play, *Medusa*, was the 2010 winner for Best Play from the Chile Drama Critics Circle, 2012 winner of the Municipal Literature Prize from the City of Santiago, and received Special Mention in the 2012 Casa de la Americas prize in Cuba.

Medusa received its world premiere at Sala Lastarria 90, Santiago, Chile, on April 11, 2010. It was directed by Sebastián Vila with the following cast:

Mariana   Carmina Riego
Carmen   Nona Fernández
Nina   Ximena Carrera

After its world premiere, *Medusa* transferred to Sidarte Theatre, then to Mori Bellavista Theatre. The play received a fourth production at the Santiago a Mil International Theater Festival (2011) and a fifth production at GAM (Gabriela Mistral Cultural Center, 2013). It has also been produced in several regions in Chile, Brazil, Mexico, and Argentina.

The play was named the winner of "The Best National Play 2010" by the Chilean Press Circle Awards. It also received an Honorable Mention from the "Casa de las Américas" Awards, Cuba, 2012, and won the "Best Play" award given every year by the Council of the City of Santiago, Chile (2012).

The play was published in Chile by Ceibo Ediciones (2013).

Characters

Mariana, *late 20s*
Nina, *late 20s*
Carmen, *late 20s*

Setting

1970s, Santiago, Chile. A living room of a downtown apartment. Scant furniture: a door, an upholstered armchair sofa, three wooden chairs, a floor lamp, and a single overhead bare bulb hanging from the ceiling.

Editors' Note

Ximena Carrera completed Medusa *in 2008 in Buenos Aires, Argentina, and Santiago, Chile. Her fictional play explores the lives of three, real Chilean women: Luz Arce Sandoval, Marcia Alejandra Merino Vega, and María Alicia Uribe Gómez, who lived together in a Santiago apartment in the San Borja area during the 1970s, after they officially began working as functionaries for DINA, the dictatorship's secret police. For further information, please see the preceding essay by Inés Stranger.*

Scene One

Carmen *speaks on the phone. It's late.*

Carmen You don't wanna talk to your Mamá? (…) Fine, go play. (…) Brand new? Where did you get brand new toy cars? Your auntie gave'em to you? (…) (*Her expression stiffens*) What man? (*Beat*) Mati, I asked you a question, my love, what man gave you those toy cars? (. . .) Did he do something to you? (*Losing patience*) What do you mean "who", Mati?! The man who gave you those toy cars, did he do something to you? (*Trying to hide her bewilderment*) No, baby, I'm not angry. Let me talk to your auntie, ok? (*Holds a second*) Tatiana? (*To the point*) What man is he talking about? (. . .) (*Explains*) Matías just told me a man, a complete stranger, gave him a pair of brand new toy cars in the park … (. . .) I'm telling you he just told me! (…) Calm down? Calm down, Tatiana, for god's sake!? A stranger gave Mati some toy cars! You think it's normal? (. . .) Let me tell you: it isn't normal. If that guy approached him, it's because he knows about me. He knows he's my son. It's a message. (…) If your head hadn't been miles away, you would've realized! No one can come near my son, do you hear me? Because if anything happens to him, in less than two seconds, the moron that you have for a husband loses his job, do you underst …

From the other side of the line, Tatiana hangs up. **Carmen**, *upset, hits the handset several times against the phone. Calms down. Dials a number. Waits.*

Carmen Adolfo? (…) Hi, sorry to call you at home, but I need a favor. (…) No, nothing's wrong. It's about my son. (…) No, he's okay, for now. It's me, I can't bear this anymore. (…) Do you remember that, in the beginning, when you brought us here, you told me that someday I'd be able to bring my son too? Well, it's got to be now. (…) Yes, I … (…) No, I can't calm down. I just talked to him and he told me that a stranger went up to him at the park and gave him some toy cars. (…) No, I don't want a guard watching him. I want him to live here with me. (…)

Dark.

Scene Two

Past midnight. Outside in the hallway by the entrance to the apartment, women's voices can be heard. One of them, **Nina**, *is humming a song.*

Carmen (*sotto voce, to* **Nina**)   Berta, please, shut up!

Nina   Don't call me "Berta" and let me sing! I'm happy!

Carmen   Sshh! You're gonna wake everybody up. (*To* **Mariana**) Would you please hurry?

Mariana   I can't find the keys, I don't have them.

Carmen   What do you mean "you don't have them"? I gave them to you when we were leaving. Before getting into the car. I said …

Mariana   No, you didn't give them to me. I don't have them.

Carmen (*to* **Mariana**)   Give me your purse. Let me check … (*Regarding Nina*) Hold her, she's gonna fall.

Nina   I'm fine. I won't fall.

Carmen (*finds the keys*)   So I didn't give them to you? What's this then?

The three women enter. **Nina** *continues to hum.* **Mariana** *crosses the room and steps out to the kitchen.*

Carmen (*to* **Nina**)   What does it take for you to shut up!

Nina   Gimme one and I'll shut the fuck up.

Carmen   Give you what?

Nina   A cigarette.

Carmen   Don't have any.

Nina   Yes, you do.

Carmen   Yes, I do. But they've just been given to me.

Nina   I'm asking just for one.

Carmen   I give you one and you'll end up smoking the whole pack.

Nina   Well if we run out, just ask Schiller! Sorry: "Adolfo"!

Carmen   Why don't *you* ask him?

Nina   Cause the old man is crazy for you, not for me.

From the kitchen, Che, the cat, meows in pain as if he had been kicked. **Nina** *jumps up and exits toward the kitchen.*

Nina (*to* **Mariana**)   What did you do to him?

Mariana   He attacked me.

Nina   He doesn't attack anyone. (*Looks at the cat*) Is he limping because of you?

Mariana   No.

Nina   Yes! He's limping! Carmen! Look!

Carmen   He's always been like that.

Nina   No.

Carmen   Yes, since he tried to kill himself,

Nina   When did he try to kill himself?

Carmen   When he jumped from the balcony. No cat jumps from a balcony if he doesn't deliberately want to kill himself.

Nina   He didn't jump, he fell. That's very different.

Mariana   If I were in his shoes, I'd also try to kill myself.

Carmen   The poor thing is hungry.

Nina   I feed him.

Carmen   Bones! He's not a dog.

Nina   It's the only thing I can get! (*Looks at Che with love.*) I don't want him to die on me.

Carmen   I think he misses his former owners, that's why he keeps jumping from the balcony, over and over and over.

Nina   He doesn't jump, he falls! He falls!

As **Nina** *stands up, she stumbles.*

Carmen   Look at you. You drank a bottle of red on your own. That's your problem, you don't know when to stop, Berta.

Nina   Here, inside these walls, I'm not Berta! How many times do I have to say it? My name is Nina! Nina!

Carmen *and* **Mariana** *stare at her.*

Nina   We go out once a month … what do you want? I feel happy, I can't help myself, I … when the end of the month is near I get happy just to think that instead of a shitty loaf of bread, I'm gonna have a plate of wontons or a Cantonese pineapple duck. Or that I'll be able to see other faces instead of the usual ones …

Mariana   Like the guy sitting at the table next to us?

Nina   What guy? I talked to no one.

Mariana   I didn't say you had talked.

Carmen   What guy?

Nina   Nobody.

Carmen Mariana?

Mariana Good night. (*Exits.*)

Carmen *stares at* **Nina** *waiting for her to speak up.* **Nina** *stares at the floor. Suddenly,* **Nina** *stands up as if she had been expelled from her chair. Looks for her purse.*

Nina Look! I wanna show you something … (*Looks around*) Where did I leave it …? (*Finds inside her purse*) Here! (*Takes out of her purse a pair of golden earrings*) Look, do you like them? Huaso bought them. For me.

Nina *gives* **Carmen** *the pair of earrings.* **Carmen** *gives them a quick look and hands them back to* **Nina***.*

Carmen They're used.

Nina No, they're not.

Carmen Look at that.

Carmen points out a brown spot on each of the earrings.

Nina (*looks at it*) What is it?

Carmen What does it look like?

Nina Looks … brownish.

Carmen 'Cause it's dry.

Nina (*throws the earrings far*) Gross!

Carmen Next time Huaso gives you a present, tell him to clean it first. (*Beat.*) What guy?

Nina (*avoiding the subject*) What?

Carmen What guy?

Nina Not important.

Carmen If it's not important, there's nothing wrong in telling me.

Nina (*caught*) He was … was sitting at the table next to us. (*Beat.*) He spent all night watching us. Well, I don't know if the whole night, but … didn't you notice him?

Carmen And?

Nina When I stood up to go to the ladies room, he followed me.

Carmen Followed? What do you mean he followed you? Why didn't you say anything?

Nina I mean, we bumped into each other, by the bathroom. And he asked me if I was Irish.

Carmen Irish?

Nina Yes. He must have thought I looked Irish. You don't know what it was like … his voice … I could barely speak … I said: "*da*" … "*yes*" …

Carmen I don't understand, why did you tell him you were Irish?

Nina I don't know, Carmen, I don't know. Not everything is so logical. I liked that he thought I looked Irish. Anyway, he ended up realizing I was Chilean.

Carmen You spoke, then. (**Nina** *doesn't answer.*) What? Did you go into the bathroom with him?

Nina No. Of course, not.

Nina *remains silent.*

Carmen What, then?

Nina Promise me you won't be angry.

Carmen Okay, I won't.

Nina First I asked for his phone number, but he said he couldn't give it to me and he pointed to his family waiting for him at the table. His wife works with him, apparently she's his secretary. So I … I gave him my number.

Carmen *Your* number? *Your* number?! *Our* number!

Nina Calm down, it's alright.

Carmen What do you mean "it's alright," Nina? We can't give out our number just like that. Are you stupid? What d'you know about him?

Nina Nothing, I mean … why is it so wrong? As soon as I go to headquarters, I'll check him out and that's it. I got his name.

Carmen Oh, right, you got his name. You have everything.

Nina I bumped into him by the bathroom, what did you expect? Should I have taken his fingerprints?

Carmen I expected you wouldn't talk to him. When will you understand there are things we simply cannot do!

Nina He didn't look dangerous. I mean, he was there with his children, his wife … he seemed decent. I know it's difficult to believe, but there was something in him, in his eyes … you could tell, Carmen. You can tell when somebody is a good person on the inside. Do you understand?

Carmen "Good"? "Good"? You were turned on. Period. If he calls, what're you gonna do? Will you go to the movies together? Have coffee? Go to the park together?

Pause.

Carmen If this guy calls …

Nina His name is Ignacio …

Carmen I don't give a damn what his name is! If this guy calls, you'll say it's a wrong number.

Nina But . . .

Carmen Or I'll tell Schiller. You choose.

Mariana *enters, barefoot. She's wearing a slip.*

Nina You? Weren't you asleep?

Mariana I came to get a glass of water.

Nina *stares at* **Mariana***'s slip. There's a large spot, like she has wet herself.*

Nina You peed yourself …

Mariana (*looks at herself for a few seconds*) Yes.

Nina *exits to the kitchen.* **Mariana** *notices the bulb hanging from the ceiling.*

Mariana This is such an ugly light! We should put something on it … I don't know, a scarf, a tablecloth or … something that makes this a bit more cozy. The feminine touch …

Carmen Mariana! (**Mariana** *looks at her.*) Are you alright?

Mariana (*looking at her as if she has asked a very strange question*) And you, Carmen? Are you feeling all right?

Carmen I don't get it.

Mariana You don't get me. No, of course you don't get me. I don't even get me.

Nina *enters with a cup of water for* **Mariana**.

Nina Something happened?

Mariana Something? Something like what?

Nina I don't know. A hard day …

Mariana A long day … yeah, maybe that was it. (*Pause.*) Today … today, I was invited to a café.

Nina Why?

Mariana Why what?

Nina Why were you invited to a café?

Mariana I don't know. I guess they wanted to have a coffee. I guess. (*Thinks.*) And at the table next to me, there were two girls studying and discussing a text written by Bouvier …

Carmen Who?

Mariana Bouvier, a French philosopher from the seventeen hundreds who was the first to elaborate … it doesn't matter. And they discussed and worked hard to understand it and they talked and talked. (*She smiles.*) You wouldn't believe what they were saying, the poor things didn't understand a word, and I wanted … I was dying to correct their mistake, in five minutes I would've been able to explain everything and they would have really understood. Honestly, no more than five minutes. Even less. Tito was outside buying cigarettes and Huaso was in the bathroom.

Carmen   Wait, they left you alone?

Mariana (*nods*)   For several minutes, yes. (*Pause.*) I should've done something, right?

Carmen   I didn't say that.

Mariana   But you're thinking it. Anyway, there was no point in escaping. It didn't even cross my mind. Maybe it was the smell of the coffee. I don't know. They trust me more than I trust myself. (*Pause.*) Funny thing. Being an open book for everyone else and a closed door for myself. (*She stares into nothing.*)

Carmen   Mariana!

Mariana   Huh?

Carmen   The girls!

Mariana   Which girls?

Nina   You were talking about these two students sitting next to you.

Mariana   The girls! Yes. (*Pause.*) I'm so tired! (*Pause.*) I stood up, I approached them and I stood between them, not saying anything, with my mouth open. They looked at me, then at each other and pretended … pretended I wasn't there. As if I didn't exist. Ignoring me. So I hit the table.

Carmen   You did, what?

Mariana   I hit the table and the coffee cups flew off. And you know what they did? They laughed. I don't know why. I only wanted to correct their mistake, so they could understand that, what Bouvier calls man's total degradation refers to "the being" in respect to "the animal," because, for him, the boundary is in the animal condition taken as the ability or rather the inability to relate to each other through "the verb." According to Bouvier, as soon as spoken language takes shape in man, it establishes in him … oh, my head! (*Picks up again.*) As soon as spoken language takes shape in man, a boundary is established … and it's not like that, it's not the development of spoken language that defines the boundary … (*It's a discovery that she reveals to the world.*) Because there's simply no boundary …!

Nina (*to* **Carmen**, *lowering her voice*)   What's gotten into her?

Carmen   I don't know.

Mariana (*unaware of everyone, for herself*)   … But they shouldn't have laughed, they should've realized how lucky they were, that the only thing I wanted was to be sitting beside them, to be one of them, and after that coffee to go back home safe and sound as they would have done, if they hadn't … (*Stops abruptly.*)

Carmen If they hadn't … what?

Mariana (*barely audible*) If they hadn't laughed.

Carmen *and* **Nina** *look at each other.*

Carmen What did you do, Mariana? Mariana!

Mariana *stands up and exits towards the bathroom.*

Nina Mariana!

Nina *tries to follow her, but halfway there she bumps into* **Mariana** *who returns bringing a large piece of the dress she was wearing before. She climbs, with certain difficulty, on the arm of the sofa and tries to arrange the fabric of the dress as a lamp shade over the bulb hanging from the ceiling.*

Carmen Get down! You're gonna fall!

Mariana Let me.

Mariana *defends herself from the other two using the piece of fabric to keep them away.*

Nina What did you do? You tore it apart?

Mariana It wasn't my size.

Nina It was new!

Mariana *tries to put the piece of fabric around the bulb to soften the light.*

Mariana (*to* **Carmen** *and* **Nina**) What do you think? Looks better this way, doesn't it? Berta, help me with this so Carmen can see how nice it looks.

Nina *doesn't move. She and* **Carmen** *stare at* **Mariana** *unable to react.*

Mariana Sorry, Nina . . . Uh, shit! I don't know what to call you sometimes … Tell me! Tell me how it looks! Better, doesn't it?

Nina (*looking at* **Carmen**) Yes, Mariana, it looks better. Now get down.

Mariana (*imitating her*) "Yes, Mariana, it looks better. Now get down." You don't have the slightest idea. (*Nina stares at the piece of fabric.*) Do you like the little dress? Here. It's yours. Although it's useless now.

Mariana *throws the torn dress on the floor and looks very closely at the light bulb.*

Mariana There's nothing we can do. This is the light we deserve.

Dark.

Scene Three

Same room. **Carmen** *and* **Nina** *are correcting some exams. But* **Carmen** *is distracted.* **Nina** *watches her.* **Carmen** *stands up and walks towards* **Mariana**'s *bedroom.* **Nina** *stops her.*

Nina (*showing her one exam*)   Can you read this? I don't understand the writing.

Carmen (*looks at it, trying to figure it out*)   "That all ... " no ... "That all subversibs are" (*Upset.*) The spelling of these apes ... to write subversive with "b"

Nina   It is spelled with a "b".

Carmen   And "v". Sub-versives.

Nina (*realizes and hides it*)   Sure. But the first one is "b".

Carmen *looks at her for one second and then picks up again what she's reading.*

Carmen   ". . . are individuals who, in the short term and in different ways, try to corrupt and break down the nation's established order." (*Smiles.*) There's no way he came up with this sentence. This guy copied. Flunk him and then inform his superior.

Nina   Are you crazy? You think I'd do something like that?

Carmen   Don't you dare?

Nina   I'm not informing on anyone. If he wants to copy, it's his problem.

Carmen   We are not there just to teach them Marxism lessons. We're also there to teach these beasts how to behave.

Nina   I didn't see anything.

Carmen   You just admitted it.

Nina (*sharply*)   I'm telling you I saw nothing! I can't accuse him of something I didn't see.

Carmen   They won't send you back to the 'Chicken Coop'[1] for turning him in. Not for that, no.

Pause.

Carmen   She's still sleeping?

Nina   I guess. The doctor said that she would go on till tomorrow, didn't he? She'll rest the whole weekend and on Monday she'll go to work as usual.

Carmen   As usual, right.

Nina   What's wrong?

Carmen   I'm tired.

Nina   Go to sleep.

Carmen   Can't.

Nina   Carmen, it's okay. Nothing happened.

Carmen   "Nothing happened"? She nearly died right here in our apartment.

Nina   But she didn't. We were lucky.

Che enters and walks towards **Nina**. *Jumps over her lap.* **Carmen** *looks at him.*

Carmen   That cat is thinner every day. He will die if he eats just bones. Don't complain if it kicks the bucket one of these days.

Nina   Don't be such a downer.

Carmen   I don't like cats.

Nina   I do.

Carmen   Enjoy it while it lasts.

Nina   What do you mean?

Carmen   If I were you, I'd start enjoying this beautiful apartment, yeah. Take a one-hour bath if you want, eat whenever you want to, walk around in your birthday suit on the balcony, do whatever you want. It wouldn't surprise me at all if on Monday we are back in the 'Chicken Coop.'

Nina (*going pale*)   Why?

Carmen   Do you think this little performance by Mariana will go unnoticed, like a casual illness?

Nina   I don't get it.

Carmen   If they wanted to kill us, they would've done it themselves. They want us alive, not dead. Those were their terms, am I wrong?

Nina   Accidents happen.

Carmen   She swallowed the whole bottle of tranquilizers. That's not an "accident". You saw her yourself. Do you think it was an "accident" that she tore that dress apart just because it was too big for her?

Nina (*lowering her voice*)   You're gonna wake her up!

Carmen   I don't care! An "accident" what she did to those two girls?

Nina   She can't take it anymore!

Carmen   We can't afford that!

Mariana *enters. She's wearing the same slip she was wearing last night.*

Nina   What are you doing up? Go to your bed. Get some sleep.

Mariana (*weakly*)   My head is aching.

Nina   Probably because you hit your head pretty hard. The doctor said it's likely just superficial. Anyway, you need to …

Mariana Doctor? What doctor? I don't remember anything.

Nina 'Cause you were unconscious. You had to have your stomach pumped. You overdosed.

Carmen (*to* **Mariana**) Why did you do it?

Nina (*to* **Carmen**) Give her a break, she just woke up.

Mariana I'm not feeling well. (*Tries to walk to the kitchen.*) I'm thirsty.

Nina Stay there. I'll bring you something.

Nina *starts to walk towards the kitchen.*

Carmen Why did you do it, Mariana?

Mariana Do what?

Carmen Did you want to kill yourself?

Mariana Kill myself?

Carmen Yes, Mariana. Kill yourself.

Mariana No.

Carmen So?

Mariana I don't know. Sometimes I need a bit more to get some sleep. I take one pill, then another, and another, and I keep turning in my bed. I'm gonna ask them to give me stronger ones. Maybe they just gave me the expired ones. Sometimes, I have to take four at a time in order to …

Carmen It wasn't four, Mariana.

Mariana Oh, my head!

Nina Shouldn't we call the doctor?

Carmen Again? And ask Schiller to send him once more just because our "little princess" has a headache? No! (*To* **Mariana**) Get a grip! Do you realize what would've happened? Do you realize?

Nina (*to* **Carmen**) Give her a break! It's over!

Carmen (*to* **Nina**) No! (*To* **Mariana**) What on earth were you thinking?

Mariana Nothing! It was an accident! I overdid it, for God's sake! It can happen to anyone! Why can't it happen to me?

Nina It's all right, it's all right. You overdid it. Nothing wrong with it. This isn't easy. Not easy at all.

Carmen Yeah, sure, she overdid it. She sent two girls to the slaughterhouse.

Mariana What?

Carmen   What? You don't remember that either? Yesterday you told us that you sent two students to the 'Chicken Coop' just because they laughed at you.

Mariana   That's not true.

Nina   Calm down. You shouldn't get excited.

Mariana   I didn't do anything. You have to believe me.

Nina   We believe you.

Mariana   Carmen, you have to believe me, please. (*Pause.*) I . . . I . . .

Nina   Don't say a word. Whatever you've done, it's over.

Mariana   No, it isn't over. 'Cause I was going to turn them in, but they left before Tito and Huaso arrived.

Nina   Even better then, 'cause nothing happened.

Pause

Mariana   I don't know.

Carmen   You don't know? What do you mean?

Mariana   I saw him. Alejandro.

Beat.

Nina   Your Alejandro?

Mariana   He's no longer "my" Alejandro.

Carmen   Wasn't he out of the country?

Mariana   It's possible. Maybe he was in hiding, I don't know. But it was him. I'm positive it was him.

Carmen   When was the last time you saw him?

Mariana   I don't know. More than two years ago.

Nina   You were … alone?

Mariana (*shaking her head "no"*)   In the car, with Huaso and Tito. But I guess they didn't see him.

Carmen   How come? Did they see him or not?

Mariana   I can't remember clearly. (*Thinks.*) At that moment, they were teasing some school girls who were walking on the other sidewalk.

Carmen   Those two are really disgusting!

Nina   Yes, I think they are so mean, because they are so disgusting! Liars …! (*To Mariana*) Did I tell you Huaso gave me a pair of earrings that were supposed to be new but weren't? Does he think I'm so stupid I wouldn't know …

Mariana I don't like it that he's here.

Nina Who?

Mariana Alejandro. They know about our relationship.

Nina And?

Mariana I don't know. I don't think it's a coincidence that I saw him yesterday.

Carmen You've just said that they didn't notice.

Mariana Now. And next time? What will happen next time?

Nina Nothing.

Mariana And those girls? I nearly turned them in just because they laughed at me.

Nina But you didn't.

Mariana Not because I didn't want to, I told you.

Nina Well, if you'd done it, they would have let them go two hours later! Those who get arrested …

Mariana Those who get arrested get that way because of us!

Carmen Does the whole building need to know?

Beat.

Mariana Sorry. I don't feel well.

Nina (*to* **Mariana**) You don't feel well because you haven't eaten. Want some breakfast?

Mariana Not hungry.

Nina But you need to eat something. The doctor said that you had to try to …

Mariana (*raising her voice*) I said I'm not hungry!

Nina Fine. Whatever.

Carmen Maybe, what you need is help.

Mariana Help? Of course I need help.

Carmen See a psychologist. That's why he is there. For a crisis like this one.

Mariana A crisis. I wish it were just a crisis. (*Beat.*) Girls, I can't go on.

Nina We have no choice.

Mariana There's always a choice.

Carmen Which one? To toss down the whole tranquilizer bottle? Mariana, don't start. We know it's not the first time that you panicked. I don't blame you. I understand you. But you need to be more careful. What happened yesterday …

Mariana   What happened yesterday was an accident, I told you. I'm sorry but I'm not like you! It doesn't seem normal for me to do this! It doesn't seem normal to make a living like this!

Nina   Mariana!

Carmen (*to* **Mariana**)   It's either this or be dead. What? Would you rather be dead?

Nina   Girls!

Mariana (*to* **Carmen**)   It's easy for you to say. How long since they've taken you to the streets?

Carmen (*to* **Mariana**)   Don't know.

Mariana   Don't know?

Carmen   Three months.

Mariana   Three months!

Nina   We have an agreement.

Carmen   I know it's hard for you, but the only thing we can do right now, is to keep doing what we do and if we turn somebody in, let it be someone peripheral, who doesn't have too much information. That's what we've always done.

Carmen *takes her things to leave.* **Mariana** *follows her.* **Carmen** *exits.*

Mariana (*to* **Carmen**, *who has already exited*)   What for? So they can electrocute him to death because he has nothing else to say? To be squeezed like a dry lemon and end up being shot or run over by a pickup truck once, twice, even three times, because he had nothing to say?

Nina   Would you shut the fuck up?! We have an agreement. We don't talk about "that" in here.

Mariana   I can't take this anymore. Don't you get it? I can't. Every person I see ends up dead. I've had it!

Nina   It's a matter of time. Just the other day I heard that this is going to end soon, really soon.

Mariana   Don't be naive! This isn't going to end soon. On the contrary, more and more people will be caught every time. When they are finished with party members, they'll start with the sympathizers and when they're through with the sympathizers, they'll go on to anyone.

Nina *exits toward her bedroom the same way* **Carmen** *did before.* **Mariana** *stays, talking into the air alone.*

Mariana   Don't you get it? Yesterday, I was going to turn in two girls just because they were laughing at me. Because they laughed. And how were they supposed not to laugh if they had a crazy woman like me standing in front of them, a stupid look on her face, unable to say a single word?

Carmen *enters.*

Carmen We have to be patient.

Mariana Patient? Patient?

Carmen To keep gaining ground and when they feel they can trust us, we ask them to let us out.

Mariana And meanwhile what? What do we do? What do I do? Tell me! Should I lock myself in my bedroom and wait for the days to go by? Or like Nina, who drinks a whole bottle every time so she can just go to sleep 'cause she can't bear the nightmares? Or like you, Carmen, begging for a phone call with your son once a month just to know if he still remembers who his mother is?

Carmen Don't try to take it out on me, Mariana. I didn't get you in here.

Mariana You know I'm right. For you, things can go on just as they are.

Carmen It's not about that!

Mariana Then what?

Carmen There's a guy stalking my son. Alright? Something can happen to my son at any moment and I'm not with him. And that, makes me feel rotten inside. Every minute away from my son makes me feel rotten. But in the meantime, the only thing I can do is stay here, be patient, and wait.

Mariana For more people to get caught. That's it. Let's stay locked up in here, giving them "peripheral names," 'cause "as long as it's not us …" I wonder, how "peripheral" your son is.

Carmen What's that? A threat?

Mariana A threat? Me? How?

After a minute, **Carmen** *exits while* **Nina** *enters. She goes to the ashtray and looks for a cigarette butt.*

Nina What you said about me isn't true. (*Looks at* **Mariana**.) I can't stand the cold. You know that.

Mariana Don't listen to me.

From the apartment above them, the first notes of the single "Te amaré, te amo y te querré" sung by Mari Trini.[2] **Nina** *looks at the ceiling. Listens for a moment. It's like a balm for forgetting.*

Nina It's three o'clock already?

Pause.

Nina I'd bet anything that right now, my old man is listening to this song. And my mom, of course, is telling him to stop it because it sounds like … like … (*remembers*) a bus driver's music.

Nina *looks at* **Mariana**. *She is staring into the air.*

Nina (*trying to make* **Mariana** *imitate her mother*)   What did she used to say?

Mariana   I don't want to, Nina.

Nina   "*Oh, Valentín, this music sounds like ...*

Mariana   Do you miss them?

Nina   "*... what a bus driver would listen to ...* "

Mariana   I asked you a question.

Nina   No. I can't do it like you. (*Charmingly.*) Do it, just once.

Mariana   I can't, Nina. I need you to answer.

Nina   Of course I miss them. What kind of question is that? When I get out of here, when my life in this apartment comes to an end, I will ...

Mariana   This isn't living.

Nina (*avoiding, looks up to the ceiling*)   Have you ever seen him? I haven't. I know he's a man, 'cause of his voice. Must be the same age as my old man. I picture this guy just like him, sitting on his sofa, playing the same record over and over again ...

Mariana *begins to exit.*

Nina   It is living. It's a much better life than putting up with people coming in at any time, with people coming in to do whatever they like, don't you get it? In this place we only hear normal people, living their normal lives. Like the widow downstairs who spends the whole day yelling at her kids. Or like the neighbor above, who, every blessed Saturday listens to that really corny ... song.

Pause.

Mariana   We're not getting out, Nina. Not alive.

Nina   Don't talk like that.

Mariana   You know it's true.

Nina   If this disgusts you so much, why don't you ask them to transfer you back to the 'Chicken Coop'?

Mariana   At least I'd know where I stand.

Nina   I know quite well where I stand.

Mariana   Over a pile of corpses.

Nina *is about to leave, but* **Mariana** *manages to stop her.*

Mariana (*almost begging*)   Wouldn't you give anything to be able to hug them again, instead of calling them on the phone once a month, never saying a word and only hearing their voices?

Nina To my old man and my mom, I'm dead. And it's better that way.

The telephone rings. **Nina** *is startled.*

Nina D'you see? D'you see? They are all over us. They heard everything we said. (**Mariana** *moves to pick up the phone.*) No, don't … or yes, tell them … tell them this isn't serious. Please, Mariana, tell them you don't know what you're saying, that I have nothing to do with this.

Mariana Would you please calm down? What, do you think there are microphones here?

Mariana *answers the phone.*

Mariana Hello? Yes? (. . .) Berta? (*Looks at* **Nina**) Schiller is that you? (. . .) Who is it? (. . .) Sorry, could you please repeat your name? (*Listens. Covers the receiver. To* **Nina**) It's a man, Ignacio Martínez, says he wants to talk to you.

Nina (*happy, almost inaudible*) He called me!

Mariana Who is it?

Nina *takes the phone from* **Mariana**.

Nina Hello? Hi, it's me, . . . Berta. What a surprise! I didn't think you would call me … (. . .) Sorry, sir, but … (*Flirting*) I don't know you well enough to address you in such a familiar way … (…) Tomorrow? Where? (. . .) If it doesn't bother you, sir, I would (…) If it doesn't bother you, Ignacio, I'd rather stay at home, I have a cold (*coughs*), but if you want, you can drop by my apartment.

Mariana *tries to pull the telephone from her.* Nina *stops her.*

Nina (*To Ignacio, staring directly to* **Mariana**) Can you write something down? Marcoleta seventy-seven, twelfth tower, fifth floor, apartment "C". (…) Right there. (…) See you tomorrow. (*Hangs up the phone*)

Mariana Who is this guy?

Nina The one I met at the restaurant.

Mariana Why did you tell him to drop by?

Nina I don't know, thought it was safer than going out.

Carmen *enters.*

Carmen Somebody called?

Nina No.

Mariana Yes.

Carmen *looks at each of them.*

Nina Wrong number.

The doorbell rings. The three women are on alert. **Carmen** *approaches the door and looks through the eye hole. She locks the security chain and slightly opens the door.*

Carmen Yes? What is it? Now? Just a moment.

Carmen *closes the door to unlock the chain and then opens the door again. Goes out. After a few seconds, she comes back.*

Carmen Get dressed. We have to go out in five minutes.

Nina Where are they taking us?

Carmen They found a house. We need to identify some bodies. There are detainees too.

Mariana Detainees? Who are they?

Carmen I don't know. They didn't tell me.

Nina Why are they taking us?

Carmen We need to identify some bodies, I just told you.

Nina But, why us? They never take us to identify bodies. That's not part of our …

Carmen I don't know! That's all he told me. What do you want? This seems strange to me too. Get dressed. Quickly.

They exit. Lights off.

Scene Four

Same room. The place is in darkness. After a few seconds, the three women enter. They do so in silence. They are exhausted. **Nina** *carries a bottle of Pisco. They let themselves fall on the chairs.*

Nina   Felt like I was going to puke my guts out. (**Carmen** *looks at her.*) I'd never been on a helicopter.

Mariana *takes her purse.* **Nina** *and* **Carmen** *watch her while* **Mariana** *takes out a handkerchief and cleans her nose.*

Nina (*while pouring a bit of the liquor in a glass*)   It's hot in here, isn't it? (*Pause.*) Should I open the windows?

Carmen *makes an expression of indifference. Che appears and jumps over* **Carmen**'*s lap. She screams.*

Carmen   Get it off me! Get it off me! Take it away! Throw it from the balcony or I'll do it myself! Piece of shit!

Nina *grabs Che away from* **Carmen** *and exits with him.*

Nina (*off-stage*)   Here is your milk and your bone. Eat now. (*Enters.*)

Carmen   I don't get how you can feed him after what we …

Nina   What do you want? To starve him to death?

Nina *pours a glass of Pisco and offers it to* **Mariana**.

Mariana   What is it?

Nina   Drink it.

Mariana   Where did you get it?

Nina   Huaso gave it to me. It'll make you feel better.

Mariana   He stole it from the house, didn't he? (*Pushes it aside.*) I don't want it.

Nina   I'll leave it here.

Nina *returns to her place. Pours herself a glass and another one for* **Carmen**.

Mariana   The good thing was he wasn't all bloody … he looked like he was sleeping, right? If only he hadn't had his eyes wide open, staring at the sky full of stars. You can see so many stars outside Santiago! I had forgotten. I almost had the feeling he was smiling. As if he was going to tell me something. (*Pause. Looks at* **Carmen**.) In which car did they take him? Did they take him? Carmen!

Carmen   I don't know, Mariana.

Mariana   You were there too. Who did he leave with?

Carmen   What does it matter?

Mariana   Someone has to close his eyes. I don't know if I did. I was going to, but I got distracted looking at the stars and afterwards … I don't know if I managed to close his eyes.

Carmen   You did.

Mariana   Yes?

Next, **Mariana** *lifts up her glass to make a toast.*

Mariana   To Alejandro. (*Pours the content of the glass directly onto the rug.*)

Nina   Mariana …

Mariana   What's wrong? Somebody's got to make a toast for the dead. He won't even have a funeral. He'll surely be thrown into the sea.

Nina   Mariana …

Mariana   Or onto the Andes. Who's gonna find him there?

Nina   Enough, please!

Mariana   No trace of him. Or the others. As if they had never existed.

Nina   Will you please shut up?!

Carmen   Let her talk. She needs to let it all out. If you don't like it, go to your room.

Nina   I don't want to.

Carmen   Why? Are you afraid a ghost will come and haunt you?

Carmen *drinks a large sip of Pisco.*

Mariana   He said what he most loved about me were my eyes. My eyes! And it was these eyes that killed him! (*Looks at* **Nina** *and* **Carmen**.) As if it was the first time I'd ever been out. I tried, I swear, I tried not to, but I couldn't help it. As soon as I saw him, I started trembling like a leaf.

Carmen   Someone else got him caught. You said that neither Huaso nor Tito had seen him.

Mariana *looks at them. Then slightly shakes her head no.*

Mariana   We were supposed to return to headquarters, but Huaso drove around the block with the excuse of looking for a pharmacy. He stopped the car and got out. It wasn't more than a minute. Came back laughing. Said he had remembered he needed to call his mother to wish her a happy birthday. And Tito said: "But you haven't got a mom." And Huaso continued laughing.

Pause.

Nina   You couldn't know …

Carmen   It wasn't your fault.

Mariana Whose then? (*Nobody answers.*) Whose?! Tell me! If I hadn't seen him, he'd be alive. But I saw him! What a party those sons of bitches must be having! How happy Schiller and the rest must be! Did you see the satisfaction on their faces? Did you see it? As if ... as if they had won the lottery!

Carmen *takes a medicine bottle out of her purse. Then, takes a pill. Offers it to* **Mariana**.

Carmen Take this.

Mariana What is it?

Carmen It'll be good for you.

Mariana Do you know what'll be good for me?

Mariana *stands up. Crosses the room and takes* **Carmen***'s purse. Sticks her hand in it.*

Carmen Don't do it, Mariana. We'll call a doctor again, they will pump your stomach and you'll wake up again. Give me those pills.

Mariana *throws the pill bottle to her.*

Mariana Take your pills! I don't want them!

Mariana *grabs a bunch of keys and walks towards the door.*

Carmen If you step out that door, they kill us.

Mariana Tell them you didn't know anything.

Nina That doesn't matter. Even if they realize we don't know anything they'll need to get even with someone. If it isn't with you, it's gonna be us.

Mariana No. That's not true. You ... you are different.

Carmen So different that they won't put a bullet in our heads for letting you escape? No, Mariana, we're not different. We are useful. But if you step out that door, we won't be any longer.

Nina So much. We've done so much. I mean ... (*Shakes her head*) I don't know what I mean, but we are better each time. No, not better. Further away, much higher.

Carmen We can't give up now. We have to keep going till the end.

Mariana There's no end, Carmen. This is an endless pit.

Nina (*near the phone, picking up the receiver*) Give the keys to Carmen, Mariana.

Mariana Nina ...

Nina Give her the keys, you little piece of shit! Or I call headquarters right now. They're right across from us, they'll be here in no time.

Mariana Are you really so fond of that guy?

Nina It's got nothing to do with him. Give her the keys.

Mariana Really? You'd do anything to get that guy into your bed ...

Carmen (*to* **Nina**) What's she talking about?

Nina No idea! Give her the keys!

Mariana No idea? (*To* **Carmen**) Didn't she tell you we're having a guest tomorrow?

Carmen *looks at* **Nina** *waiting for an explanation.*

Nina He called.

Carmen Who?

Nina Ignacio. The man I met in the ...

Carmen Yes, I know who Ignacio is. And?

Nina I invited him to come over, tomorrow.

Carmen Didn't I tell you that if he called, you should tell him he had a wrong number?

Nina I couldn't.

Carmen So, are you stupid or what? How on earth could you invite a stranger in here? What if he's armed?

Nina He won't be. Not everybody wants to kill us ...

Carmen Give me the telephone.

Nina What for?

Carmen I'll tell Schiller to arrest him if he shows up.

Nina No, please, don't do that.

Carmen Don't you see? It's too dangerous. You know nothing about him!

Nina But I want to see him! Please! I know I don't know him, but he must be a good guy ... He's gotta be a nice guy!

Carmen Really? A married man coming here to have sex with another woman? Yeah, sure, he must be an angel.

Nina Please, don't ... don't do anything. I don't want him to get arrested.

Mariana I didn't want Alejandro to be caught either.

Nina (*to* **Mariana**) It's not the same! It's not the same! (*Almost crying. To* **Carmen**) Please, I beg you, don't tell them anything.

Carmen That guy will not set foot in this apartment.

Nina I'm begging you ...

Carmen (*threatening her*) Should I call?

A beat.

Nina (*gives* **Carmen** *the telephone*)   Okay, okay. He won't set a single foot in this apartment.

Carmen   It's for your own good.

Nina (*crying. To* **Mariana**)   Happy? Are you happy now?

Mariana   I'll be happy when I get out of this place.

Carmen   Mariana, cut it out. I know it's been a rough day, especially for you, but …

Mariana   Rough? Rough? It's hell. I killed him, Carmen. I killed him! What do I do now? How on earth do I go on? He was the only thing I had promised myself not to betray and I did.

Carmen   I'm sorry, Mariana, believe me I'm truly sorry. But there's nothing we can do. Alejandro is already dead.

Mariana   Yes! We can, it's a matter of wanting to! The three of us together!

Nina   What?

Mariana   We'll have no guards tomorrow.

Carmen   Forget it.

Nina   What's she talking about?

Mariana   What time do they call tomorrow?

Carmen   You're not thinking, Mariana.

Nina (*insists*)   What is she talking about?

Mariana   What time do they call tomorrow?

Carmen   At ten.

Mariana   After we talk to them, we leave.

Nina   Leave? We can't even go to the shop on the corner to get bread by ourselves, and we're just leaving?

Carmen   It's suicide.

Mariana   No! We can go to the church. The priest, the one who helps the widows, what's his name?

Carmen   Father Graciano; but that piece of shit just wants to see our faces in court.

Nina   They would find us, and, even if we managed to escape, how are we supposed to make a living? As whores? Begging on the streets? Think—this, at least, is a refuge.

Carmen   I'm not alone. I have a son.

Mariana   Your sister can keep taking care of him like she has done till now.

Carmen Not anymore. I asked Schiller to … let me bring Matías to live with me. (*Beat.*) Here.

Nina When?

Carmen A few days ago. (*To* **Mariana**) Before you swallowed that entire pill bottle.

Nina When is he coming?

Carmen I don't know yet. He told me it would be alright as long as you two agreed. There's a guy stalking him.

Mariana You want to bring the kid here? To this apartment?

Carmen He's my son.

Nina And what are we? His godmothers?

Carmen I'm not asking you to understand what it means to be a mother.

Nina I am supposed to understand you and accept you bringing your child in here, and on top of that I have to live a nun's life? Tell me Carmen, why don't you go straight to hell?

Carmen It isn't the same. My son is not dangerous.

Nina It's not about that, Carmen. I don't want a kid running around in here. Period. End of discussion.

Carmen Even in jail women are allowed to live with their sons.

Nina But this isn't a jail.

Mariana No?

Nina No. Whatever it is, it's our home.

Carmen Just think. A kid around here can make this a bit … easier.

Mariana How can this life be easier, Carmen?! How?! Giving people up during the day and reading "Little Red Riding Hood" to your kid at night?

Nina You can't do this to us, Carmen.

Carmen I don't want him to be kidnapped and killed! Is that so hard to understand?

Nina Sorry.

Carmen Nina …

Nina Ah! Look how fast my real name comes to your head! No. If you were so eager to play "house" with your son, you should've opened your mouth before coming to live with us.

Carmen I had no choice. None of us did.

Mariana There's always a choice, Carmen. There always is.

Carmen (*To* **Mariana**)   Stop it! Enough! I don't want to listen to you anymore!

Carmen, *in long strides, goes to the door and holds it wide open.*

Carmen   I don't give a shit! If you want to go, go!

Mariana *looks at the door. Doesn't move.*

Carmen   What're you waiting for? Go!

Mariana *walks toward the open door. Stays in the doorstep.*

Carmen   It isn't so easy, is it?

Mariana *moves away from the door.* **Carmen** *closes it.*

Carmen   Good night.

Carmen *takes her purse and exits towards her bedroom.* **Mariana** *can't even look at* **Nina**, *who's staring at her. Just takes her purse and leaves towards her bedroom.* **Nina**, *alone, takes the bottle of Pisco. Sits in the armchair. Drinks all that's left in the bottle. Turns off the light. Dark.*

Scene Five

Nina *is on her knees searching for Che.* **Carmen** *enters.*

Nina Have you seen Che?

Carmen Why should I have seen your cat?

Nina He disappeared. I've been calling him to give him his breakfast but he hasn't shown up.

Carmen Maybe he's in the apartment next door.

Nina (*shaking her head*) He never goes over there. (*Beat.*) Maybe you're right. Maybe he couldn't bear it anymore and he threw himself over the balcony. I didn't get to say goodbye.

Carmen Did you look over the balcony?

Nina I can't bring myself to look.

Pause.

Carmen Nina, we have to talk. What happened yesterday—

Nina (*interrupting*) I've got nothing against your kid. It's just that I don't like them. Never have. They've got that look like … like they're not hiding anything, you know what I mean?

Carmen (*nodding*) Ok. We'll talk later.

Pause.

Nina What're you looking for?

Carmen My glasses.

Nina You wore them yesterday.

Carmen Not those. The real ones. Adolfo wants me to … (*Corrects herself*) Schiller wants me to start working on his memoir. I can't see anything without my glasses.

Nina You're not teaching anymore?

Carmen I don't know. Don't think so.

Nina I thought you liked teaching. That you and I would go on teaching …

Carmen I'll do what he orders me to do. If he wants me to teach, I'll teach. If he wants me to write his memoir, then I'll write his memoir. If he wants me to serve him a cup of coffee every fifteen minutes, I will serve him a cup of coffee every fifteen minutes. (*Pause.*) And you? Are you planning on going to work dressed like that?

Nina I'm waiting till she comes out of the bathroom.

Carmen Who?

Nina   Mariana.

Carmen   I was in the bathroom.

They look at each other for one second. Then, both of them exit rapidly towards the bathroom and other bedrooms. A second later, they both enter.

Carmen   Why didn't you tell me she was not in her bedroom?!

Nina   I thought she was in the bathroom! What? Am I her bodyguard?

Carmen *takes her purse and throws its contents onto the rug looking for the keys.*

Nina   She did it. How? When?

Carmen (*barely audible*)   I don't know.

Carmen *stands up. Goes towards a spot in the room and stops. Then, she goes to another and stops again. It's as if all of a sudden, she's lost her place in the world.*

Carmen   We don't have to be afraid. We've done nothing wrong.

Nina   When they realize she isn't here, they'll take it out on us. (*Looks at* **Carmen**, *terrified.*) On me.

Carmen   Don't say that.

Nina   What? Do you think Schiller is going to let them lay a finger on you?

Carmen   It isn't my fault.

Nina   Nobody likes me. That's all.

The telephone rings. **Carmen** *picks up.*

Carmen   Hello? Yes? (…) It's me … (…) Commander! How are you doing? (…) May I know why? (…) No, not at all. It's just that we are not ready yet. Give us fifteen minutes. (*Hangs up.*)

Was it Schiller? (**Carmen** *nods.*) And?

Carmen   They're coming to pick us up now, in fifteen minutes.

Nina (*puzzled*)   It isn't even nine. We still have more than an hour.

Carmen   That's what he said.

Nina   I don't get it. Why this change of plans?

Carmen   He didn't say. He gave me no explanation. The only thing we have to do is be ready 'cause they'll be picking us up in fifteen minutes.

Nina   And Mariana? (**Carmen** *doesn't answer.*) Carmen! I asked you a question! What do we do about Mariana?

Carmen   I don't know! I don't know! I don't know!

Carmen *bends over in pain. She holds her stomach.*

Nina They're going to send us back to the 'Chicken Coop' right? (*As if they had any choice.*) No. I can't go back in there. The things they yelled at us … I understood that we weren't going back in there. That once we were here, working … (*Gets closer to* **Carmen**.) Fuck, Carmen, that's what they told us!

Carmen The three of us together, Nina! The three of us or none.

Nina Wait! They don't know anything yet. When they come, we go down, just you and me. We say Mariana is in the bathroom. When they see she isn't coming, they'll come up and look for her and then they'll realize she's missing. The only thing we have to do is pretend we know nothing and look surprised when they tell us she's missing.

Carmen (*looks at her*)   They already know, Nina.

Nina What do you mean, "they already know"?

Carmen Why do you think they are picking us up earlier?

Nina Did he tell you that?

Carmen No need to. We let her escape. It was our responsibility and she escaped from us.

Nina I'm sorry, Carmen, but she isn't my responsibility. You're in charge of the keys, not me. There's a reason why they gave you the keys instead of me.

Carmen How do I know it wasn't you who let her escape?

Nina Why would I do that?

Carmen I don't know. Weren't you very good friends? As a child, Mariana spent a lot of time in your house. You were like sisters. Must be hard to say "no" to a sister. How do I know that she didn't ask you to shut your mouth while she escaped in front of you?

Nina I did nothing, Carmen. I swear. Nothing.

Carmen I'd like to believe you, Nina.

In an outburst, **Nina** *takes the telephone and puts it on* **Carmen**'s *lap.*

Nina Tell him. Tell Schiller what happened. Tell him she stole the keys away from you when you were sleeping and escaped without us realizing.

Carmen What for?

Nina So they know we have nothing to do with this.

Carmen Do you know what they would do to her if they find her?

Nina I don't care. It's her problem.

Carmen If I call Schiller and tell him … but, do you realize what this means?

Nina Call him, Carmen! I told you: I won't go back to the 'Chicken Coop'!

Carmen *starts dialing a telephone number. Somebody knocks at the door.*

Mariana (*offstage*)   Girls! Are you in there?

Carmen *gets close to the door. Puts on the chain and opens only as much as it can.*

Carmen   Are you by yourself?

Mariana (*offstage*)   Yes.

Carmen *closes the door, unlocks the chain and then opens the door. Takes* **Mariana** *by one arm and forcefully pushes her into the apartment.*

Nina   How could you, Mariana? How could you do this to us! (*She jumps on* **Mariana** *and tries to hit her but* **Carmen** *stops her*) Selfish! Motherfucker! Do you realize, you stupid bitch? Do you realize what they would've done to us if they found out you were gone?

Mariana   I went to see Father Graciano. As soon as he saw me, he recognized me. He didn't even want to talk to me. He treated me badly. Even tried to kick me out of the church, but I didn't move. I asked him to help us in exchange for information. And he accepted.

Carmen   What?

Mariana   The only thing we have to do is testify in front of some lawyers, point out some meeting points, clandestine centers …

Nina   What for? So that they can hang us out to dry in court?

Mariana   He gave me his word. If we cooperate, they'll leave us in peace.

Nina   Leave us in peace? Yeah, they're gonna shoot us in the middle of the street.

Mariana   No, they would provide asylum for us in an embassy. The Swedish embassy probably because the priest they killed was Swedish. And then, to Sweden.

Nina   Sweden? They'll send us to Sweden?

Mariana   Yes, Nina.

Nina   I know nothing about Sweden. Is it cold there?

Mariana   I don't know, Nina, how could I know. I guess so. And hot too maybe. Come on, pick up your stuff, we can't carry too many things.

Nina   Now?

Mariana   He's downstairs waiting for us in a car.

Carmen   So hard. I worked so hard. The only thing I wanted was a way out. I dreamed that at some point, I would be able to take his hand and walk him to school. Just that. And when that happened, I would stay there, standing next to the janitor during the whole class day. And when he came out and saw me, his face would light up 'cause I'd be standing there, where I never am. And he would introduce me to his classmates as his mom. And then, I would buy him some candy, some popcorn … the things they sell outside school! And after that, (*as if she could see it happening in front of her*) I would hold his hand and we would both walk together back to our house. Like everyone does. (*The glimpse of a smile disappears from her face.*) I believed in that.

Mariana   And it will happen. Didn't you hear what I've just told you?

Carmen   I heard you, Mariana, I heard you perfectly. But you know none of that's going to happen. You know what they do to traitors.

Mariana   They don't have to know anything.

Carmen   They already know! They know everything!

Pause.

Mariana   You told them.

Carmen   As if we needed to.

Mariana   So? I don't get it. Tell me, what's happening?

Carmen   Tell her, Nina, tell her what's happening.

Nina   Before you came, Schiller called. They will pick us up in fifteen minutes. He didn't say why, only that we've got to be ready. (*To* **Carmen**, *as a last hope*) Maybe it's about something else.

Carmen   If they send us back to the 'Chicken Coop,' consider yourself lucky.

Mariana   Let's not waste any time. These fifteen minutes can save our lives! (*To both*) What're you waiting for?

Carmen   I'm not going anywhere. I've got a child. Did you forget that?

Mariana   And I told him about your son. From here we'll go and pick him up next.

Carmen *looks at* **Mariana** *for one second.*

Carmen   And my sister? And my brother in law? And my nephews? Can I bring all of them to the embassy? (*Looks at Nina.*) And Nina? Can she take her parents with her? (*Mariana doesn't answer.*) Tell me, Mariana! Did you tell him about Nina's parents?

Mariana   Let's not waste time right now …

Carmen   Did you talk about them, yes or no? No, right? Because you are only thinking of saving your own skin. But if I put one single foot in that embassy, do you know how cruel they would be to my sister, to her family?

Mariana   I'm not thinking of my own skin, Carmen! I'm thinking of all of those other skins we'll save if we stop collaborating with those pieces of shit! Right now, downstairs there's a man risking his own life to save ours and many others. That doesn't count?

Carmen I didn't ask him to do anything for me! (*Pause.*) If you wanna leave, then leave. I'll take my chances.

Mariana No. The three of us or nothing. Those are Father Graciano's terms.

Carmen (*with a defeated smile*) We are still a "package".

Mariana (*desperate, she turns to* **Nina**) Nina …

Nina I don't know, Mariana, I don't know. It's too complicated. If we plan it better, with more time, we can …

Mariana We don't have any time. If we don't go down in five minutes, Father Graciano will leave. Do you get that? He leaves. This is our last chance. If we don't go down in five minutes, he'll think that I lied to him. I know it's too little time, but just think a bit, it could work. And if it does, we're going to be free and not just that. We'll be able to repair at least some of the damage we've caused.

Nina Don't say that! They make us do it! We have no choice!

Mariana Now we do. Now we have one, Nina. We can choose.

Carmen If we can choose, I choose to stay.

Mariana Carmen …

Carmen What's the use of a dead mother to my son?

Mariana What's the use of an absent mother to your son?

Carmen At some point, this will come to an end.

Mariana And you think that, at that point, you'll be free? When their party is over, and it will be over, what will happen to us? They're gonna kill us, Carmen. And if *they* don't do it, the *others* will. And even if that does not happen, we'll be looking over our shoulders every second of our lives. You think you'll be able to go out and buy bread like everyone else? That you will be able to walk with your son to school like everyone else? No, Carmen, because none of us have the right to have a life. Not you with your son, (*to Nina*) nor you with your parents. We will go down into history as traitors.

Carmen What do I care about history.

Mariana Because it hasn't happened yet, Carmen. But at some point it will, and what are we going to do then? Supposing we get to be alive at the end of this nightmare, what are we going to do? Will they believe our tears of repentance?

Beat.

The three women look at each other. **Mariana** *approaches the door slowly and opens it.* **Carmen** *and* **Nina** *look at it as if it were opening for the first time. The bulb hanging from the ceiling is having surges and dips in voltage. The three of them look at it. It happens once more. The women look at each other. The voltage dips until reaching complete and total darkness. End of play.*

Notes

1 The 'Chicken Coop' (*el gallinero*) is a euphemism for a clandestine torture center during the Chilean dictatorship.
2 Mari Trini (1947-2009) was Spanish singer and songwriter.

Hilda Peña:

Unconventional Motherhood, Grief, and Subjectivity

Coca Duarte

English translation
Constanza Brieba

Hilda Peña by Isidora Stevenson Bordeu portrays a woman who has suffered the loss of her son in a police shooting marked by excessive force following a bank robbery in Santiago, Chile, committed by the armed militant group Lautaro in 1993.[1] The play unfolds through Hilda's narration, interweaving memories of her relationship with the boy who became her son after she took him into her home, with the moment she learns of his death and how this transforms her life. Hilda recalls that she never wanted children, nor did she have a partner—she lived peacefully in her solitude. However, a boy who lived on the street gradually caught her attention. She recounts how she went from offering him tea and bread to inviting him to stay in her home—how he first slept on the floor, then got his own room, went to school, completed military service, got a job, and how his girlfriend eventually moved in with them. These events unfolded almost unnoticed, naturally, despite the fact that he was not her biological son.

On the day of the O'Higgins Bank robbery, carried out by the Lautaro group, the couple had gone out to exchange a pair of pants Hilda had bought for her son's girlfriend as a Christmas gift. While preparing lunch, Hilda sees a bag on the news that had been left behind in the bank, and, although she doesn't want to believe it's the same one, the police visit her that afternoon to confirm that both her son and his girlfriend were killed in the shooting. This woman, who had never wanted children, cannot come to terms with losing him and asks the cemetery workers to leave the niche where he is buried open. In exchange for oral sex, they allow her to enter every day to see her son's body. Hilda needs to observe this body, to recognize the moment it emptied her son, to study the stages of its decomposition—and toward the end of the narrative, she asks a healer to wake him up before he rots.

Although the play is not intended as a documentary, it is set against the historical event known as the Apoquindo Case or the Apoquindo Massacre. After the robbery of the O'Higgins Bank by the Lautaro Youth Movement, officers of the Chilean police force, the Carabineros, surrounded a passenger bus in which the assailants were fleeing. Witnesses claimed that, once surrounded, the members of the Lautaro group disposed of their weapons and were willing to surrender. However, the police response was to fire indiscriminately into the bus. As a result of the shooting, three of the assailants and three passengers died at the scene, and twelve others were wounded. The actions of the Carabineros are considered a human rights violation due to the disproportionate use of force and the killing of both members of the movement and innocent victims.[2]

The case occurred in October 1993, just a few years after the return to democracy following the civil-military dictatorship of Augusto Pinochet, during a period known as "the transition to democracy." This period was marked by the persistence of key authoritarian elements in Chilean political life, such as the appointment of Augusto Pinochet as Commander-in-Chief of the Army and the lack of reforms to the 1980 Constitution, which had been created under the dictatorship. These conditions enabled the continuation of violent practices similar to those of the dictatorship, such as abuses of power by the elite and the police. From the perspective of social coexistence, there is a tension between the fear of reliving the past and the need to address unresolved conflicts. However, "in the name of governability, the emphasis is placed on a possible future at the expense of a past of conflict,"[3] leading to a politics of consensus aimed at achieving balance and social peace. In this context, addressing the human rights violations committed during the dictatorship is perceived as an unresolved issue—one that must, nevertheless, be approached gradually so as not to disrupt the balance achieved among political forces.

From the perspective of its dramaturgical strategies, *Hilda Peña* can be understood within what I define as *Narrativity*, understood as "a contemporary tendency in which the performer does not enact actions on stage but rather narrates, evoking past events, revealing his inner world, and directly addressing the audience in an ambiguous enunciative situation that does not construct a fictional time/space, but rather alludes to the here and now of the stage/audience relationship."[4] I understand *Narrativity* in theatre as emerging within the context of a broader questioning of representation—and specifically of history—giving rise to the vindication of memory discourses and the emergence of testimony as an alternative to traditional language operations used both in the social sciences and in art. *Narrativity* draws on the communicative agreement of testimony—that is, the encounter between the witness and their listener—while working from within fiction, with the audience positioned as direct recipients of a confession made by a character. This approach has the capacity to highlight the uniqueness of a subjective experience that has been excluded from official narratives, and to create an intimate encounter between the audience and the reality portrayed.

In *Hilda Peña*, Stevenson Bordeu uses language as if it were poetic verse, establishing rhythm and linguistic fragmentation to give voice to her protagonist: Hilda speaks to us in the first person, recounting her experiences and gradually revealing the mechanisms and details that shape her. It is through this unfolding that her singularity, complexity, and contradictions emerge. When she appears before us, we understand that she is a survivor and that loss is the place she now inhabits.

I . . . I was not like this before.
(Silence.)
I was different before.
I mean, I was always skinny. Always had all my teeth.
But I didn't bite my nails.[5]

Grief has left a mark on her body, transforming her forever, which in her work at the beauty salon has relegated her to a lesser role.

I didn't bite my nails before.
They were long, like in the dream.

> In the salon I worked, washed hair, waxed, and cleaned.
> Now that my hands are like this they don't let me. Because of the image. The beauty salon. I just clean.
> The girls tell me not to bite them, but I can't. I don't know.
> In any case, it's not that I'm hungry.[6]

This silent gesture reveals the character's present anguish—the need to mutilate herself in order to dull another pain. As the author recounts, this was the first image that inspired the play: "I see, at the door of a hair salon . . . a woman smoking . . . and her nails were very bitten . . . the first question I asked that image was: why would someone mutilate their body like that? And . . . it seemed so logical, inflicting one kind of pain to cover another."[7] The character's journey—and the one we follow as spectators throughout her story—mirrors Stevenson Bordeu's initial inquiry: a descent into the unveiling of a mystery. Who is she? What happened to her to bring her to this point? What more will she reveal about her grief?

We come to understand all of this through what Hilda herself shares from her unique perspective. Hilda has no shame in expressing opinions that go against conventional norms, and in that sense, she resists the social expectations imposed on women, such as having a partner and children: "I never wanted children ... I don't like babies ... It sounds bad but it's true ... We don't all have to be born. What for? No shortage of people."[8] "Easier that way. More practical. Them with their men drinking beer and their children they have to bathe on Sunday night ... Them with their work at work and their work at home. Them with their lives, and me with mine."[9] However, despite these convictions and her comfort with solitude, she encounters the boy who would later become her son.

> I always see those kids and I don't care.
> That sounds ugly. But it's true.
> I mean I look at them, I feel sorry and move on.
> That's not caring.
> Caring is doing something.
> Moving on is not caring.
> I don't know.
> *(Pause.)*
> They sleep near the City Hall.
> I don't know, this one mattered to me.[10]

A new kind of motherhood is thus constructed—one born from the meeting of two lonely people, not based on convention: "So that's how he stayed. And became my son. (Pause). He was my son. I don't know if I was his mother. I never asked him."[11] Although not biological, Hilda's unique form of motherhood seems aligned with the image of the Latin American woman who, alone and through great effort, manages to raise her children. This echoes the description by anthropologist Sonia Montecino of the family model that has prevailed in Chile since colonial times, shaped by mestizo culture: "the mother-centered family," where "the core unit is a mother and her children"[12]; "children made vulnerable by the absence of the father or of both parents."[13]

2 Hilda Peña (Paula Zúñiga) grieves for her deceased son in *Hilda Peña* by Isidora Stevenson Bordeu, directed by Aliocha de la Sotta, Centro Cultural Matucana 100, Santiago, Chile, 2014. (Photo: © Diego Carrasco)

Perhaps that is why Hilda's way of experiencing motherhood feels so familiar in its excess—because it is centered entirely on her son, regardless of the fact that he is not hers biologically or what others might think when she takes him into her home: "The girls told me not to. That something could happen to me. I wasn't afraid. I didn't know him from before, they said."[14] Once she decides to protect him, her way of expressing affection extends even beyond his death. She grieves in a way that is consistent with the person she has revealed herself to be: she refuses to accept the loss of her son or their physical separation. She is capable of carrying out an extraordinary act in order to continue seeing him even after he has been buried, and in her need to soothe the pain of loss, she remains attentive to the possible decomposition of his body, ultimately seeking out a healer to bring him back from the dead.

Hilda's complexity lies in the contradictions and paradoxes that define her: she is a hairdresser, but one who no longer works with clients; she is a mother, though not biologically. She performs a tremendous act of generosity by taking in a street child as her own, yet she struggles to express her love: "Sometimes he looked sad, as if thinking. Quiet. I so wanted to hold him, to cuddle him. I didn't. I couldn't."[15] In my view, the contradiction that gives the most meaning to her story is that, despite having always avoided attachments and emotional bonds, she becomes a victim of loss: "I didn't want a child and suddenly I had this one."[16] This paradox keeps us in a state of constant tension, one with no easy resolution, and leads us to wonder whether it was worth leaving behind her solitude, only to return to it now through a sense of emptiness she had never known before. At the same time, it raises broader questions about emotional bonds—and the benefits and risks they carry.

This contradiction also drives her to speak to us, as if trying to make sense of the details that give meaning to her experience, though without success. Hilda reveals the knots of her pain gradually and in fragments, weaving together past and present events in an effort to untangle them. However, her aim is not to determine whether her son was actually involved with the Lautaro group or to uncover the specific cause of his death; instead, her reflection centers on this paradox of emotional bonds—something profoundly human.

Returning to the narrative structure of Stevenson Bordeu's theatrical text, the story is intimately woven around a journey that, as previously mentioned, reveals Hilda's identity, her unconventional view of the world, and her deepest secret: her refusal to separate from her son's body and her attempt to bring him back to life. It also offers us a glimpse into the particular details of the encounter between two lonely people, intertwining past and present events to reconstruct a unique relationship between a mother and her son. Through this narrative, which sensitively delves into the subjective experience of a woman facing loss, we are confronted with the inherent conflict of human emotions. Ultimately, by portraying the pain of this indirect victim of police violence rooted in the dictatorship, the play allows us to access a significant period of Chile's recent history from a unique and intimate perspective.

Notes

1. The Lautaro Youth Movement, an armed organization and youth guerrilla movement during Chile's military dictatorship, named after Lautaro, the leader of the indigenous resistance against the Spanish, was founded in 1982.
2. V.V.A.A., Los tribunales militares y el caso Apoquindo (Compilation of Press Articles), Archivo Chile, 2024.
3. Lechner, Norbert, and Pedro Güell. "Construcción Social de las Memorias en la Transición Chilena." Archivo Chile, 1998, p. 1.
4. Duarte, Coca. *Escribir la escena, trazar el presente: estrategias dramatúrgicas del teatro chileno 2007-2017*. Editorial Cuartopropio, 2023, p. 134.
5. Stevenson Bordeu, Isidora. *Hilda Peña*, in *Dramaturgas Chilenas: Plays by Chilean Female Writers in the Early 21st Century*, edited by Coca Duarte, Anne García-Romero and Inés Stranger, Methuen Drama, 2025, p. 71.
6. Ibid., 71.
7. Stevenson Bordeu, Isidora. Personal Interview. 19 October 2023.
8. Stevenson, *Hilda Peña*, p. 72.
9. Ibid., 73.
10. Ibid., 74.
11. Ibid., 77.
12. Montecino, Sonia. *Madres y huachos: alegorías del mestizaje chileno*. Sudamericana, 1991, p. 54.
13. Ibid., 61.
14. Stevenson, *Hilda Peña*, p. 75.
15. Ibid., 76.
16. Ibid., 78.

Further Reading

Brncić, Carolina. "El monólogo y la ficcionalización del testimonio en el teatro chileno actual: *Hilda Peña*." *Revista de humanidades* no. 49, 2024, pp. 313-39.

Duarte, Coca. *Escribir la escena, trazar el presente: estrategias dramatúrgicas del teatro chileno 2007-2017*. Editorial Cuartopropio, 2023.

Grumann Sölter, Andrés and María de la Luz Hurtado, editors. *XVI Muestra Nacional de Dramaturgia 2014: Prácticas creativas, discusiones, registros*. Santiago, Consejo Nacional de la Cultura y las Artes, 2015.

Rojo, Sara. "Memoria del horror: *Las brutas*, de Juan Radrigán; *Hans Pozo*, de Luis Barrales; e *Hilda Peña*, de Isidora Stevenson." *Revista Culturas* no. 13, 2019, pp. 107-18.

Hilda Peña

Isidora Stevenson Bordeu

English translation
Constanza Brieba

Isidora Stevenson Bordeu, born in Los Ángeles, Chile in 1981, is a playwright, director, and educator. She received a degree in theatre and acting at the Universidad Arcis. As a playwright, she has developed numerous plays since 2012, including *Campo* (2013), *Hilda Peña* (2014), *Réplica* (2018), *Informe de una mujer que arde* (*Report from a woman who burns*, 2021), *Soledad Escobar* (2020), *Niebla* (*Fog*, 2021), *Mi corazón es un ancla* (*My heart is an anchor*, 2021), *Fin* (*End*, 2022), and *Amanda Labarca* (2023), among others. Her play *Hilda Peña* won entry into the 2014 16th National Playwriting Festival in Chile and received the City of Santiago 2015 Playwriting Prize. Her play *Réplica* won the City of Santiago 2018 Playwriting Prize. As a director, she founded the company Teatro La Nacional, where she has directed numerous works. She has also directed plays by Luis Barrales, Sergio Gómez, Manuela Oyarzún, and Carla Zúñiga. As an educator, she has taught at Universidad Academia Humanismo Cristiano, Instituto Arcos, Universidad de Playa Ancha, Escuela de Cine de Chile, Universidad de las Américas, Universidad Arcis, and Universidad Bolivariana. From 2019 to 2020, she served as co-artistic director, with Marco Antonio de la Parra, of the 19th National Playwriting Festival in Chile.

Hilda Peña received its world premiere at Matucana 100, 16th National Playwriting Festival, 2014, directed by Aliocha de la Sotta, with the following cast:

Hilda Peña   Paula Zúñiga

Subsequently, the production received numerous performances throughout Chile, including Sala Los Andes, Concepción (2015), Corporación Municipal de Los Angeles (2015), Sala de artes escénicas de Valparaíso (2015), Teatro de Coyhaique (2015), Quilicura Teatro (2016), Cine Artes de Viña del Mar (2016), Cámara Chilena de la Construcción, Antofagasta y Ovalle (2016), Teatro UC (2017), Centro GAM, Fitam, (2018), Teatro Ictus (2018), Centro GAM (2015-2018), FEDAM región del Maule (2019), and Festival Cielos del Infinito (2019).

In Latin America, the play was presented at Festival de Artes Escénicas FAE, Lima, Perú, (2016), Teatro Cervantes, Buenos Aires, Argentina, (2016) and Feria de Artes escénicas, Uruguay, (2018).

At the 16th National Playwriting Festival, Chile, Isidora Stevenson Bordeu won the Emerging Writer award in 2014. Subsequently, *Hilda Peña* won the "Best Play" award given every year by the Council of the City of Santiago, Chile (2015).

The play was published in Chile by Punto de Xiro (2018) and Ediciones Oxímoron (2024).

Characters

Hilda Peña, *40s*

Setting

Christmas, 1993. Santiago, Chile.

Playwright's Note

On October 21, 1993, an attack on the O'Higgins Bank at the Apoquindo Lighthouse, a middle-class shopping area on the northern side of Santiago, ended in eight deaths. In this fictional work inspired by the actual event, one of the dead is the son of Hilda Peña. From there onward all is sorrow. The play unfolds as a delirious account, the desperate memory of a woman who cannot accept the idea of letting go of her dead son.

Scene One

Hilda   No. Wait.

(*She wipes her mouth.*)

I don´t know how to start.

I forgot what it was like.

(*Closes her eyes.*)

I'm in a lake.

I'm in a green lake. It's so green it doesn´t seem like water.

(*Pause.*)

It's raining but there's no clouds and it's not cold.

I don´t know where the rain comes from but I don't think about that in the dream.

I know I'm in the South. I've never been to the south, but in the dream I know it's the south.

I can't swim, but in the dream I can.

I go into the water naked.

The water is not cold.

It´s delicious.

I lie back like this and the rain falls on my face.

The water is so green I can't see my feet.

It frightens me.

Not seeing your feet is weird.

Feet are feet, you have to see them.

That frightens me in the dream.

In life too.

(*Pause.*)

I told someone about the dream before. They said there is a green lake.

That it's in the south. Something Los Santos.

I'd never heard of it. It doesn't ring a bell.

I'm floating in the green water and in the lake plastic bags start floating.

I see them and I feel like throwing up.

Instead of a dream it's becoming a nightmare.

I know plastic bags are not frightening in life. But there they are.

I don´t know where they come from but there are so many. They are all alike.

Thousands of bags move in the water like jellyfish.

I don´t want them to touch me.

And I remember that I have to find a bag.

I begin to look for it but they are all alike.

I touch them and I'm frightened. It´s more frightening than not seeing my feet.

I don't know.

I cry.

(*Pause.*)

I cry in the green lake and the rain gets mixed up with my tears.

Like crying in the shower.

I cry loudly. Noisily.

I wake up and stop crying.

Scene Two

Hilda   I had the idea of telling them to try on what I got for them.

It was the day before Christmas.

I don't know, I just had the idea.

His size I know, so everything was alright.

For her I got pants size "S." 'Cause I think she's skinny.

(*Pause.*)

I am skinny too but I wear "M."

The following day they were going to exchange it. Pants were too small.

Had to be an "M" too.

The jacket fit her well.

Because if you buy a jacket and pants for your son, you buy a jacket and pants for your daughter in law. One should be fair.

I've never given socks for Christmas. Christmas is Christmas.

Christmas is not like a birthday. It's different.

(*Pause.*)

He had to run errands first.

Then off to exchange it.

I was expecting them for lunch.

I had bought chicken for supper.

So just rice and cabbage for lunch. (*Pause.*)

It always makes me laugh when I say cabbage. I don´t know. It's a sort of funny name. (*Pause.*)

It was hot.

I was expecting them for lunch.

On TV they said something about the Lautaro.

The Apoquindo Lighthouse Mall.[1]

The O'Higgins Bank. Eight dead.

I was just listening. Not looking. I was chopping cabbage.

Two police officers were arrested on the spot for reckless use of their service weapon, said the voice of the journalist. I looked just then.

I don't know. I just looked.

I didn't understand.

(*Pause.*)

Lying on the floor of the bank. There was the bag.

The same bag made of the same paper for the "S" pants.

What was it doing lying there and not in her hand?

How many bags like that one are there in the world?

How many made of the same paper?

(*Pause.*)

The Apoquindo Lighthouse Mall. I don't even know which bus goes there.

(*Pause.*)

Errands are run downtown. Not at the Apoquindo Lighthouse Mall.

When the police arrived, I explained that he had not arrived.

They said they knew that.

I told them he was not with the Lautaro.

They came because of something else they said. Because of the bank.

They had not come looking for him.

They came to let me know.

They were at the bank.

Both of them.

(*Pause.*)

The bag on the floor of the bank was her bag. There are no two identical bags.

4 million pesos were stolen.

(*Pause.*)

Lautaro is a Mapuche[2] name.

Apoquindo is a Mapuche word.

Apumanque is another Mapuche word.

I don't know what they mean.

Scene Three

Hilda   I . . . I was not like this before.

(*Silence.*)

I was different before.

I mean, I was always skinny. Always had all my teeth.

But I didn't bite my nails.

They were pretty before. Long.

On weekends I painted them to go out.

(*Silence.*)

The lady psychologist from the clinic told me I have to do my things, go out, have fun.

I do my things, I have always done them.

That's who I am, I don´t know.

I joined the neighborhood group, I did.

It was the psychologist's idea though.

Veterinarians go there.

Eye doctors.

I have to wear glasses, they said.

I don't like them, there they are.

They gave them to me.

They're nice, with a golden frame. But I don't like them.

To see everything with a square around is weird. I don't know.

They do bingo, hot dog nights.

They all go.

Sometimes I go too.

(*Silence.*)

I don't have a dog. I don't like animals. They frighten me, they do.

A dentist was there once.

Never came back.

Sometimes there's a lady who helps people to read or write.

She teaches those of us who don't know.

I knew before, but because I never do it I began to forget, I became sort of incoherent.

Sometimes I forget to write the little wave over the "ñ"[3] and it stays an "n".

I just laugh, you see, I'm Peña. Not Pena. Not Sadness.

I don't know, but it makes me laugh.

But I don't get confused with numbers. It must be because I have to do the receipts at the hairdresser's.

Receipts are all numbers.

Put the date. Write down the money.

I like numbers.

I don't know.

There's so few of them, and can add up to so much.

(*Pause.*)

Everything happened so fast.

I didn't realize.

Suddenly I was like this.

I don't know how to be different anymore.

Before I never used to think about the way I was. I just was.

I was alone and didn't care.

I did my things and because I was alone I never thought of anyone else.

(*Pause.*)

I never wanted children, I didn't, I was not interested.

I don't like babies.

It sounds bad but it's true.

It's not bad.

Whenever I said it to the girls at the salon they told me off.

Their crying.

I don't know.

You can't work.

The body gets, like, different.

(*Pause.*)

We don't all have to be born.

What for? No shortage of people.

Lots of people. Lots of hunger.

(*Pause.*)

I didn't have a man either.

I had.

I was not like this before.

I had one but he left.

They took him. I don't know.

I never knew.

We were not married. Nor did we save for a house. We just lived.

He liked to go to the street market. He liked getting his knick-knacks.

I cried the day he left. After that I never cried again.

I threw away all his stuff.

It's as if he had never been here.

I'm not complaining.

I'd already had a man.

One man in life is enough.

(*Pause.*)

I hadn't had children, period.

In any case, it didn't make me sad.

Anyway, the girls invited me to parties in their homes, with their people.

Me there.

Easier that way.

More practical.

Them with their men drinking beer and their children they have to bathe on Sunday night.

Them with their relatives who have lunch and don't wash the dishes before leaving.

Them with work at work and work at home.

Them with their lives and me with mine.

Sometimes they'd tell me to find someone.

I was fine like that.

(*Silence.*)

A few children sleep in front of the City Hall. Those types.

When I started working across from the City Hall, I saw them every day.

Because the Hair Salon moved to the plaza.

The shopping arcade was no good. Very few people.

Too many foreigners said the owner.

The owner leased a place on the plaza. The girls were happy.

Not me.

The plaza was ugly like that. No trees. Just cement.

They put up a sculpture.

Ugly.

I don't understand it.

It's not something. Any one thing.

The salon is in front of the City Hall.

The ugly sculpture is in the middle of the plaza.

You can't not look at it.

I always see those kids and I don't care.

That sounds ugly. But it's true.

I mean I look at them, I feel sorry and move on.

That's not caring.

Caring is doing something.

Moving on is not caring.

I don't know.

(*Pause.*)

They sleep near the City Hall.

I don't know, this one mattered to me.

I kept thinking about him. I felt sort of guilty. I don't know.

Going around in dirty clothes.

Going around with his dirty hair. Smelly.

Reeking of glue sometimes. Of booze always.

Sometimes I gave him bread. Gave him tea.

And little by little that's how it happened. I don't know.

It happened.

We didn't talk much.

We sat there drinking tea and eating bread with something.

Cold cuts, egg.

After a while he was living in my house.

(*Pause.*)

I don't know. It happened.

I didn't have children. I didn't have a man. I lived alone.

It was my home.

It is my home.

First he slept on the floor. On a blanket.

He didn't want to sleep on the couch. "Just here," he'd say.

The girls told me not to.

That something could happen to me.

I wasn't afraid.

I didn't know him from before they said.

From there he moved to the couch. After a while. He was happy.

I made him shower.

The neighbor gave me a mattress.

After a while I got him a bed.

Got it at the street market.

And so on.

I don't know.

It sounds weird, but that's how it happened.

Nothing strange happened. Not for him or me.

In the back room we arranged his bedroom.

He'd never had a bedroom he said.

He started going to school.

He'd never been. He liked it.

He did his homework in the dining room.

He didn't have a medical record at the clinic either.

We never talked about his family. Nothing.

I didn't want to pry. If he didn't want to talk, I wasn't going to ask.

To each their own.

Sometimes he looked sad, as if thinking. Quiet.

I so wanted to hold him, to cuddle him.

I didn't. I couldn't.

I didn't pry.

It was his stuff.

I never knew.

(*Pause.*)

Sometimes I'd like to know. But I don't want to.

I don't know how.

Sometimes I don't sleep thinking about his family.

What is it like?

Who could I ask? I don't know anyone.

And then I feel like a rage.

Where is the body that bore that child?

(*Silence.*)

I took him to the clinic.

He was skinny. Sick too.

I lied to the doctor. I didn't want to humiliate him.

I blamed myself. I saw he was ashamed.

He gained weight.

We drank tea and watched TV when I came home.

He brought cold cuts. Sweets. He worked sometimes. He earned his share.

I didn't ask for anything, just that he didn't steal from me.

And that if he left, he should never return.

That's all I asked.

So that´s how he stayed.

And became my son.

(*Pause.*)

He was my son.

I don't know if I was his mother. I never asked him.

I don't know what he is now.

I think of his body.

Fresh—bloated—rotten—dry.

I think how cold he was in winter.

I think how cold he must be now.

I think how cramped he must be in there. With a glass right here.

(*Silence.*)

Once he won a TV in neighborhood bingo.

He was happy that day. It was a color TV.

He gave it to me. "For everything," he said.

That day he was happy. It was the only time I saw him cry. It wasn't sadness.

(*Pause.*)

He went to school and I didn't help him with homework. I just don't know.

He began to learn.

And he talked of the things he learned.

I just listened.

I wasn't ashamed. We don't all have to know.

We can't all be doctors.

Someone has to cut hair or cook.

He finished school. There was a ceremony.

Diplomas, carnations, photos.

It was nice, the two of us there.

(*Silence.*)

After he served in the military he went on to have a girlfriend.

He served a long time.

I thought about him.

The days went by slowly.

I had tea on my own and got bored watching TV.

Went for a walk in the afternoon.

I met stray dogs that followed me.

I don't like them but I didn't say anything to them.

Whenever he came home he brought roast chicken.

He didn't like fries, made him sad. I never asked.

I would like to know now.

I won't leave you alone again, he said when he returned from the service.

He grew his hair. I used to cut it sometimes. The tips.

I liked cutting it.

It was like cuddling him.

I didn't want a child and suddenly I had this one.

(*Silence.*)

I got him a job in a processed meats factory, not far from here.

He was so fond of beer salami.

I don't know. I just thought it was the place for him.

I don't know if he liked it but he didn't complain.

I think he was used to it.

(*Pause.*)

I was used to him already. With her, too, later on.

They met at work, those two.

Both worked in the processed meats factory.

She worked there before. She was from the South.

She came over for tea and then he'd walk her to the bus.

During the Telethon[4] her boarding house caught fire.

I offered for her to come and stay in our home for a while.

She never left again.

There were always sausages at home. Because of the factory. They got them at cost.

(*Pause.*)

He didn't want to pursue a military career. He didn't like it.

I didn't meddle in his stuff.

If he didn't want it, he just didn't.

I thought it was good because he'd have healthcare.

Insurance.

The only time he started swearing here at home was when he said "fucking soldiers."

I just laughed.

He apologized. Never talked about it again.

Us three, we lived here, with his girlfriend.

The three of us together.

They were in their room, at the back.

I called her my daughter-in-law, even though they weren't married.

She called me ma'am.

(*Pause.*)

When I heard them laugh at night it made me want to laugh. I don't know.

And I laughed alone. Quietly.

You can't hear laughter and not laugh.

I had already purchased the gifts.

It was our first Christmas together.

Us three.

There they are still.

Under the tree, they are. I'm still paying for them.

I bought them in installments.

It's all there, but the pants they were exchanging that day.

Both jackets and his pants.

Her jacket, his jacket, and his pants.

The bag her pants were in, I saw it lying on the floor of the bank.

On TV they showed the inside of the bank from the entrance.

No bodies were visible. People walked from one side to another and the bag there lying on the floor.

(*Pause.*)

I didn't understand.

I stopped cooking to understand.

Was it where they went?

But errands are run downtown.

What was the bag doing there?

She had it in her hand. They were just exchanging it and coming back.

What were they doing in the bank?

Money order, check, bonus. I don't know.

I didn't know they had to go to the bank.

I thought it could be another bag.

A similar one, but not the same.

The same one, same store, same paper, but not the same.

I got scared.

I went over to the neighbor. She said there are many similar bags.

They didn't come to lunch.

I burned the rice.

In the afternoon police arrived.

(*Silence.*)

I went to identify him.

His body.

I had to go look at him. There.

Lying on that metal. He was cold.

Taking his hand was like touching a glass.

Bodies are not like glasses.

Bodies are bodies and glasses are glasses.

What was my boy doing there as a glass?

(*Silence.*)

That's the last thing I remember.

That whole night was erased.

(*Pause.*)

We had a wake for him at the neighborhood group.

People came from the factory. From the military.

They all heard it on TV.

(*Pause.*)

On TV they said it was those Lautaro.

I never turned it on again.

There it is.

(*Pause.*)

Her family came from the South.

They offered to hold a service together.

I said no.

I never saw them again.

I think they were evangelical.

I wanted to tell them about the pants and the jacket.

That the shop was not at the Lighthouse.

That I didn't send them to the bank.

That I don't know what errands they were running.

That my boy was not Lautaro.

That we decorated a tree.

That it was her idea.

That it turned out pretty.

That it didn't have a star, just little balls.

That they laughed at night and I liked to listen.

(*Silence.*)

I didn't want children and I ended up having this one.

Scene Four

Hilda Sometimes I dream they left me a grandson and that I have long nails.

The boy doesn't have a face though.

I mean he does, he's not a monster. He has one but I don't see it. I mean I see it but now I can't remember what it's like.

Some other times I dream I am in the South, that I go to a lake and swim.

I can't swim, but in the dream I can.

The lake is so green that I can't see my feet.

It frightens me not to see my feet.

It's weird. I don't know.

Feet are feet. You have to see them.

I've never been to the South, the furthest I've been is Departamental.[5]

I've never been to the sea either.

But that's different.

The sea is different.

(*Pause.*)

I didn't bite my nails before.

They were long, like in the dream.

In the salon I worked, washed hair, waxed, and cleaned.

Now that my hands are like this they don't let me. Because of the image. The beauty salon. I just clean.

The girls tell me not to bite them, but I can't. I don't know.

In any case, it's not that I'm hungry.

Scene 5

Hilda   I'd like to know if you can do something.

I've seen you in the newspaper. What you do.

I have kept your articles.

People believe in you.

I too want to believe.

Not that I don't believe.

(*Silence.*)

The day we held the wake was the day they put him in the casket.

Get out, they said. I didn't want to. I wanted to look at his glass body.

We dressed him in a shirt he didn't like.

He had to be buried in fancy clothes they said.

I wanted him to wear his Colo soccer shirt.

I don't know. I did what they said.

(*Pause.*)

Sometimes at night I can't stop thinking he didn't like that shirt. That I can't change it anymore.

That he'll wear it forever.

(*Pause.*)

I folded the soccer shirt and put it in his hand.

I covered his legs with a blanket. Because he was always cold. I got this weird feeling.

The undertakers arranged him and everything.

I saw how they put cotton in his mouth.

I saw how they glued his eyes.

Because they can't be open like that, they said.

Glue. Eyes. Some things should not be said together.

(*Pause.*)

When he was ready they said they would seal it.

That the casket had to be sealed because of the health code.

That we could look at him if we opened the lid. That it had a glass.

(*Pause.*)

I threw up while they sealed it.

Maybe because I ate an unwashed pear.

I've never had a pear again.

(*Silence.*)

I am alone here.

The Peñas are from the North. They don't live here.

I don't know where they live.

I don't have their addresses or phone numbers.

I lost a notebook where I had all that.

I just know they live up North.

(*Pause.*)

The Peñas have a mausoleum here.

All I had from them was a sheet of paper stating that a niche in the mausoleum is for me.

The Peñas left me a niche.

They don't live here but their dead are here.

That's weird.

(*Pause.*)

I don't know the Peñas.

Do they also forget to write the little wave over the ñ?

That niche in the Peña mausoleum was where they were going to put me.

(*Silence.*)

When we laid him in the niche I vomited again.

I don't know.

That pear I think.

The guy from the cemetery helped me. He walked me outside.

He gave me water and offered me a cigarette.

I don't smoke. I don't like it. I smoked that day.

I vomited and smoked.

I told him not to close the grave. That the next day I'd come back to say goodbye quietly.

(*Silence.*)

There was no Mass.

Just people talking about my boy.

(*Pause.*)

My glass boy with the shirt he didn't like.

With his legs covered.

Cramped inside that casket.

(*Silence.*)

When I got home I poured myself some tea.

The girls offered to stay. I just wanted to be alone. Lying on his bed. With his stuff.

I don't know what time I fell asleep. At six I was awake again.

When I opened my eyes I thought it was a nightmare.

Like it wasn't true.

For a second I thought I heard them laugh and I thought nothing had happened.

(*Pause.*)

They gave me time off at the Hair Salon.

I went to the cemetery.

(*Silence.*)

At first they said no.

That it was not allowed.

I pressed them.

The graves have to be closed, they said.

They can't be left like that.

I offered them money. They said no.

I explained that I just wanted to look at him.

They were astonished.

He's going to get ugly they said.

Fresh—bloated— rotten—dry, I said.

They looked puzzled. One of them laughed.

I don't know. He just laughed.

Open the lid, look at him and then close it. Just that, I said.

They shared a look.

(*Pause.*)

I kneeled in front of him.

I didn't even think about it.

I didn't care.

I just did it.

In the end …

He knew what I was offering right away.

He did the rest.

(*Pause.*)

The other one watched.

He watched for a long while. Opened his fly and waited.

(*Silence.*)

I'm not ashamed.

(*Silence.*)

I go every day.

(*Silence.*)

I go inside.

I am with them.

I rinse my mouth with a drink I buy at the entrance.

(*Pause.*)

I open the lid.

I clean the glass.

I look at him.

(*Pause.*)

His body behind the glass.

You can see him down to here.

Fresh—bloated—rotten—dry.

(*Silence.*)

I hear his silence.

I talk to him a little and go off to work.

I keep his picture here all day.

(*Silence.*)

The body is strange.

It's like it was emptied.

The girls say that goes to God.

They know nothing about what I do.

I don't know.

It's private.

It's not shame, it's private.

I see him empty.

I see him but without him.

I see how he is but different.

Fresh—bloated—rotten—dry.

(*Pause.*)

I try to imagine him inside. Like in the drawings in his books.

It's weird because those drawings show things separately.

And inside it's all together.

It's all dark and cramped.

Afterwards it becomes different.

Fresh—bloated—rotten—dry.

He doesn't frighten me.

I don't think he's ugly. Weird, yes. Different.

(*Silence.*)

When he bloated up I felt sad.

He looked tight.

There are days in which he is different colors.

At first he was kind of yellow.

Pale.

Greenish.

Purple.

Bloated.

(*Silence.*)

I know now the rotting comes next. I read it in his book of Natural Sciences.

The decomposition of the dead has four stages:

Fresh—bloated— rotten—dry.

(*Silence.*)

At the cemetery they don't understand.

They say I'm weird.

That this is wrong.

They're the weird ones who like to get a blow job from someone they don't know.

(*Pause.*)

I don't speak to them. I do what has to be done and I go see my boy.

They help me with the door.

Then they leave.

I open it on my own.

(*Pause.*)

I didn't think he would get like that so fast.

Fresh—bloated—rotten—dry.

(*Pause.*)

When I took him chocolate eggs, ants ate them.

I don't know why it made me so sad. I started to cry. I cried a long time.

If ants ate his eggs, are they going to eat him too?

(*Pause.*)

I talk to him.

I tell him the things I have to do during the day.

Sometimes I clean the glass. It fogs up.

But most of the time I'm quiet. Listening to his silence.

Looking at what his body has become.

Does it hurt?

Can his body hurt if it's empty?

If it's empty, where did the inside go?

Where did he go?

(*Silence.*)

Once I saw on TV a program about saints.

There are very ancient saints.

Some of these saints don't rot.

As if they were made of plastic.

Or ceramic. I don't know.

They open the casket and they still are like when they were buried.

They are so good, the little saints don't rot.

(*Silence.*)

My boy was not a saint.

I don't know what saints are like.

But if my boy were a saint I think I'd know.

If he were a saint he wouldn't be like he is.

He wouldn't have turned that color.

(*Silence.*)

So, I wanted to ask you something.

Before more time passes.

Ask you if you could do that thing you do.

What you said once in the newspaper that you did.

I have the article here. Look.

That story of the girl from Coñaripe.[6] That you awoke.

Please.

Try to see if he wakes up.

Try to see if you can do it now.

Please try to see if you can take away the cold from my boy.

That color.

Try to see if my boy wakes up.

Please.

You see he is going to rot afterwards.

It won't be possible to do something later.

I read in the newspaper that you have powers. That you've done it before.

That you are like a wizard, sort of esoteric.

That you take assignments.

Please.

Can you do this?

You can still wake him up. I think.

Please try.

Please give it a try.

Please my glass boy.

Please my bloated child.

Please my yellow, pale, greenish, purple child.

Please.

You see if he rots then it won't be possible anymore.

End of play.

Notes

1. The Apoquindo Lighthouse Mall is a commercial center in Las Condes, an area in the northern part of Santiago. The attack at the bank was led by the Lautaro Youth Movement, a Chilean armed organization founded in 1982.
2. The Mapuche are indigenous communities in south-central Chile. Lautaro was a sixteenth century Mapuche warrior who led the resistance against the Spanish conquest of Chile. Apoquindo is the name of a river and a settlement in the area of Santiago now known as Las Condes. Apumanque means "Chief Condor" in the Mapuche language. Apoquindo and Apumanque are also names of avenues in Las Condes.
3. The Spanish letter ñ is pronounced "en-ye"
4. The Telethon is a yearly charity event broadcast on Chilean television during the first week of December.
5. Departamental is an avenue that travels across southern and southeastern Santiago.
6. Coñaripe is a Chilean town in the Valdivia province.

School for Girls:

Student Protests, Political Victims, and Temporal Paradox

Inés Stranger

English translation
Christine Ann Hills

In her play *School for Girls*, Nona Fernández stages and examines a series of Chilean high school protests. The play references the 2006 student protests, known as the Pingüina revolution,[1] which marked the first protests carried out by students after the return to democracy in Chile in 1990. The play also addresses subsequent protests, as students have mobilized almost every year since 2006. However, the play is most likely inspired by the events of 2011, a later wave of protests that included university students and achieved significant changes and propelled their leaders into the public eye. Among these young leaders was the recent President of the Republic, Gabriel Boric (born 1986). What is striking about this play is how it connects these more recent, post-dictatorship student protests with those that took place in the 1980s. During that decade, high school students opposed the Pinochet regime and faced severe repression for doing so.

The plot of *School for Girls* unfolds on two levels. The first can be described as documentary-like. This level centers around a character known as the Aged Youth, who tells the story of four high school students who died during the 1980s. The second level of the work presents a fictional story set in 2015. It takes place in the science lab of a girls' high school, where three women dressed in school uniforms appear before a teacher. These women have been hiding in the tunnels beneath the school since a student protest, the date of which they cannot recall.

Fernández explains how the inspiration for this play "had been turning over in my head after the Penguin Revolution of 2006, and then it was in 2011 when the writing began to weave itself together."[2] She goes on to say how struck she was by hearing students in the street shouting the same slogans that her generation had shouted in their own youth when protesting during the 1980s. Fernández draws attention to that moment when the idea came to her, "the idea of encapsulated time, having that feeling of time standing still. Once again, young people were on the streets; though they were different bodies, they were still the same ideas circulating."[3] This led her to visualize "the image that evokes the text: the image of Carmina Riego, the actor, emerging from a ventilation duct in a high school. A woman in a school uniform."[4]

With these initial ideas, the text began to take shape. Fernández developed endearing and recognizable characters and explores themes such as loyalty, betrayal, friendship, dreams, and various other moral conflicts that typically arise within the school environment. Anticipating that artistic expressions could overshadow and complicate the main political ideas proposed by the text, the author cautions: "This play must be performed with the naivete and conviction of someone who dares to journey to the stars."[5]

The play is divided into nine scenes, referred to as periods, which mirror the structure of a typical school day. Each period ends with the school bell ringing. In addition, there is an appendix containing the play that one of the characters, Fuenzalida, had been writing in her theatre workshop.

First period. The Aged Youth. The action begins with the introduction of a character whose status is undefined; he is a ghost-like figure known as the Aged Youth. He enters a laboratory where there is a poster of Yuri Gagarin (1934-1968), the Russian cosmonaut, with his spacecraft and a blackboard with the equation for the Theory of Relativity written on it. The youth, dressed in a school uniform, has his back to the audience. He looks at the equation and writes "Suck dick, Carvajal." He turns to face the audience, and we see a fresh bullet wound on his forehead.

The Aged Youth will appear in every other scene, without interacting with the rest of the characters. He narrates the story of four different student leaders who, in the second half of the 1980s, decided to take up arms and were killed by the dictatorship.

Second period. Gama Casiopea. The teacher enters, talking on his cell phone. He is clearly in the throes of a panic attack. He unbuttons his shirt, looking exhausted and unwell. It becomes apparent that he is talking to his wife. He tells her that he was with the other teachers when he suddenly started feeling this way. He says it is not because of the student protests, and eventually, he admits that he has not taken his medication for the last three months.

The teacher hangs up and leaves his phone on the lab table. He hears a female voice calling out to him from somewhere. The teacher realizes that there is a woman behind the grate of a ventilation shaft, shining a flashlight on him; she has heard everything he has just said. She addresses him as "sir," as if she were one of his students. He tries to identify her, but the name Maldonado does not ring any bells for him. She explains to him that she has been hiding since the last school occupation. The teacher helps her out. She is a woman around 45 years old and is dressed in a school uniform. The scene ends when she hits him with an iron bar taken from her bag. He falls unconscious.

Third period. Pegasus 51: The Aged Youth enters; he looks lost in space. He tells us that a friend named Pegasus 51 invited him to join the militia. However, he, Alfa Centauro, replied that he preferred to continue fighting as a student leader. He mentions that Pegasus 51 always carried a small revolver, referred to as a "cat killer," for protection, and that he and some other friends had decided to rob a bakery, but they were ambushed by police. These police officers had killed his brother, and then they murdered him in a police van, throwing his body onto the street next to his brother. Through this text, Alfa Centauro implies that these events pushed him to join the armed struggle. This story is inspired by the deaths of the Vergara Toledo brothers in 1985, Eduardo (1965-1985) and Rafael (1967-1985), an emblematic case in the student struggle against the dictatorship.

Fourth period. Beta Andromeda and Epsilon Sagittarius. The teacher is lying unconscious on the laboratory floor. We see the beams of two flashlights approaching from behind the grates of another two ventilation ducts. These flashlights belong to two women, Riquelme and Fuenzalida, both a little over 45 years old. They shine their flashlights on the teacher, who wakes up with a start. They introduce themselves, saying they are students at the high school, and ask about a classmate who just left through a grate. The teacher says that he saw her, that Maldonado hit him, and left. Fuenzalida,

3 Riquelme (Roxana Naranjo), Fuenzalida (Nona Fernández), and Maldonado (Carmina Riego) defy the Teacher (Francisco Medina) in *School for Girls* by Nona Fernández, directed by Marcelo Leonart, Teatro de la Universidad Católica de Chile, 2015.
(Photo: © Maglio Pérez)

who cannot speak, communicates by writing messages in a notebook. The teacher is confused; he questions them about whether this is a joke to unnerve him, a scheme to get him fired, or a trick by Carvajal. The students reassure him, saying that they would never form an alliance with that traitor and that, as seventeen-year-old students, they have no intentions of becoming coordinators or taking his job. The teacher grows increasingly perplexed as they begin to question him about his life. Clearly upset, the teacher starts talking about his job, family, debts, efforts, and his anguish. The students tie him to a chair: they have, after all, heard him talking to someone who is not present in the laboratory. It dawns on the teacher that the women do not know what a cell phone is. They believe it to be a detonator for explosives.

Carvajal, the school's Vice Principal, calls the teacher on the phone and instructs the teacher to leave the premises. The teacher replies that he intends to stay and work, but he realizes that Carvajal does not believe him and hangs up. There is a knock at the door. It frightens them as it might be Carvajal. However, it turns out to be Maldonado. She informs them she has been outside and seen a student protest. "Everything's the same, this thing hasn't moved forward one bit in all the time we've been inside there."[6] She then confesses that they have spent more time in hiding than they thought, at least five months, since graduation is upon them tomorrow. She regrets not being able to go to the party with Alpha Centauro. They talk about the play they had been rehearsing and how their parents are going to punish them.

After listening to them and seeing how lost they are, the teacher musters the courage to ask them about the occupation and the revolt they led. They recount their proud achievements in the student struggle. It is revealed that, on that occasion, Carvajal called the cops, and Alpha Centauro ordered them to hide. However, the police took him and Fuenzalida into custody, and both left quietly in tears. The teacher asks when this happened, and Fuenzalida writes July 10th, 1985.

Fifth period. Zeta Neptune: The Aged Youth appears with a sheet of graph paper, speaking as if he were giving a speech at a funeral. He reads a letter written by a student from Zeta Neptuno High School, "We're young, we value life, and we're fighting for a better future for ourselves. It's for that love that we take up arms and are not afraid to die."[7] This text is inspired by a letter written by student activist Mauricio Maigret Becerra (1966-1984) on December 28, 1983, in Santiago. Mauricio Maigret Becerra was shot down in a square in Pudahuel on March 29, 1984.

Sixth period. A true constellation: Maldonado, Fuenzalida, and Riquelme are sitting at the lab tables, taking notes with pencils and notebooks. The teacher is teaching them and, using a very gentle approach, he tries to explain to them that really much more time has passed than they believe they have been in hiding. He talks to them about the theory of relativity. Maldonado is happy to be back in class; however, Riquelme, while finding the lesson very interesting, wants to know how things are on planet Earth. She says they have a group of people waiting for them, and they need to return with answers. The teacher hands them a newspaper to show them a news story. They pass it around until Fuenzalida ends up ripping it up to prevent her classmates from seeing the date. We find out that after she was taken prisoner, Fuenzalida had returned to hiding at the school.

The school principal calls, worried. She says the teacher's wife has called her. The teacher responds that there is no crisis; he is just doing some grading. This is when the revelations come to light. Fuenzalida speaks. The women believe it is a miracle that she can speak. Fuenzalida asks them to come back and forgive her, saying it is better not to know the truth. Finally, the teacher encourages them to look at their reflections in the window. "Who are . . . those women . . . who are looking at us from the other side of the glass?"[8] Through the reflection, they come to understand that they are now adult women.

Seventh period. A black hole. Alpha Centauro enters as if lost in outer space. He explains that he was taken prisoner for killing a police officer.[9] He was tortured and held in a black hole. He tells us how, in that dungeon, he dreamed of his last day at school, and of being like Yuri Gagarin. Finally, he takes on the role of an astronaut trying to communicate with Earth.

Eighth period. Alpha Centauro. Maldonado and Riquelme come to terms with their situation: life has passed them by, and now they are old. They question Fuenzalida. She explains that after she was released by the police, she managed to get into another school, finish her studies, and go to university, only to become disillusioned with life. She wanted to come back to this high school because it is the only time in her life that she remembers fondly. That is why she returned to the hideout.

They discuss whether they should return to the hideout to tell their classmates the truth. They are distraught. Maldonado wants to know what happened to Alpha Centauro, and Fuenzalida explains that he was arrested for killing a police officer. Later, he was taken to a hospital, from where he was rescued by his comrades in an operation. Several people were killed during the rescue, but he got away. He managed to hide in the house of someone who had helped him in the past, but now that democracy had been established, that person felt compelled to turn him in. This is how Alpha Centauro was arrested and killed.

The phone rings. It is Vice Principal Carvajal warning the teacher that they are coming to pick him up in an ambulance: they have been watching him on the lab cameras and have noticed he has been talking to himself for a long time. Clearly, he is not well. As a final gesture, the teacher decides to join the women in hiding; he does it because he is the responsible adult. "Young ladies, I think that the best thing to do, before Carvajal's gorillas arrive, is to enter that place from which you've come and to tell your comrades what is happening."[10] With that, all the characters disappear through the ducts. This is followed by a scene called "A Normal Family," the play that Fuenzalida was writing for the theatre workshop. It shows a normal mealtime in a normal family, in which the father is preparing to hand over Alpha Centauro to the police.

School for Girls is a major theatrical work. Fernández uses the character Alfa Centauro as a documentary device to provide background information on the deaths of four young students. By doing so, she remembers and pays tribute to these young people whom history has tended to forget. Additionally, she constructs a theatrical fiction through the dramatic interaction between a science teacher confronted by three women dressed as schoolgirls whom he accepts and treats as students. The growing awareness of the time that has passed for the characters Maldonado and Riquelme unfolds over at least two lengthy scenes in the play. This recognition process is very dramatic and perhaps goes beyond the political theme of the play. Maybe we can all empathize with these women's realization that we are no longer young, and we have not managed to do what we dreamed of doing; that life has passed us by without us even noticing.

Finally, the teacher is undoubtedly the play's most endearing character. He is in the middle of a profound existential crisis. He is grappling with panic attacks, financial troubles, marital problems, and a longing to be a father, but even so, he is capable of empathizing with the women. He treats them as the students they believe themselves to be, with tenderness and tact. In this interaction, the teacher recognizes that these times are not his either. He accepts the final call of his vocation as a teacher and decides to go with them into the school's underground hideout to face the truth of their lives. This act effectively signifies his abandonment of this world and perhaps his death. After the developmental reading we held in Chicago,[11] Ricardo Gamboa, the actor playing the teacher, provided an important key for interpreting the play. He suggested perhaps the entire work is the dream of a teacher who is reaching the limits of his physical and moral strength. This is just one possible interpretation. Through a seemingly simple metaphor, Fernández addresses the nostalgia we feel for bygone times when notions of good and evil seemed more clearly defined.

Notes

1 The "Revolución Pingüina" (Penguin Revolution) was an important student movement in Chile that took place in 2006. It got its name thanks to the uniforms worn by the

secondary students, which made them look like penguins. The main reason for the protests was the privatization of education in Chile: the students demanded quality public education that was free for everyone.
2 Fernández, Nona. Personal Interview. 18 October 2023.
3 Ibid.
4 Ibid.
5 Fernández, Nona. *School for Girls*, *Dramaturgas Chilenas: Plays by Chilean Female Writers in the Early 21st Century*, edited by Coca Duarte, Anne García-Romero and Inés Stranger, Methuen Drama, 2025, p. 101.
6 Ibid., 117.
7 Ibid., 125.
8 Ibid., 136.
9 The story of Alfa Centauro is based on the real-life events of Marco Ariel Antonioletti (1969-1990), who was a militant in the Movimiento Juvenil Lautaro (MJL, Lautaro Youth Movement). He was assassinated on November 15th, 1990, by officers of Chile's Investigative Police just one day after he was rescued from Sótero del Río hospital, where he had been transferred from prison needing medical treatment. The rescue operation resulted in the deaths of four prison officers and one police officer. In addition, a female MJL activist was shot in the spine and left disabled for life.
10 Fernández, *School for Girls*, p. 144.
11 "*School for Girls* by Nona Fernández, translated by Andrea Thome," developmental reading directed by Susan E. Bowen, University of Notre Dame Law School, Chicago, IL. 31 March 2025.

Further Reading

Palacios-Valladares, Indira. "Internal Movement Transformation and the Diffusion of Student Protest in Chile." *Journal of Latin American Studies*, vol. 49 no. 3, 2017, pp. 579–607. https://doi.org/10.1017/S0022216X16001905
Puga, Ismael. "The Stranger the Better: Support and Solidarity in the 2011 Students' Protests in Chile." *Social Movement Studies*, vol. 15, no. 3, 2016, pp. 263–76. https://doi.org/10.1080/14742837.2015.1070337
Rocco Núñez, Bernardo and Zurita Hecht, Federico. "Representación de la historia del fracaso nacional en El taller y Liceo de niñas de Nona Fernández." *Latin American Theatre Review*, vol. 53, no. 1, 2019, pp. 101–20. https://doi.org/10.1353/ltr.2019.0024
Tapia Marín, Felipe. "Elementos de la ciencia ficción como suscitadores de problemáticas políticas contemporáneas en *Liceo de niñas* de Nona Fernández." *Apuntes de Teatro*, vol. 149, 109–24. https://doi.org/10.7764/apuntesdeteatro.149.64997.2024

School for Girls

Nona Fernández

English translation
Andrea Thome

Nona Fernández Silanes, born in Santiago, Chile, in 1971, is an actor, novelist, and playwright. She received her degree in acting from the Pontificia Universidad Católica de Chile School of Theatre. Her novels include *The Twilight Zone* (2002), winner of the Municipal Literature Prize; *Space Invaders* (2013), finalist for the National Book Award; *Voyager* (2015), winner of the Best Published Work at the National Book Council; *La Dimensión Desconocida* (*The Unknown Dimension*, 2016), winner of the Sor Juana Inés de la Cruz prize, selected by the Guadalajara International Book Festival, and finalist for the National Book Award; *Preguntas Frecuentes (Frequent Questions, 2020)*; *Voyager* (2023); and *¿Cómo recordar la sed? (How to remember thirst?, 2023)*. Her books have been translated into numerous languages, including English, Italian, French, and German. Her plays include *El Taller* (*The Workshop*, 2012), winner of the Altazor prize and the Nuez Martín prize; *Liceo de niñas* (*School for Girls*, 2015); *Paren la Música* (*Stop the Music*, 2021), winner of Best Play from the Chile Drama Critics Circle; *El Difunto Imaginario* (*The Imaginary Dead Man,* 2023), produced by Theater Basel, Switzerland; and the theatrical adaptations of *Space Invaders* (2022) and *Voyager* (2024). From 2017 to 2018, she served as co-artistic director, with Pali García, of the 18th National Playwriting Festival in Chile.

School for Girls received its world premiere by La Pieza Oscura at Teatro de la Universidad Católica de Chile, Santiago, Chile, on October 23, 2015. It was directed by Marcelo Leonart with the following cast:

Teacher	Francisco Medina
Maldonado	Carmina Riego
Riquelme	Roxana Naranjo
Fuenzalida	Nona Fernández
The Aged Youth	Juan Pablo Fuentes

After its world premiere, *School for Girls* was produced in 2018 at the Teatro Nacional Chileno by La Pieza Oscura, directed by Leonart. In 2022, the play was produced in Germany at Teatro de Dormut, directed by Anna Tanti.

The play was published in Chile by Ediciones Oxímoron (2016).

For Marco Ariel Antonioletti

Characters

Teacher, *30s, Graduated from the University of Chile with a major in Physics. He is the Head Teacher of Section B of the Senior Class. He is the Educational Coordinator for the high school. To keep his job, he conceals the panic attacks that he's been suffering from lately.*

Maldonado, *45, Secretary of the student body and member of the high school's theatre troupe. Alias: Gamma Cassiopeia.*

Riquelme, *45, President of the student body and director of the school's theatre group. Alias: Beta Andromeda.*

Fuenzalida, *45, Student with disabilities. Playwright of the school's theatre group. Ex-principal singer of the school choir. Alias: Epsilon Sagittarius.*

The Aged Youth, *20s, Spokesperson of the Federation of High School Students. Future or longtime member of the Lautaro Movement.[1] Alias: Alpha Centauro.*

Setting

2015. Chile. The science lab of a public high school for girls.

Playwright's Note

This play should be staged with the ingenuity and conviction of those who dare to make a voyage to the stars.

First Period

The Aged Youth

The school science lab is visible in shadows. A poster of Yuri Gagarin and his spaceship, the Vostok 1, hanging on a wall. A large blackboard. In the center of the blackboard, we can see, written in white chalk, the formula for the theory of relativity, $E=MC^2$.

An **Aged Youth** *examines the formula. He wears a school uniform and is only visible from behind. After a moment he takes a piece of chalk and starts writing on the blackboard. Once he's done, he steps back a bit to examine what he's written.*

SUCK DICK, CARVAJAL is written in white letters.

The **Aged Youth** *turns around and shows his face.*

On his forehead, we can see the fresh bullet hole. It's a perfect circle. Blood and raw flesh on the face of an ancient child.

The bell rings, indicating the start of classes.

Second Period

Gama Cassiopeia

*The door to the Lab opens. The **Teacher** enters quickly, talking on his cell phone. He unbuttons a few buttons on his shirt, he seems overwhelmed, sick. He sweats. He doesn't feel right. He walks and speaks with difficulty. He's in the middle of a panic attack.*

Teacher   My chest feels tight, I'm seeing little white spots. (. . .) I don't know, I don't know. . .there's nowhere to look at myself.

*The **Teacher** goes up to one of the windows. He pulls back its curtain a bit and looks at the reflection of his face in the glass.*

Teacher   Yes, my pupils are dilated. (. . .) Yes, I feel my legs shaking. (. . .) No, I have no idea why it's happening right now. (. . .) No, Nancy, it has nothing to do with the protest, that's over by the Alameda, nothing's happening over here. (. . .) I was sitting there, with the rest of the teachers, grading, when I started to feel like this. . .drowning. (. . .) How could you even think that I'd ask for help! If Carvajal sees me like this again he's going to make it his mission to fire me. (. . .) Please, Nancy! I know I'm having a panic attack, why do you think I'm calling you. (. . .) I'm not letting anyone know, that's why I called you, for support. (. . .) What? The pills?

*The **Teacher** remains silent for a moment. He doesn't respond.*

Teacher (*uncomfortable*)   Yes, I heard you. (. . .) I haven't taken them. (. . .) It's that. . .I ran out. (. . .) No, I haven't bought more. (. . .) Yes I know, Nancy, I know that's why I'm having these attacks, but it's just that. . . I don't want to take them anymore. (. . .) They're not good for me, they make me swollen, they make me sleepy, make me stupid, and I don't want to go around like that, you know? (. . .) I haven't taken them for a while now. (. . .) A while. (. . .) Three months. (. . .) Don't get like that, Nancy! (. . .) I can handle it, trust me. (. . .) Nancy? Nancy?

*The **Teacher** turns his phone off. He sits on a laboratory bench and tries to breathe deeply and calm himself, without success.*

Teacher (*to himself*)   Relax . . . this will pass.

Soon, as he keeps inhaling and exhaling, he hears a female voice coming from somewhere.

Maldonado   Psst . . . Mister Teacher. Teach . . .

*The **Teacher** looks around him. The laboratory is completely empty.*

Maldonado   Psst . . . here, Teach . . . here . . .

*The **Teacher** seems disconcerted. The voice makes him uneasy. He breathes deeply.*

Maldonado   Here, Teach . . . down here, down here . . .

*From the grate of an air duct shines the beam of a flashlight. The **Teacher** sees it and becomes even more uneasy.*

Teacher Shit.

Maldonado Are you okay now? Do you feel better?

*The **Teacher** sees what seems to be a high school student on the other side of the grate. He peers at her from a distance but can't see well.*

Teacher Who are you?

Maldonado Can you breathe? Are you feeling calmer?

Teacher How long have you been spying on me?

Maldonado I'm not spying on you.

Teacher Then what are you doing there, hidden, listening to private conversations?

Maldonado Did the cops leave? They're not arresting people anymore?

Teacher Arresting?

Maldonado That bald-ass Carvajal still around there?

Teacher Young lady, more respect towards the Vice Principal.

Maldonado He's a rat, Teach.

Teacher Come out of there at once.

Maldonado I'd like to, sir, but first I need you to give me some guarantees.

Teacher Guarantees of what?

Maldonado That you're not gonna rat like Carvajal.

Teacher What are you doing there? How'd you get here?

Maldonado Those pills you stopped taking . . . what are they for?

Teacher So you were spying on me.

Maldonado Don't get mad, Teach. In times like these, the only way to trust in someone is by exchanging intel. I'm not here, you get me? You've never seen me or heard me. If you keep my secret, no one will ever know that you're like that, kinda . . . "cuckoo."

Teacher Young lady, I am not crazy, more respect, please.

Maldonado So then why do you take pills? Why are you having a breakdown? Why are you hiding and talking to yourself?

Teacher I wasn't talking to myself!

Maldonado Come closer, Teach, please.

*The **Teacher** comes closer to the grate.*

Teacher Yes . . .?

Maldonado (*flirty*) What nice eyes you've got, Teach.

Teacher (*uncomfortable*)   What do you want, miss?

A screwdriver is thrown from the grate. The **Teacher** *seems more freaked out each minute.*

Maldonado   I need you to open this grate and help me get to the street without anyone seeing me. I don't want them to arrest me.

Teacher   Young lady, the march is at least ten blocks away. No one is going to arrest you here.

Maldonado   How can I be sure?

Teacher   Because the school is empty, there are no students, only a few teachers. The police won't come here.

Maldonado   Excuse me, Teach, but when I crawled in here, the school was completely taken over by cops. They took Hinojosa, Garrido, Torres, la Chica Pérez. Why do you think I'm in here?

Teacher   Where are you exactly? How long have you been there?

Maldonado   Since the cops swarmed the school.

Teacher (*surprised*)   Since the last occupation?

Maldonado   What do you mean last? Mister, don't try to confuse me. I know exactly how things went down. I've had more than enough time to think about it.

Teacher   How long have you been in there?

Maldonado   I prefer not to get into the details, mister. Besides, I'm not too clear on that myself.

Teacher   Days?

Maldonado   Mm . . . weeks.

Teacher (*surprised*)   Weeks! You're not serious, are you? What's your name, miss?

Maldonado   The less you know, the better, mister.

Teacher   At least tell me what grade you're in.

Maldonado   What for, mister?

Teacher   I've never heard your voice, you know?

Maldonado   That's because we don't have any classes together.

Teacher   I'm the Physics teacher for the whole high school.

Maldonado   I'm in the Humanities.

Teacher (*thinking, confused*)   I don't have a single student named Hinojosa, you know that? Or Pérez, or Torres, or . . . Guajardo.

Maldonado   Garrido, sir.

Teacher   I don't have anyone with those names.

Maldonado   They're my classmates, sir. They were detained. Them, and some of the ones who showed up from other schools. (*Treading cautiously*) Alpha Centauro, for example, they took him, too. Have you heard anything about him? Do you think they've released him?

Teacher   Alpha Centauro? What kind of name is that?

Maldonado   He's one of our leaders. Curly-haired, really handsome. Do you know him?

Teacher   This is a girls' school, young lady, there's no "Alpha Centauro" here. And if any of my students were detained, I'd know about it. In fact, if any of my students were stuck inside there since the last occupation.

Maldonado (*correcting*)   The only one, sir.

Teacher   The only one, the last one, same thing. If one of them had disappeared, I would have found out. Their guardians, their family members would have come, the Police Investigators, the press . . .

Maldonado (*interrupting*)   Mister, stop making things more confusing and get me out of here. Many comrades are depending on this operation.

Teacher (*taken aback*)   Comrades? Are there other students with you?

Maldonado *is silent for a moment. The* **Teacher** *insists.*

Teacher   Young lady, I'm asking you a question. Are there more students with you?

Maldonado   Yes, sir.

Teacher   How many?

Maldonado   Many, sir.

Teacher (*shocked*)   Many! But that's impossible, young lady. How can there possibly be a group of students stuck in a hole in the wall!

Maldonado   Sir, this hole, as you call it, is just one way out.

Teacher   One way out of where?

Maldonado   From the place we're in.

Teacher   But what place is that?!

Maldonado   A hideout.

Teacher   Whose hideout? From what?

Maldonado   Mister, I don't want to get you in trouble. I just need you to get me out, understand?

Teacher   Get you out of this hole which, according to you, is the exit to a hideout where you, and a group of fellow students, have supposedly been for weeks since the last occupation?

Maldonado Exactly.

Maldonado Forgive me, but I'm not going to fall for this ridiculous nonsense. You'll have to find someone else if you don't want to tell me the truth.

*The **Teacher** heads to the door, resolute, and opens it to leave.*

Maldonado (*shouting desperately*) Mister, I'm telling you the truth!

Maldonado *sticks her hand through the grate. She reaches it out to the **Teacher**, who watches her from a distance.*

Maldonado (*begging*) Please don't leave me here.

*After a moment, the **Teacher** seems convinced. He closes the door. He comes closer, picks up the screwdriver and starts to remove the screws from the grate of the air duct.*

Teacher What is your name, young lady?

Maldonado Gamma Cassiopeia, sir.

Teacher I'm being serious, miss. What's your name?

Maldonado I can't tell you the real one, mister. It wouldn't be wise for either of us.

Teacher It's the least I should know if I'm going to get you out of there.

Maldonado *takes a moment to respond.*

Maldonado (*reluctantly*)   . . . Maldonado, sir. Beatriz Maldonado.

Teacher There's no Beatriz Maldonado in this school.

Maldonado The screw, sir. You've got one screw left. Loosen it, please.

*The **Teacher** loosens the last screw and he passes it to **Maldonado**. The grate falls. From inside emerges **Maldonado**, a woman wearing a schoolgirl uniform. She's wearing a navy blue jumper, a white shirt, and a little tie with the school's insignia. She's around 45 years old, or more. Her uniform looks shabby, dirty, and old. It's probably a bit too small for her. She's carrying an old leather schoolbag. The **Teacher** looks at her speechless, bewildered.*

Maldonado (*looking at him*)   Your eyes really are nice, Teach. Forgive me, it's nothing personal, but in times like these, as I told you, one can't trust anybody.

Maldonado *takes a metal bar from her bag and hits the **Teacher** violently on the head. The **Teacher** falls to the ground, unconscious. The bell rings, signaling the end of a class period.*

Third Period

Pegasus 51

As if lost in the middle of outer space, the **Aged Youth** *is in light surrounded by complete darkness. He seems prepared to teach a class. The scar of a bullet wound still on his forehead.*

Aged Youth   Pegusus 51 was the first one to propose it to me. "Alpha Centauro," he said. "Why don't you get involved in the militias?" And I, who wasn't so convinced at the time, told him no. That I preferred to keep fighting at school with my high school comrades, that actually, the truth was . . . I was scared. "Now you're scared, Alpha, but sooner or later you're gonna join us. Occupations aren't enough, marches aren't enough. We've got to arm ourselves, they give us no other option." That's what he told me.

Pegasus 51 had been expelled from school and no other school wanted to take him. Thing is, he had a rep for being this subversive kid because he'd been a student leader and he'd been thrown in jail a few times. See, Pegasus, since he was little, chose a more radical struggle. That's why he was always plotting things. That's why he carried a small revolver.

The **Aged Youth** *shows a small revolver that he takes out of his bag.*

A shitty weapon, like this, a "catkiller," to protect himself, that's what he said. (*He puts it away.*) That's also why one night, there in the Villa Francia, with his brother and four more comrades, it occurred to them to rob the bakery on the corner of Cinco de Abril and Las Rejas. It's just—they had to fund the militias, because the militias, like everything else in life, have to be funded in some way, they don't fund themselves.

And so that's how Pegasus set out, with his brother and his buddies, walking down the street to the bakery, when a truck full of cops appeared behind them and lit up Pegasus with its headlights. He was there for just two seconds, all lit up, motionless, wondering what the hell to do. "Shit, fucking motherfuckers, we haven't even robbed anything and they're already onto us," he must have told himself.

The group dispersed. Pegasus and his brother, without noticing that they were being followed, went into a passageway and suddenly found the cops there, out of nowhere. On one side, a cop in an armored truck. On the other side, more cops on foot. And Pegasus and his brother between them. They all looked at each other. They all observed each other for a minute. Cop. Militant. Militant. Cop.

If things had been civilized, Pegasus could have said, "Dudes, what's up, why are you following us? We were just walking down the street." But things hadn't been civilized for a while, for anyone. The chief cop, a big solid man with a sinister look who watched him with crazy eyes, was a sub-lieutenant from the Alessandri police station who'd had them pegged for a while. He had searched his house in Villa Francia, followed his family, harassed his parents, the only thing he wanted was to catch him, so Pegasus knew that that conversation, that night, was not going to be possible.

According to the cops, what followed was a confrontation. They were all shooting to kill. (*He gestures as if shooting a gun*) Pow ... pow ... A cop gets shot in the chest and falls to the ground. But it's from a Taurus pistol, the kind his colleagues use. Pow ... pow ... Pegasus receives a shot in the back and also falls to the ground. Pow ... pow ... Pegasus' brother also gets shot, but this is more serious, it's to the heart. "Damn," thinks Pegasus. "This wasn't the plan, they're gonna let me have it when I get home." Pegasus drags himself, he wants to embrace his brother, to see if he's still breathing, but a policeman stops him by bashing a rifle into in his face. "What's wrong with you, fucking pig, it's my brother, I just want to see how he is." Without listening, the policemen cuff him, they grab him by the hair, by the legs, and throw him into the truck.

The rest of their comrades watch, hidden, from afar, without any idea of what's happening inside. They don't know that Pegasus is there. They don't know that they've got him on the floor, crushed under a cop's heavy boots. They don't know that one of the policemen fires a bullet into the back of his neck. (*He makes a shooting gesture.*) Pow ... They don't know that they take the corpse out of the truck and throw it on the ground, next to the body of his brother. They don't know.

That's where they left the two brothers.

Pegasus was 18 years old and was never able to finish high school.

A schoolbell rings. End of class period. .

Fourth Period

Beta Andromeda and Epsilon Sagittarius

We see the **Teacher** *lying unconscious on the floor of the lab. Everything is in shadow. Through the grates of two other air ducts, two flashlight beams get closer and closer.*

The screws from the other two grates fall to the floor. The grates fall with a bang. From inside the air ducts emerge two women dressed like schoolgirls. They're around 45 years old, or more. They are **Riquelme** *and* **Fuenzalida**. *They act like guerrilla operatives. Bandanas hide their faces. They inspect the place with their flashlights. They illuminate and shine bright on the* **Teacher**, *who wakes, frightened.*

Teacher   No, please! No!

Riquelme   Mr. Valdebenito?

The **Teacher** *nods, surprised.*

Riquelme   Don't be scared, we're students here. I'm Beta Andromeda and my comrade is Epsilon Sagittarius. Obviously those aren't our names, but that's what you can call us. We're looking for a comrade.

Fuenzalida *looks toward the grate that* **Maldonado** *emerged from and shows* **Riquelme**.

Riquelme   You must have seen her, sir. She came out through here, through this grate.

Teacher   Maldonado?

Riquelme *and* **Fuenzalida** *look at each other uneasily.*

Riquelme   She gave you that name, sir?

Teacher   Yes.

Riquelme   I can't believe it! What else did she say, mister?

Teacher   What is this? Some end of the year prank? Did you all get together and agree to make a fool out of Mr. Valdebenito?

Riquelme (*disconcerted*)   I don't know what you're talking about, sir.

Teacher   Whose idea was it? Carvajal's? Let's confuse Mr. Valdebenito until he proves what a screwup he is and then fire him . . . is that it?

Riquelme *and* **Fuenzalida** *look at him perplexed. They don't seem to understand what he's saying.*

Teacher   Let me tell you something, I've worked hard to get here. I've done training courses, seminars, pedagogy workshops, psychological tests, medical exams. I've built a Teaching Portfolio unlike any of my colleagues because I've laid out convincing evidence of my work. I've taken part in educational projects, in extracurricular programming, I've met with the people from the Department of

Education, with the people from the universities. I've done entrepreneurial coaching sessions in the evenings, English brush-up courses on Saturday mornings.
Extra meetings with the director, extra meetings with the teachers, extra meetings with the inspectors, with the whole student body, with their parents and guardians, and all while I keep on religiously teaching classes here, in the lab, coordinating curricula, grading exams, turning in grades punctually, completing student evaluations on time. I've passed all my peer evaluations with flying colors. It hasn't been easy, it's cost me time, health and energy, but I did it, therefore I am not going to give up being Educational Coordinator so easily, and even less because of a ridiculous ambush like this. Tell that to Carvajal. I earned this position and neither he nor anyone else is going to take it away from me.

Riquelme   Sir, don't misunderstand. We never, hear me clearly, never would establish even the most minimal tie with the disgusting traitor pig Carvajal. And we don't want to take away your job, either.

At a sign from **Riquelme**, *she and* **Fuenzalida** *pull down their bandanas and show their faces.*

Riquelme   Look at us, we're teenagers, we're sixteen years old, why would we want to work as Educational Coordinators?

The **Teacher** *looks at them, disconcerted.*

Teacher   How far do you want to take this? What kind of joke is this?

Fuenzalida *writes something on a page from a school notebook. Then she pulls out the page and hands it to the* **Teacher**.

Teacher (*reads the paper*)   WE ARE NO JOKE. (*He looks at them uneasily.*) What is this?

Fuenzalida *writes on another notebook page, tears it out and hands it to him.*

Teacher (*reads*)   I AM A STUDENT WITH DISABILITIES.

Riquelme   It's true, Mister. Our comrade Sagittarius recently lost her ability to speak. (*Just to him*) It's been a sensitive topic for her.

The **Teacher** *looks at them, bewildered.*

Teacher   All right, all right . . . I won't ask you any questions, I'm not even going to try to understand what is happening. I'm just going to go out this door so that you can go on with this . . . game, but without me. Sound good?

Fuenzalida *and* **Riquelme** *suddenly and violently block the door. They forcibly immobilize the* **Teacher** *and sit him in a chair.*

Riquelme   No, sir. Please excuse us, but you're not going anywhere.

The women tie him up to keep him from moving.

Teacher   But what is this! Let me go! Help!

Riquelme Collaborate and this will be much easier for us all.

Fuenzalida *writes on another notebook page. Then she tears it out and holds it in front of his eyes so he can read it.*

Teacher (*reads*) WHAT HAPPENED TO MALDONADO? (*He looks at them and responds.*) I have no idea what happened to Maldonado. I helped her get out of the ... wall, she hit me, she knocked me unconscious and that's all I know.

Riquelme She didn't say where she was going? What she wanted to do?

Teacher No.

Fuenzalida *writes on a page and shows it to the* **Teacher***.*

Teacher (*reads*) DON'T LIE! (*looks at them*) I'm not lying, she said nothing else.

Riquelme Did she talk about Alpha, mister?

Teacher Alpha Centauro?

Fuenzalida *and* **Riquelme** *look at each other, uncomfortable.*

Riquelme What did she tell you about him, mister?

Teacher Nothing, that he was young, a leader, very handsome.

Riquelme Handsome?

Fuenzalida *writes on a page and shows it to him.*

Teacher (*reads*) WHAT DO YOU KNOW ABOUT HIM? (*looks at them*) Nothing, I know nothing about him, I already told you.

Fuenzalida *writes on a page and shows him.*

Teacher (*reads*) WHO IS NANCY? (*looks at them*) What does that have to do with you?

Fuenzalida *writes on a page and shows him.*

Teacher (*reads*) WHO IS NANCY?! ANSWER! (*looks at them*) My wife.

Fuenzalida *writes on a page and shows him.*

Teacher (*reads*) HOW LONG HAVE YOU BEEN MARRIED? (*looks at them*) Nine years.

Fuenzalida *writes on a page and shows him.*

Teacher (*reads*) DO YOU HAVE CHILDREN? (*looks at them*) That's none of your business!

Riquelme He has kids!

Teacher No.

Fuenzalida *writes on a page and shows him.*

Teacher (*reads*)   WHY NOT? (*Uncomfortable*) Well . . . things haven't worked out.

Riquelme   What things?

Teacher   She thinks it's not the right time yet. She's got . . . other plans.

Riquelme   What plans?

Teacher   Well . . . her work. Her work is very important to her.

Fuenzalida *writes on a page and shows him.*

Teacher (*reads*)   WHAT DOES SHE DO? (*Looks at them*) She's a secretary at a garment factory.

Riquelme   And that prevents her from having kids?

Teacher   It's complicated . . . we need income. As a teacher at this school I don't make that much, I have to take other work, give private classes, take on more duties . . .

Riquelme   Educational Coordinator.

Teacher   Exactly. And besides, if my wife were to get pregnant now, it's likely the same thing will happen to her that happened to all her colleagues when they had kids.

Riquelme   What happened to them?

Teacher   They've been fired. They come back from maternity leave and they hand them their severance. And that's the ones that are full-time employees, but Nancy, my wife, is an independent contractor, they'd let her go immediately, and the way things are, we can't afford that luxury. We bought an apartment, you know? We've got to pay the mortgage and the maintenance fees, which are out of control. I knew it would be unnecessary to have an apartment with a gym and event space. Do you think we've ever used those, even once? We leave home at seven in the morning and we get back around nine pm. You think that with that schedule we feel like going to work out? But now we have to pay for those services every month. And then there's the car, because Nancy bought herself a car, because don't you know she works far away. She has to cross the whole city and she can't squeeze onto the subway every morning, because she's already been robbed, been groped. I mean one time a guy practically pulled down her underwear, excuse me for saying it so crudely like that, but that's what happened. And of course, Nancy won't stand for that kind of treatment, she's a decent woman. Nobody could stand it. So we also have to finish paying off the car before we can even think of having a family.

The **Teacher** *falls silent. Absorbed in his thoughts.* **Fuenzalida** *writes on a notebook page and shows it to him.*

Teacher (*reads*)   AND WHERE IS MRS. NANCY NOW? (*to them*) At her job at the factory.

Riquelme   But if she's there, why did we hear you talking with her here, in the lab? Do you talk to yourself, mister?

The **Teacher's** *cell phone rings on one of the lab tables.* **Fuenzalida** *and* **Riquelme** *look very alarmed. After the second ring,* **Riquelme** *shouts frantically.*

Riquelme (*shouting*)   Agh! What is that!

The **Teacher** *stares at them without understanding why they're so panicked.*

Riquelme (*shouting*)   It could be a bomb!

Teacher   A bomb?

Riquelme   Mister Teacher, don't act so naïve! It must be a trick.

Teacher   Whose trick?

Riquelme   The cops, Central Intelligence, that fascist Carvajal.

Teacher   Young ladies, it must be my wife. Let me answer it.

Riquelme   They've already tear gassed us in the middle of classes, this could be dangerous.

Teacher   It's not at all dangerous.

Riquelme   Mister, we've got comrades who they've blown up in their own apartments with devices like this.

Teacher (*freaked out*)   What are you talking about!

Riquelme (*desperate*)   About Omega 21. They blew him and two more comrades to high heaven right in the middle of Villa Portales.

Teacher   Who are "they"?

Riquelme   They said that they were making a bomb, that they found ten kilos of ammonia gelatin explosive among the remains, but that isn't true! Do you know how much ten kilos of ammonia gelatin is?

Teacher   No.

Riquelme   With just one kilogram you can blow up a high voltage power station—what were they gonna do with ten kilos? Only a pack of madmen would store so much in their own home, and Omega was no madman. Besides, they found weapons and documents that implicated him in terrorist attacks, and the most curious thing is that the only thing that wasn't burned in the fire were those weapons and papers. How strange, right? Now do you see how far they'll go? This could be the same kind of thing!

The **Teacher** *looks concerned by this information. The phone stops ringing.*

Teacher   They hung up.

Riquelme *gets closer and carefully examines the cell phone.*

Teacher (*still affected by the information*)   Who are you talking about, young lady? What is the name of that young man who they blew up with an explosive?

Riquelme (*focused on the cell phone*)   This is high-end technology. It has numbers... and buttons... and lights... I've never seen something like that, so sophisticated...

The phone rings again. **Riquelme** *and* **Fuenzalida** *throw themselves on the floor, shielding themselves from danger.*

Riquelme   No...!

The **Teacher** *inches forward with his chair and with great difficulty manages to answer the phone.*

Riquelme   Don't do it, sir!

Teacher   Stop this nonsense and let me answer! (*he answers*) Hello? (...) (*surprised*) Carvajal...

Riquelme (*alarmed*)   What are you doing, mister?

The **Teacher** *gestures for her to be quiet.*

Teacher   I'm here, in the lab... (...) No, I'm not feeling bad, I just came to check on a couple of things. (...) Yes, Carvajal, I'm sure I'm not ill. (...) (*surprised*) Leave in your car? All of us with the Principal? (...) It's just, I was thinking of staying to work longer, I'm still not done grading. (...) Everything's cut off. (...) Barricades. (...) Tire perforators. (...) Water cannons. (...) I won't be able to get out alone. (...) Yes, yes, I'm here. (...) No, don't worry, there's no reason to come get me, I'll be there soon. (...) Yes, of course, Carvajal...

The **Teacher** *hangs up the phone, nervous.*

Teacher   Carvajal noticed.

Riquelme   Why do you talk to yourself on that device?

Teacher   It's a telephone, young lady, I was not talking to myself, I was talking to Carvajal.

Fuenzalida *and* **Riquelme** *examine the device, uneasy.*

Riquelme   If you were really talking on... that thing... with that disgusting traitor pig Carvajal, why didn't you tell him about us? Why didn't you tell him that we took you hostage?

Teacher   I'm a hostage?

A knock at the door. All three look at each other in terror.

Teacher (*to himself*)   Carvajal...

Fuenzalida *and* **Riquelme** *quickly secure the door. They act as if they're completing a mission. They try not to be heard from outside. They urge the* **Teacher** *to speak.*

Teacher (*to the door*)   Carvajal, I told you it wasn't necessary to come. I'll come up in a bit.

Before they can react, there's another knock on the door. From outside, we hear the voice of **Maldonado**.

Maldonado   Teach, it's me . . . let me in please.

They all look at each other in surprise. **Riquelme** *quickly opens the door, and* **Maldonado** *appears. She's soaking wet, disheveled, her uniform dirty.*

Riquelme   Why the hell did you leave, you crazy bitch?

Teacher   Young lady, please, watch the language! We are in an educational institution!

Riquelme   I'm sorry, sir. (*To* **Maldonado**) Do you realize what could have happened?

Maldonado   Don't yell at me! I needed to know about Alpha and the rest of our classmates.

Riquelme   And did you find anything out?

Maldonado   No, nothing.

Riquelme   Where'd you go?

Maldonado   Out to the street.

Teacher (*horrified*)   You went out on the street like *that*?

Riquelme   And what happened?

Maldonado   You wouldn't even believe it . . .

Maldonado *looks at them, disturbed.*

Maldonado   Everything's the same, this thing hasn't moved forward one bit in all the time we've been inside there. There was a giant ruckus, they arrested two comrades from Aplicación and five comrades from High School Number Five. The cops forced them into the van, kicking them and hitting them with rifle butts. Water canons, armed trucks, tear gas. Look how these sons of bitches left me!

Fuenzalida *writes in her notebook, rips out the page and hands it to* **Riquelme**.

Riquelme (*reads*)   WE HAVE TO STAY HIDDEN. (*responds*) Of course, comrade.

Maldonado   I don't think it's a good idea to keep waiting.

Riquelme   Do you want the same thing that happened to our other comrades to happen to you?

Teacher   To who? To the young men you were talking about recently? The ones with the explosive?

Riquelme   Do we want to change this country? Well then, let's wait for our historical moment. Those were the instructions we were given.

Maldonado   It's that there's something we didn't realize, chiquillas.[2] (*She looks at them uncomfortably*). Chiquillas . . . sit down.

Riquelme *and* **Fuenzalida** *sit.* **Maldonado** *looks at them nervously.*

Riquelme   Talk.

Maldonado   Chiquillas, since we went into hiding, more time has passed than we thought.

Riquelme *and* **Fuenzalida** *look at each other, confused.*

Riquelme   What do you mean . . . more time?

Maldonado   A long time.

Riquelme   How long of a time?

Maldonado   Chiquillas, when I got out of here and I crossed the schoolyard, I peeked into the gym, and you wouldn't believe what I saw.

Riquelme   What did you see?

Maldonado   All the chairs are in rows in front of the proscenium. And they decorated the stage with the school's flag and shield, with balloons and shiny gold tinsel letters that say . . .

Riquelme (*guessing what's coming*)   That say what?

Maldonado   Senior graduation!

Riquelme *and* **Fuenzalida** *despair.*

Riquelme   Fuck me to hell! (*To* **Teacher**) Sorry, sir.

Fuenzalida *writes in her notebook, tears out the page and gives it to the* **Teacher** *to read.*

Teacher (*reads*)   WHEN IS GRADUATION? (*to them*) Tomorrow.

They all lose it.

Maldonado   Chiquillas, it's December, five months have passed since we went into hiding. (*She counts*) August, September, October, November, and December. We've been in there for five months! Five months, completely lost!

Riquelme   My Papá is going to kick my ass.

Maldonado   My Mamá's never going to speak to me again.

Riquelme   Five months! But how could we not even notice!

Maldonado   It's that time passes really weirdly when you go into hiding you get lost, get confused. I could have sworn we were there, I don't know . . . a couple of weeks.

Riquelme (*realizing something*)   And the play? (*To* **Teacher**) We're part of the theatre group, we were rehearsing our play for the graduation ceremony. Sagittarius had finished the script. Right, Sagittarius?

Fuenzalida *agrees.*

Riquelme It was looking amazing!

Maldonado I'm sure we fucked up. They're going to put on the chorus singing the Farewell Song.

Riquelme And the party? (*To the* **Teacher**) Is there going to be a graduation party?

Teacher Of course.

Maldonado Where?

Teacher At La Cuca of Huechuraba.

Riquelme No!

Maldonado (*lamenting*) And I wanted Alpha to go with me.

Riquelme Now it's too late for us to find a decent dress, or to invite anyone . . . It's too late for us to organize anything, comrades!

Maldonado At this point, we've probably all flunked out!

Riquelme (*realizing*) That means that the University Entrance Exam . . .

They look at each other, even more disturbed.

Maldonado We're screwed!

Riquelme We didn't even register for it.

Maldonado No! After working so hard to keep up my GPA! What for? For nothing?

Riquelme I was going to study law, do you realize that? I was going to be a national congresswoman when democracy finally returns.

The **Teacher** *listens, confused.*

Teacher When what returns?

Riquelme Democracy, sir. Because one day this country will be free and sovereign again, even if we have to spill blood.

Maldonado And we are the ones to count on for that moment.

Riquelme Chile needs the next generation and here we are, ready to take over.

Maldonado That's why we organized our glorious occupation, Mr. Teacher!

Riquelme That's why we've been here, hidden, awaiting the day when we'll emerge to gain freedom!

Teacher (*interrupting*) Young ladies, forgive me for interrupting this ecstasy of yours, but which heroic occupation is that, please?

The three women look at each other, perplexed.

Riquelme I'm surprised, Teach. What planet are you living on?

Maldonado Do you honestly not know anything about our takeover?

Teacher No.

Maldonado *moves the chair that the* **Teacher** *is tied to. She leaves him looking at the blackboard as if it were a stage. The students prepare to perform.* **Fuenzalida** *writes on the blackboard: July 10, 6:00am.*

Riquelme Winter, fog, darkness. Everything indicated that the day would be tense, difficult.

Maldonado We met up at the subway exit. That was the meeting point. All the area high schools were summoned.

Riquelme We were more than two hundred comrades. We didn't know each other, many of us had only seen each other, but we all knew why we were there.

Maldonado "This is unbelievable," said Alpha Centauro with that plump little mouth of his, because he really has gorgeous lips. "We never imagined this level of participation, comrades, this is totally unprecedented," he said, and we like, started to laugh. *(She laughs.)* A nervous laugh, though.

Riquelme Along with Alpha Centauro, we climbed up on a bench and started to organize the situation.

Maldonado Alpha has lips to die for, Teach. He's the voice of our movement. He speaks like the gods.

Riquelme "Are you ready, comrades?" asked Alpha . . .

Maldonado And we shouted "Yes!"

Maldonado and Riquelme Yes!

Riquelme And then Alpha Centauro blew a whistle . . .

Fuenzalida *blows a whistle.*

Riquelme . . . and we started off en masse down the street to take over the school.

Maldonado Some teachers started panicking when we got there. "Let us go, you little shits, what have we got to do with this nonsense!"

Riquelme That's when that disgusting traitor pig Carvajal called the Principal at home to let her know what was happening. She was sick, in bed, so she was spared from seeing the glorious entrance into her office that we had prepared. But she still demanded to speak with one of us over the phone, so Gamma Cassiopeia did it.

Maldonado I covered the receiver with my bandana and made up an exaggerated voice that would throw them off, that wouldn't let them identify me, and which, also, would scare them, you understand? (*changes her voice*) "Hello," I said, "this is one of the movement representatives."

Riquelme (*imitating the Principal*) "What's going on, Maldonado?" answered the Principal.

Maldonado I stayed silent.

Riquelme (*imitating the Principal*) "Do you have something to do with this, Maldonado?"

Maldonado I took the handkerchief off and went back to my usual voice. I told her yes, I told her what our goals were with the occupation, that we had a long list of demands, and that inside there were lots of people from other schools, that it wasn't just our idea.

Riquelme (*imitating the Principal*) "Are you actually stupid or are you just acting that way, Maldonado? Do you realize that everything you're doing is pure bullshit?"

Maldonado Excuse me, Ms. Principal, but I'm not going to let you curse at me, I haven't disrespected you.

Riquelme (*imitating the Principal*) "You haven't disrespected me, Maldonado? You barge in with your people kicking and shoving, you lock up all the adults, I'm sure you're breaking windows, writing on walls, tearing up the place, and you have the gall to tell me that you're not disrespecting me? Go to hell and stay there for a while!"

Maldonado When the initial euphoria passed, Alpha gave the order to go up to the roof. We grabbed all the benches and chairs we could and we barricaded ourselves up there.

Riquelme We hung a banner that we had painted, we hung our flag and there we stayed, celebrating the occupation on the very top of the school.

Maldonado At ten a.m. the first van full of cops showed up. (*To* **Teacher**) Guess who had called them?

Teacher Carvajal.

Riquelme Little by little, more cops started coming, and then more, and more.

Maldonado All of a sudden we heard a voice from a loudspeaker. "Students, you must leave the school now."

Riquelme Alpha responded that in order to come out and end the occupation, we had a list of demands that had be met.

Maldonado The cops responded that we could stick our list of demands up where the sun don't shine and that we better come out once and for all if we didn't want them to come in by force.

Riquelme "There's no fucking way you'll get us out!" yelled Alpha Centauro, and the yell became a chorus.

The three women repeat the yell, clapping and dancing.

Riquelme and Maldonado (*yelling*) No fucking way you'll get us out, pa, pa, pa, pa, pa. No fucking way you'll get us out . . .

Fuenzalida *blows the whistle.*

Maldonado   That's what we were doing when Alpha blew the whistle to get our attention.

Riquelme   The cops were positioned in front of the school with their shields, their helmets and their police batons. A couple of them came up to the gate to cut the chains so they could come in, but it wasn't even necessary because guess who showed up with a vengeance to cut the chains.

Teacher   Carvajal.

Riquelme   Then the rain of stones started falling from the rooftop. We threw rocks at them, sticks, chairs, tables, whatever we could find to keep them from coming through.

Maldonado   A pack of cops climbed up on the roof of a van and started shooting.

Riquelme (*imitating the sound of gunshots*)   Pow . . . pow . . . The bullets flew right by us. We all threw ourselves on the floor.

The three of them throw themselves on the floor remembering what they did.

Maldonado   Garrrido got shot in the foot. "Ay," shouted Garrido, and some students from Amunátegui helped her.

Riquelme   Pissed, our comrades from High School Number One started throwing Molotovs.

Maldonado   The bombs fell right next to the cops.

Riquelme   The fire lit up a cop car.

Maldonado   And that's when everything went to hell. That set off the cops and they full-on stormed the place.

The women are lost in their memories for a moment, as if watching the policemen enter.

Riquelme   Alpha told us: "Comrades, hide yourselves. This is going to be a massacre. Take people to a secure location."

Maldonado   That's when we gave the order that everyone who could should get into the hideout.

Riquelme   One by one they started going in.

Maldonado   We squeezed them in with pliers, but still not everyone fit.

Riquelme   Alpha and Sagittarius went to the schoolyard and took care of the rest. Of the folks from Aplicación, the National, from High School Number One and Number Seven, from Amunátegui, but they couldn't do much.

Maldonado   From the hideout we could hear the shouts.

Riquelme   Sagittarius was there.

Maldonado   But once she finally could tell us about that moment, she couldn't speak anymore, she didn't have any voice left.

Riquelme   Since that happened, she only writes.

Maldonado   Sagittarius wrote that four cops grabbed her by the hair and threw her in the middle of the schoolyard.

Riquelme   She tried to defend herself, but it was useless because they kicked her, beat her with their rifles and left her dumped on the ground.

Maldonado   Sagittarius wrote that she cried on the floor of the schoolyard in front of our comrades and the police.

Riquelme   Sagittarius wrote that Alpha jumped between them all. "Fucking cops, piece of shit fascists," he said, "don't you realize that she's a woman, would you beat your daughters like that?"

Maldonado   But the cops didn't care and they kept pounding on Sagittarius.

Riquelme   So then Alpha took out his small revolver.

Maldonado   A crappy little weapon he had. A "catkiller," to defend himself, that's what he'd say.

Riquelme   And in a suicidal act he shot at the cops who were kicking Sagittarius. (*She imitates the action*) Pow . . . pow . . .

Maldonado   One of the cops fell to the ground.

Riquelme   Alpha shot his eye out.

Maldonado   Then he shot his ear off.

Riquelme   The blood bounced off the tiles of the schoolyard.

Maldonado   Everyone was shocked. The cop was dead.

Riquelme   That's when they jumped on Alpha, kicking him. They threw him on the ground next to Sagittarius.

Maldonado   What happened next is confusing and we didn't experience it ourselves. We only know what Sagittarius wrote.

Riquelme   That they took them, walking single file, to the police vans that were parked outside.

Maldonado   That they went out through a long tunnel of cops who didn't let them see much.

Riquelme   That they squeezed inside however they could, all jammed together.

Maldonado   That Sagittarius cried softly, that Alpha also cried softly.

Riquelme   That the van started its motor.

Maldonado   That they left the school behind . . .

Riquelme   . . . with the disgusting traitor pig Carvajal, with the teachers, with the people who had gathered outside, with us hidden away, waiting for the moment to come out.

The three women remain silent. They've come to the end of their performance. The **Teacher** *gazes at them for a moment, perplexed. He breaks the silence, delicately.*

Teacher (*carefully*)   The day of that . . . glorious takeover that you've told me about . . . the day on which you went inside there to wait, as you say, when exactly was that?

Fuenzalida *writes in her notebook and then tears out the page and hands it to the* **Teacher**.

Teacher (*reads*)   MONDAY, JULY 10 . . . 1985. (*He looks at them, astonished.*) You've been in there since then?

The women nod. The **Teacher** *looks at them, disconcerted.*

The bell rings, announcing the end of the class period.

Fifth Period

Zeta Neptune

As if lost in outer space, The **Aged Youth** *is in light, surrounded by absolute darkness. The scar of a bullet hole still on his forehead. He carries a letter in his hands. The paper has gridlines and is old and deteriorated. The* **Aged Youth** *reads. Maybe he's reading to his friends, as if he were in the middle of a funeral.*

Aged Youth (*reading*)   "The first time I went to a protest, I saw how the police would kick us for asking for things that we thought were just. We'd all run, we were like mice, we didn't have a way to defend ourselves. That's when I realized that all the evil things I'd seen since I was little were caused by the interest that one group of people has in sucking the rest dry, and that that group relies on violence to keep things the way they are. That's also when I understood that it was very difficult to complain about this or try to begin a dialogue, because the only thing that you get in return is a beating.

We don't like violence. It's the brutality of the system which leaves us no other choice. They condemned us to a system that's not good for everyone, but just for a few. We're young, we value life, and we're fighting for a better future for ourselves. It's for that love that we take up arms and are not afraid to die."

The **Aged Youth** *stops reading.*

Aged Youth   Zeta Neptune was inspired and liked to write. He gave me this letter so that we could publish it in the school newspaper. I didn't change a thing, only added a couple of commas, but everything else is his. "Alpha Centauro," he told me, "don't change anything on me," and I gave him my word.

Zeta Neptune was a comrade from Aplicación. Two weeks after writing this, he died in a shootout in Pudahuel. His body had two bullet wounds, one from a SIG military assault rifle and one from an UZI submachine gun.

He did not get to see his letter published.

The bell rings, signaling the end of a class period.

Sixth Period

A True Constellation

The students are sitting at the laboratory tables. They all have a notebook and pencil. They watch the Teacher attentively, who is teaching them a lesson. He's still out of sorts. The information they've told him has made him worse. He sweats, his hands tremble. Nevertheless, he tries to settle himself so that he can keep going. On the blackboard, he has erased the previous writings and has drawn the planet Earth.

Teacher Young ladies, this is our planet: Earth.

*The **Teacher** looks at them and interrupts himself. His gaze gets lost looking at the three women who watch him attentively.*

Teacher (*returning to his lesson*) On earth we live adrift in a kind of ocean of space and time. We're carried by our planet around the sun. Since its beginning, the earth has completed four billion centuries around the sun. The sun, for its part, travels through the galaxy, and for its part, the Milky Way, our galaxy, moves between other galaxies. Therefore, we've always been space travelers.

Maldonado How long did you say we've been traveling around the sun, sir?

Teacher Four billion centuries.

Maldonado *takes notes. From the objects in the lab, the **Teacher** takes out a large jar with sand. He takes out a fistful from it.*

Teacher Look at these fine grains of sand. They're derived from larger rocks through centuries of erosion. Through them we can understand that the roots that sustain our present are anchored in the past. We, then, are also . . .

*The **Teacher** looks at them and breaks off. He gazes at the three women who watch him attentively.*

Riquelme So, what are we, then . . . ?

Teacher (*reacting*) . . . time travelers.

Maldonado How cool!

Teacher But since we're trapped on earth we don't notice where we're going in space or how fast. From our limited position, it's difficult to understand the evolution of the cosmos, because what we perceive is just a tiny reality. If we just think of the insignificant number of stars that we can see, with luck, on a clear night, we realize it, how blind we are. Because there are more stars in the universe than all the grains of sand on all the beaches on all of planet Earth.

*The **Teacher** throws the fistful of sand into the air. The students watch him.*

Maldonado Invisible stars.

Teacher Invisible to us, who cannot see them.

Riquelme Excuse me, sir, I don't want to interrupt you, but . . . why are you explaining this to us? Is it for the University Entrance Exam? Remember, we already messed that all up.

Maldonado Don't interrupt him, let him continue. It's so nice to take classes again.

Teacher (*to* **Riquelme**) What was your name, miss?

Riquelme Beta Andromeda.

Teacher Did you know that's the second-brightest star in the Andromeda constellation?

Riquelme (*surprised*) Me?

The **Teacher** *draws the Andromeda constellation on the board, marking the six stars that make it up.*

Teacher Andromeda, in Greek mythology, was a beautiful young woman whom Perseus saved from a terrible monster. You knew that, right?

Riquelme Yeah, we even did a play about it with our theatre group. Right chiquillas?

Maldonado I was Andromeda.

Riquelme And I was Perseus.

Maldonado Sagittarius wrote the play.

Riquelme And she was also the monster.

The comments seem to make **Fuenzalida** *uncomfortable.*

Maldonado But go on, Teach. Go on.

Teacher (*pointing at the blackboard*) This is Beta Andromeda. You'll find it seventy-five light years away from earth. The light by which we see this star has spent seventy-five years crossing interstellar space in order to get here, you understand?

Maldonado Woah, that's a long time.

Teacher For us, but not for the stars. Imagine, in the hypothetical case that Beta Andromeda were, at this very moment, exploding out there in space, we wouldn't know about that explosion for seventy-five more years. That's how long that interesting information takes to get to Earth.

Maldonado So, a lot of the stars we see might be dead?

Teacher Exactly.

Maldonado So what we're seeing is those stars' past?

Teacher You said it.

Maldonado They're like mementos or pictures of something that's not there anymore.

Fuenzalida *writes on one of her pages and hands it to* **Maldonado**.

Maldonado (*reads*)   GHOSTS.

Riquelme *suddenly stands up, agitated.*

Riquelme   Sir, I'm sorry to insist. Your class is very interesting, but what we're doing makes no sense at all. You are the only "responsible adult" that we've come across for months and that's why we've agreed, by consensus, to let you be free, always and only if you do not reveal our hideout and our heroic mission, which is gestating under the ground of this high school. But now that we've come to this agreement, we have nothing else to do here.

Teacher   Miss, you are correct. I am the "responsible adult" at this moment and I am obliged to pass on certain knowledge to you.

Riquelme   We're running against the clock. There's a group of people hiding, who we're responsible for, and we have many decisions to make. Have you forgotten that we've been in hiding for five months?

Teacher   Those five months of confinement that you speak of, could be five centuries or five seconds in Cosmic time. It all depends on how you want to look at it.

Maldonado   Time is relative, is what Teach wants to tell us.

Fuenzalida *writes in her notebook and gives it to* **Riquelme**.

Riquelme (*reads*)   AND NOT EVERYTHING WE SEE IS WHAT WE THINK WE SEE.

The **Teacher** *takes a newspaper from a drawer.* **Fuenzalida** *looks at him with alarm.*

Teacher   Just today I read in the newspaper about the discovery of a new star. Its name is Gamma Trident and it's twenty-five light years away from our planet.

Riquelme (*interrupting*)   Is that today's paper, Mister?

Teacher   Yes, it's from today. See what Gamma Trident looks like through a telescope.

The **Teacher** *opens the paper and shows them the photograph published inside.* **Fuenzalida** *looks tense.*

Teacher   This photo is from yesterday, and the date, which you can read here in detail, is the date which will be registered in history as the date of a great stellar discovery.

Riquelme *takes the newspaper from the* **Teacher***'s hands.* **Maldonado** *comes closer.* **Fuenzalida** *seems restless. The* **Teacher** *watches them with expectation.*

Maldonado   How beautiful . . . And just to think, this star, which is like a little baby, because they just discovered it, is actually an old lady of a hundred and twenty, right, Teach?

Teacher   Mm . . . more or less.

Maldonado Maybe we aren't ready to receive the knowledge of the stars, and that's why everything gets to us late.

Maldonado *closes the paper.* **Riquelme** *takes it from her.*

Riquelme All that about the star and outer space is interesting, but I'd like to see how things are going here on planet Earth. We've spent so long in hiding with our comrades, we have no idea how things are going in the world five months later.

Riquelme *starts paging through the paper. The* **Teacher** *watches her expectantly.* **Fuenzalida** *too.*

Maldonado (*to Riquelme*) I told you everything was the same.

Riquelme (*paging through*) It's true, here are the ads for the Telethon[3] that's starting soon.

Riquelme *turns pages.* **Fuenzalida** *looks more nervous.*

Riquelme The Christmas sales . . . (*She finds something interesting*) National news: Today President Michelle Bachelet once again declined to receive student leaders in the presidential palace La Moneda. On its part, the student movement has called for a peaceful and legal march on the Alameda.[4]

Riquelme *raises her eyes, disconcerted.* **Maldonado** *too.* **Fuenzalida** *watches them, terrified.*

Riquelme and Maldonado (*to* **Teacher**) Who is President Bachelet?

Teacher (*gently*) Young ladies, what I'm going to tell you is delicate and mysterious, as is everything in the cosmos. The newspaper that you're looking at was published today and even if you didn't see the date, I have to tell you that much more time has passed than you . . .

The **Teacher** *is about to continue, but before he can,* **Fuenzalida***, very nervous, takes the paper away from* **Riquelme** *and violently crumples it up. .*

Riquelme Sagittarius, what's up with you?

Teacher Miss, are you all right?

Fuenzalida *tears the paper into many tiny pieces. She seems a little out of control.*

Riquelme Sagittarius!

Maldonado Oh poor thing! Another crisis!

Riquelme Please excuse her, sir. Since she returned, Sagittarius hasn't been well.

Maldonado She came back like that, mute and kind of nuts. Seems like all those blows to the head left her that way. It's hard for us to control her.

Teacher (*confused*) She came back from where?

Maldonado From outside, of course.

Teacher But wasn't she with you?

Maldonado They arrested her the day of the takeover, she didn't go into the hideout with us.

Teacher And when did she come back?

Maldonado I'm not sure what to tell you because we're feeling kind of disoriented when it comes to time . . .

Fuenzalida, *very restless, writes on the blackboard: LET'S GO BACK.*

Riquelme Yes, Sagittarius, but we have to come to an agreement first. How are we going to go back and just tell our comrades the truth all of a sudden.

Maldonado We have to think of a good strategy, tell them carefully, in an indirect way, so they don't die of shock on us.

Riquelme (*to* **Maldonado**) Maybe we could talk to them about space, about how strange and crazy time is in the cosmos, that could give them some context, don't you think?

Maldonado That's true! Start there, jabber on a bit, and then, very carefully, tell them the truth.

Fuenzalida, *even more restless, writes on the blackboard: NO TO THE TRUTH.*

Maldonado (*freaked out*) Sagittarius, what are you doing? Do you want to keep our comrades in the dark in there?

Riquelme Managing and restricting information is a fascist strategy only fitting for that disgusting traitor pig Carvajal, not for us.

Fuenzalida *writes on the board: TIME IS NOT THE SAME HERE.*

Maldonado (*to* **Riquelme**) That's true. Remember what Teach just said, time is relative and totally weird, that's why those five months felt like nothing in there.

Riquelme Weird as it might be, I cannot hide from our classmates the fact that they flunked the year, that they won't get to do the play, or graduate, or take the University Entrance Exam, and that their parents must have been waiting for them for months.

Fuenzalida *writes desperately: OUR CAUSE IS MORE IMPORTANT.*

Maldonado That's also true. What are five months next to the future that awaits us if we're conscientious and careful?

Fuenzalida *writes desperately: OUTSIDE THEY WON'T TAKE CARE OF US.*

Teacher (*to* **Fuenzalida**) Miss . . . What happened to Alpha Centauro and the rest of your classmates who were detained?

Fuenzalida *doesn't respond. She only underlines the sentence she just wrote.*

Riquelme Sagittarius wrote that they were all taken prisoner, that they let her out first.

Teacher (*to* **Fuenzalida**)   And how long ago was that, young lady? How long were you outside before you returned to the hideout?

Fuenzalida *hunches her shoulders.*

Teacher   You don't remember? Don't know?

Riquelme   Don't pressure her, Teach.

Teacher   Why didn't you want your classmates to read today's newspaper?

Fuenzalida *writes on a page and hands it to the* **Teacher**.

Teacher (*reads*)   NONE OF YOUR BUSINESS, FUCKING OLD BASTARD.

Maldonado (*worried*)   Sagittarius, please!

Riquelme   See, you shouldn't pressure her. You don't know what it's like to be detained, you have no idea how a person ends up after that.

Teacher's *cell phone rings. They all look at it in surprise.* **Maldonado** *screams in fear.*

Maldonado   Agh! What is that?

Riquelme   Relax. It's a phone, the teacher already explained it to us.

Maldonado   But how can *that* be a phone?

Riquelme   A lot of things have happened in five months, you see?

Teacher *answers the phone. He doesn't seem to recognize the number.*

Teacher   Hello?

Riquelme (*to* **Maldonado**)   See, it's a phone.

Teacher (*surprised*)   Principal, ma'am . . . (. . .) Yes, yes, I'm doing well, ma'am.

The women make signs telling him not to mention them. He nods, understanding.

Teacher (*surprised*)   Who called you? (. . .) Nancy, my wife? (. . .) She's worried about me, she's worried something serious could happen to me . . . (. . .) (*pretending*) Oh but it's so silly of her to call you, I'm perfectly fine here, just finishing some grading. (. . .) No, why would you think that, I'm not having another breakdown. (. . .) (*nervous*) She told you I would say that? (. . .) (*emphatically*) What I'm saying is true, that's all over, it's treated, I don't know why my wife would call and bother you saying she's worried about panic attacks that I don't get. (. . .) No, ma'am, I'm fine. (. . .) No, ma'am, I don't need help. (*yells out of control*) There's nothing wrong with me, I'm telling you! (. . .) (*he controls himself*) Excuse me, ma'am . . . please excuse me. (. . .) Yes, ma'am, of course, ma'am . . . I'll be there immediately, madam Principal. (. . .) Yes, immediately.

The **Teacher** *hangs up, overwhelmed. The women look at him.*

Riquelme   The Principal realized that you're not okay?

The **Teacher** *nods.*

Riquelme Mrs. Nancy told her . . .

The **Teacher** *nods.*

Riquelme And that could cost you your job.

The **Teacher** *nods.*

Riquelme That's so wrong what your wife did, Teacher. She practically turned you in. Is Carvajal your wife's last name?

Teacher *nods.*

Riquelme For real? her name is Carvajal?!

Teacher No, come on.

Maldonado It's that there's always some disgusting traitor pig Carvajal in each of our lives, Teach.

Teacher Young ladies, as the "responsible adult," I wanted to orient you and help you with your space-time problem, but . . . I'm going to have to leave and evacuate the facility with the rest of the teachers.

Riquelme Sir, we depend on your silence.

Teacher Don't worry, I won't say anything.

The **Teacher** *starts walking towards the door.* **Maldonado** *stops him.*

Maldonado Teach, wait. It's not all lost. Come here, let us spruce you up a bit so that you go to your bosses looking more presentable.

Maldonado *sits him down.* **Riquelme** *takes out a comb and combs his hair.* **Maldonado** *fixes his clothes, ties his tie, tidies him up.* **Fuenzalida** *just watches.*

Maldonado You look better like this, see?

Riquelme Less like a crazy person.

Maldonado See you're good looking, all you have to do is look at the Principal with those eyes of yours, and that lady will believe everything you say.

Riquelme A person who looks good is a person who's feeling good. It's an attitude thing. You reflect what you have inside. Do you have a mirror?

The **Teacher** *shakes his head no.*

Maldonado But there's the window, you can look at yourself in the reflection.

Riquelme *stands the* **Teacher** *before one of the classroom windows. The window is covered by a curtain.*

Maldonado Smile. The Principal needs to see you as a calm, sane person. Look at yourself . . .

Riquelme *stands by the* **Teacher**. **Maldonado** *goes to open the curtain so that he can see his reflection. Before she can do it,* **Fuenzalida** *gets between and grabs the curtains, closing them.*

Maldonado (*bothered*)   Sagittarius!

Fuenzalida *grabs* **Maldonado** *and* **Riquelme** *and takes them over to the open grate of an air vent. She motions at it vigorously.*

Riquelme   Yes, Sagittarius, we'll go back to our comrades, but we're helping the teacher.

Maldonado   He has been the only "responsible adult" who's been cool with us and he needs support. Look at the state he's in!

Fuenzalida *grabs* **Maldonado** *with strength and tries to force her through the grate. Her efforts are desperate.*

Maldonado   Sagittarius . . . .! What's going on with you? No! Andromeda, do something! She's gone totally nuts on us!

Riquelme   Sagittarius that's enough! Let our comrade go! Let her go, damnit!

Riquelme *tries to stop the action, to no avail. The* **Teacher** *watches, affected.*

Riquelme (*forcefully, as an order*)   Stop, Sagittarius, for motherfucking sake! (*to* **Teacher**) I'm sorry for cursing, sir.

Riquelme *stops the out of control* **Fuenzalida**, *who seems to react to her yelling.*

Riquelme   What is going on with you? I understand that we're all a bit shook up, but we cannot lose control, comrade. We owe each other respect and care. As intense as the things we experience may get, we only have each other. We can't go around attacking each other. That is impermissible! Look what you did to poor Maldonado.

Maldonado   Do you remember when you first got to the hideout? Do you remember what awful shape you were in? Who helped you? Who took care of you? Well, let us fix up the Teacher for a bit too.

Riquelme   Both he and we need to appear calm if we want to go speak with someone. He with the Principal, and we with our comrades.

Maldonado *fixes her clothes and hair that were messed up during the tussle with* **Fuenzalida**.

Maldonado (*to* **Riquelme**)   How do I look?

Riquelme (*she combs her hair a bit*)   Good . . . and me?

Maldonado *takes out some lip gloss and puts it on her friend. She does the same.*

Maldonado   You look gorgeous. Look at yourself . . .

Maldonado *is about to open the window curtain so that* **Riquelme** *can see her reflection. Before she does,* **Fuenzalida**, *exhausted, speaks in a thin thread of a voice.*

Fuenzalida (*tired and in despair*)   Chiquillas . . .

They all stare at her, shocked for a moment.

Riquelme   Sagittarius?

Fuenzalida   Why . . . do you . . . want to see yourselves?

Maldonado and **Riquelme** *gaze at her in happy amazement.*

Riquelme   Sagittarius, you're talking! Do you realize it?

Maldonado   It's a miracle.

Riquelme   Hold on, say something . . .

Fuenzalida (*confused*)   I . . .

Riquelme (*interrupts*)   It's your voice! Your beautiful voice!

Maldonado   I can't believe it, it's like I had forgotten Sagittarius's voice.

Riquelme   It must have been from the nervous shock.

Maldonado   I've read that strong emotional blows can take away or give back your voice just like that, in a flash.

Riquelme   Our classmates are going to go wild in there, they're going to ask you to sing something.

Maldonado   Sagittarius sings, Mr. Teacher.

Riquelme   She's the lead voice of the school choir.

Maldonado   She blows everyone away at open mics and festivals.

Riquelme   In the plays, she sings more than anyone . . . You should have seen her when we did *Grease*! She was John Travolta!

Maldonado   And I was Olivia!

Fuenzalida (*shyly*)   Not everything we see is what we think we see.

Riquelme and **Maldonado** *look at her with some discomfort.*

Riquelme   Yes . . . of course, Sagittarius . . . Let's see, try saying something else.

Fuenzalida (*shyly*)   Time is relative.

Maldonado (*excited*)   Perfect! It comes out perfect!

Fuenzalida   Information takes a long time to arrive.

Maldonado (*to* **Teacher**)   She's repeating your lesson like a parrot, Teach. Your class made her better!

Riquelme   Why don't you try to sing?

Riquelme *hums something to her.*

Fuenzalida   I'd never do anything to hurt to you.

Riquelme *and* **Maldonado** *look at each other, perplexed. They don't understand.*

Maldonado   That has nothing to do with the class.

Fuenzalida   I would never betray you.

Maldonado   Neither does that.

Riquelme   Of course you wouldn't betray us, why would you say that?

Fuenzalida   Sometimes . . . there are no words to express certain things.

Riquelme (*weirded out*)   What things?

Fuenzalida *looks at them without responding.*

Maldonado   Like what happened to you at the police station when they arrested you?

Riquelme   We've never pressured you to talk about that.

Fuenzalida   Other things.

Riquelme (*insists, wary*)   What things?

Fuenzalida   Strange things . . . things that happen, the way they happen up there, among the stars. Without us being aware of them. Without anyone really caring about them.

Maldonado *and* **Riquelme** *listen, bewildered.*

Riquelme (*wary*)   Could you be more clear, Sagittarius?

Fuenzalida (*ashamed*)   Chiquillas, forgive me . . .

Fuenzalida *seems to be in great anguish. The* **Teacher** *intervenes.*

Teacher   Young ladies, until three months ago, I took pills. There were quite a few, all for different things, but the end I sought was to feel better, because as time went on, I was feeling more and more wretched. I took them for many years, and the truth is that I was doing better. Nothing that used to make me feel rage or sorrow mattered to me. I didn't despair anymore about my twelve-hour workday, or the news, or money problems, or my dramas or anyone else's. I stopped caring about my mother, who had cancer and was in a nursing home. I stopped caring about why Nancy didn't want to have children. Over time, I stopped caring about anything at all and it seemed like I was happy. One day they called me on the phone to tell me that my mother had died. I hung up and kept grading exams because I had to hand in my grades that afternoon. That evening, when Nancy and I got to the apartment, I took my sleeping pills and we went to bed. I didn't tell her. I simply forgot. That's when so much happiness started to scare me, and after my mother's burial, I emptied all the pill bottles into the toilet and I stopped taking anything. I'm doing terribly, you've seen me, I'm not going to lie, but I had no alternative. So much comfort was making me worse. I was safe, but that safety was not real. Soon, it's likely I'll lose my job, and then my life will fall apart, but at least now it matters to me.

The women stare at the **Teacher**, *not understanding.*

Riquelme Forgive me sir, but why are you telling us all this?

Teacher Since the beginning of time, man has wanted to leave the comfort of his home on Earth, in order to take the risk and travel through time to the stars. Why? Because he wants to know more. If what he discovers on this journey is strange, painful, or makes him furious, or sad, or scared . . . that's better than giving himself over to ignorance, isn't it? We all have the right to know how things are beyond the limits of our little world. (*To* **Fuenzalida**) Or isn't that true, Miss Sagittarius?

Fuenzalida *looks at the* **Teacher** *for a moment. Soon she takes her classmates' hands and turns them to face the window.* **Maldonado** *and* **Riquelme** *seem confused.*

Fuenzalida *keeps holding the hands of her comrades. She looks at the* **Teacher**. *The* **Teacher** *pulls aside the curtains, exposing the glass.*

The three women look at their own reflections in the glass for a while.

Riquelme (*perplexed*) Who are . . . those women . . . who are looking at us from the other side of the glass?

No one responds.

Maldonado Is that my Mami?

Riquelme (*insisting*) Who are . . . those women who are looking at us from the other side of the glass?

The **Teacher** *responds with great sensitivity.*

Teacher They are . . . stars, Miss. What you are seeing is a true constellation.

The three women look at their own reflection in the window glass.

The bell rings, signaling the end of the class period.

Seventh Period

A Black Hole

As if lost in outer space, the **Aged Youth** *is lit, surrounded by complete darkness. The mark of a fresh bullet hole is still on his forehead.*

Aged Youth   Alpha Centauro, aka me, was detained for having killed a policeman during the takeover of a high school. He did it with a "catkiller," a janky firearm, that he used to defend himself and to defend his friends. They locked up Alpha Centauro, aka me, in a dark room, isolated from the world, completely incommunicado. One of those two-meter-by-two-meter cells where you couldn't see much, where you couldn't hear anything, and where he knew nothing about his mother or his friends. Every once in a while the door would open and they brought him out to take him to another room where they sat him in a chair and questioned him. They asked him about his fellow militants, about his high school classmates, about his family. They questioned him and they beat him. They questioned him again and they beat him again. And they kept questioning him and they kept beating him. But Alpha Centauro, aka me, never, listen closely, *never* became a disgusting traitor pig. Alpha Centauro, aka me, never turned anyone in.

And in that way, Alpha Centauro, aka me, after each interrogation, returned to his dark room a total wreck. He spent days, or years, I don't know, locked up there.

Time is relative. Imprisonment is a black hole that sucks up everything, minutes, memories, even dreams. Alpha Centauro, aka me, in that dark room where I was or am, had a repeating dream. There, he dreamed of the last class he had at school.

The **Aged Youth** *looks at the poster of Yuri Gagarin on the wall of the laboratory. He moves towards it.*

Aged Youth   The teacher talked about the Soviet Space program that sent the first man to space. On April 12, 1961, Major Yuri Gagarin became the first cosmonaut to travel to outer space in his ship, the Vostok 1. Alpha Centauro, aka me, dreamed or dreams that I am Major Gagarin. Alpha Centauro, aka me, dreamed or dreams that I'm there, locked into Vostok 1, looking through a tiny hatch at the darkness of the Universe. What he could see or sees from there is unnameable. The stars are within arm's reach, closer than you could ever imagine. Pegasus 51, Gamma Cassiopeia, Zeta Neptune, Omega 21, Epsilon Sagittarius, Beta Andromeda. Major Yuri Gagarin, aka Alpha Centauro, aka me, closed up in his ship, freed from gravity, can float between his four walls, walk on the ceiling, jump and fly over each corner of his imprisonment. In space, the body is light, you don't feel hunger or cold. You don't feel fear either. You don't miss anyone. In the dream that I dream, Major Yuri Gagarin, aka Alpha Centauro, aka me, picked up or pick up the radio to communicate with Ground Control and inform them that everything is good, that from here you can see things with clarity, and that, just as it was recorded in History, from outer space the Earth looks blue and you don't hear the voice of any god.

Hello? Major Yuri Gagarin here, aka Alpha Centauro, aka me, communicating with planet Earth. Hello? Ground control? I have some important information to deliver. Hello? Ground control? Is anyone there? Can anyone hear me? Can anyone hear me? Can anyone hear me?

The bell rings. End of class period.

Eighth Period

Alpha Centauro

The women are sitting, lost staring at their own reflections in the glass. They seem to be in shock. A moment has passed. The **Teacher** *watches them. Silence fills the laboratory.*

Riquelme   So . . . when I go out there, people are going to call me "ma'am?"

The **Teacher** *and* **Fuenzalida** *look at each other, searching for a response. Then, they nod.*

Maldonado   So . . . when I go out there, they're going to offer me a seat on the bus, they're going to talk to me like I'm an old person?

The **Teacher** *and* **Fuenzalida** *look at each other. Then, they nod.*

Riquelme   So when I go out there, my Mamá and Papá might not be around anymore?

The **Teacher** *and* **Fuenzalida** *look at each other. Then, they nod.*

Maldonado   So when I go out there, I might no longer be able to have children?

The **Teacher** *and* **Fuenzalida** *look at each other. Then, they nod.*

Maldonado   So when I go out there, I won't be a student anymore?

Fuenzalida *nods.*

Riquelme (*upset*)   So did you go to college?

Fuenzalida *nods.*

Maldonado   What'd you study?

Fuenzalida   Advertising.

Riquelme (*horrified*)   Advertising? What happened to theatre? And singing?

Fuenzalida *shrinks into herself.*

Maldonado   And how did things go for you?

Fuenzalida   Well. Really well.

Maldonado (*angry*)   If things were going so well for you, then why'd you come climb in there with us?

Fuenzalida   It's just that . . . during that whole time that things were going well, I forgot . . . a few things. A bunch of things . . .

Maldonado   What things?

Fuenzalida   My home, for example. Or . . . my parents, or . . . my friends.

Maldonado (*upset*)   Who could forget their home, their parents and their friends!

Fuenzalida   My whole goal in life was to do really well. And things went so well that, when I finally wanted to remember everything, nothing and no one was there anymore.

Maldonado (*upset*)   And so that's why you came here?

Fuenzalida   You were the only memory I had left. I never thought I'd find you in there.

Maldonado   And why didn't you say anything to us?

Fuenzalida   What could I say?

Riquelme   That thirty years had passed, that we were old fucking ladies, that there was no reason to keep waiting to go outside.

Maldonado   And what happened to the people who were detained with you? What happened to Hinojosa, Garrido, Torres, la Chica Pérez?

Fuenzalida   They all got out. Some earlier, some later, but they all got out.

Riquelme   And where are they now?

Fuenzalida (*shoulders shrinking*)   I don't know. I suppose each one's doing their own thing.

Riquelme   Are any of them a political leader? Or congress person? Or mayor? Or president of a political party, or of something?

Fuenzalida *shakes her head no.*

Maldonado   And Alpha? Not even Alpha?

Fuenzalida *shakes her head no. There's a certain fatalism in her look.*

Maldonado   I can't believe he wouldn't come look for me. (*To* **Fuenzalida**) And you never knew what happened to him?

Fuenzalida *looks at them, nervous. She nods.*

Fuenzalida   Yes . . . but . . . from the news.

Maldonado   From the news?

Fuenzalida *looks at them nervously. She doesn't know how to begin. Then she goes up to the* **Teacher** *and speaks into his ear. The* **Teacher** *seems struck by what he hears.*

Teacher   He's Alpha Centauro?

Fuenzalida *agrees.*

Teacher   Yes . . . I remember that case.

Maldonado   Case? Alpha became a case?

Fuenzalida *speaks into the* **Teacher**'s *ear again.*

Teacher   No, miss, you need to tell them yourself.

Riquelme (*anxious*)   What happened with Alpha?

The **Teacher** *looks at* **Fuenzalida**, *encouraging her to speak.* **Fuenzalida**, *with great difficulty, begins to tell the story.*

Fuenzalida   Because of the death of that policeman here in the school, and for other things, Alpha ended up in the Public Jail.

Maldonado (*upset*)   Like us here.

Fuenzalida   It's not the same.

Riquelme   It's the same!

Fuenzalida   Time passed. A long time. One day in 1990, after the return of Democracy, the guards had to take him to an eye doctor appointment at a hospital.

Riquelme *and* **Maldonado** *look at each other as if recalling something.*

Riquelme and Maldonado (*guessing*)   The Sótero del Río Hospital in Puente Alto.

Fuenzalida *nods.*

Fuenzalida   While he was imprisoned, they beat him so much that the retina of one of his eyes detached.

Maldonado (*guessing*)   That's why he needed to get checked out. That's why he came to the hospital.

Fuenzalida *nods.*

Fuenzalida   So . . . there was Alpha, in the hospital, in the middle of his medical checkup, with the guards waiting for him outside in the hall.

Maldonado (*guessing*)   It seemed like a routine procedure, but suddenly, one of the nurses that was with him made a signal.

Fuenzalida   Yes.

Riquelme *makes a signal similar to what the nurse might have made. She and* **Maldonado** *start to act it out.*

Maldonado   It was a strange sign that Alpha didn't understand.

Fuenzalida   Yes.

Riquelme   Soon several of the medical staff that were there in the room and in the hallway unexpectedly took out their weapons and started shooting.

Fuenzalida   Yes.

Riquelme *and* **Maldonado** *imitate the action.*

Maldonado (*imitating the sound of the bullets*)   Pow . . . pow . . . the bullets were flying all over the place, meanwhile two comrades grabbed Alpha and started to run.

Riquelme It was a rescue! The most spectacular rescue

Maldonado Alpha didn't know much, but he followed their orders, and he ran and ran and ran with his fellow militants who guided him through the hospital hallways, while (*imitating the sound of bullets*) pow . . . pow . . . the gunshots came and went.

Riquelme No one understood anything. The doctors, the nurses, the orderlies, the patients, everyone threw themselves to the ground, trying to escape the gunfire.

Maldonado *and* **Riquelme** *throw themselves to the floor, imitating their actions.*

Fuenzalida People died. One policeman, I think. And some prison guards.

Maldonado (*imitating sound of bullets*) Pow . . . pow . . . The leader of the group was also shot down.

Riquelme *becomes the leader of the group. She falls to the floor, riddled with bullets.*

Maldonado While she lay on the floor, the rest of the group kept running to the hospital parking lot, where they jumped into a truck and sped away with Alpha inside.

Riquelme What happened after that is not too clear.

Maldonado The group disappeared into the city and the whole police force started looking for Alpha.

Riquelme The woman who had fallen, the leader, was the only one who knew where they were going to hide him, but since she wasn't around anymore, they had to improvise.

Maldonado They made contact with a family. It was a family that had always hidden people during the dictatorship.

Riquelme It was a "normal" family. Father and mother, "responsible adults," with their two kids. No one would suspect that a family like that would be hiding a fugitive militant.

Maldonado And that's where they left Alpha, at the home of this "normal" family, with this "responsible adult" couple, so that he would be safe. So that they would protect and take care of him.

Riquelme He hid with them, like one more son.

Fuenzalida But it didn't last long.

The women look at each other.

Riquelme One or two days later, Alpha was discovered.

Teacher But how? It's not easy to find someone who's gone into hiding.

Maldonado Unless there's a disgusting traitor pig who betrays him.

Teacher Someone turned him in?

Maldonado, Fuenzalida, and Riquelme We all have a Carvajal in our lives.

Riquelme Alerted by the rat, the police arrived at the house of the "normal" family that was hiding him.

Maldonado More than fifty detectives from the Special Forces appeared in the middle of the night.

Riquelme Alpha realized what was happening and ran out.

Fuenzalida As he was trying to escape . . . in a gunfight . . .

Fuenzalida *looks nervous. She can't continue.*

Riquelme *(finishes)* . . . a bullet, fast as a meteorite, reached him. Alpha died right there.

Maldonado *and* **Riquelme** *take each other's hands. They can barely believe the story they've told.*

Teacher Young ladies . . . how did you know that story?

Riquelme It's the plot of the play that Sagittarius wrote.

Maldonado We were rehearsing it so we could present it at graduation.

Riquelme The only thing she didn't write was that the protagonist was Alpha. That part, we didn't know.

Fuenzalida *looks at them with regret.*

Fuenzalida I went to his wake. I came up to the coffin and I saw him, lying there, full of flowers. He looked just like I remembered him, it seemed like no time had passed. He had a bullet wound here, on his forehead . . . It's strange that in the middle of a gunfight, while you're supposedly running away, that a bullet would hit you just here, right in the middle of your forehead.

It takes **Fuenzalida** *a moment before she can continue.*

Fuenzalida Sometimes I think I see him here in the school, you know? He's wearing his uniform, and talking in that way he liked to. He talks and talks, telling stories. I don't know if he's talking to himself or with someone. Maybe he's talking to me.

Silence.

The **Teacher**'s *cell phone rings. Nobody seems to notice it. It rings several times.*

The **Teacher** *approaches the phone. He looks at the screen. He responds calmly. Very calmly.*

Teacher Carvajal. (. . .) Yes, I'm still here. (. . .) Yes, the Principal spoke to me. (. . .) What? An ambulance? With paramedics? Why did they bring an ambulance? (. . .) For me? But why would I leave the school in an ambulance! You've all gone crazy! (. . .) I'm the crazy one? What are you saying, Carvajal! (. . .) I'm not having a nervous breakdown, I'm perfectly fine. (...) I don't know what you've heard over there, from the other side of the door, but I have not been locked in here talking to myself. (. . .) No! I'm with a group of students who need my help and I'm not leaving this school until I've resolved their problem. I'm not making anything up. I'm the only "responsible adult" here, and I'm going to take care of them because that is my job. I'm not going to just leave them stranded. (. . .) You're watching me? (*He looks at the ceiling of the room.*) There are security cameras here in the lab? What is this, Carvajal? An ambush? (. . .) I'm not a lunatic, Carvajal! And send your guards and nurses if you want! I'm not going to abandon my students even if it's the last thing I do!

The **Teacher** *hangs up.*

Teacher   Disgusting traitor pig! They never told me they had installed cameras!

Riquelme   Don't worry, Teach. We're not going to let them take you.

At a sign from **Riquelme**, *they each take out small revolvers and show them to the cameras.*

Riquelme   Don't worry. They're janky little weapons.

Fuenzalida   "Catkillers."

Maldonado   We only use them to defend ourselves.

Teacher   Young ladies, I think that the best thing to do, before Carvajal's gorillas arrive, is to enter that place from which you've come and to tell your comrades what is happening.

Riquelme   Sir, this is our problem, there's no reason you'd have to . . .

Teacher (*interrupting*)   I have a reason, Miss. I am your teacher, I am your "responsible adult." Therefore we are going to go in there together and talk with those women. We'll start by talking about the stars. About their light, that comes to us from the past. We'll talk of space, of distance, of black holes, and of time. That, above all: about black holes and the relativity of time.

The three women look at each other nervously. **Riquelme** *picks up the flashlights that were left on the floor. She passes one to each woman and gives another to the* **Teacher**.

Riquelme   It's dark in there, and hard to see things clearly. Let's go, sir, follow us.

The cell phone rings. They all look at it. The **Teacher** *lets it ring. We hear pounding at the door. Quickly, single file, they start to climb into the air duct with their flashlights lighting the way. They disappear.*

The bell rings, signaling the end of the class period.

The Normal Family

by

Roberta Fuenzalida[5]

FOR ALPHA CENTAURO

Theater Workshop

The Normal Family

A sign made of shiny paper, with gold lettering, has been attached to the blackboard. On the sign, we can clearly read: The Normal Family.

A television is drawn on the blackboard. And a date: NOVEMBER 1990.

The Normal Father, who will be played by **Fuenzalida**, *turns on the TV and watches it. We hear the voices of two newscasters. They're the voices of* **Riquelme** *and* **Maldonado**, *who read their scripts in front of the audience.*

Newscaster 1   For more than twenty-four hours, the terrorist who was rescued yesterday from the Sotero del Río Hospital has been on the loose.

Newscaster 2   The subversives unfurled a dramatic but bloody operation, during which four guards and one policeman were killed.

Newscaster 1   Violently breaking through every police barricade, the insurrectionists fled, and disappeared into the city.

Newscaster 2   The police and the bureau of Investigations are working intently to find them.

Newscaster 1   "Actions like this declare war on Chile's new democracy and only hinder the peaceful coexistence of all our citizens," declared the nation's President.

After a moment, the Father's wife, the **Normal Mother**, *enters, to be played by the* **Teacher**. *The wife sets the laboratory table for dinner.*

Normal Mother   Change the channel, I don't want him to see that.

Normal Father   All the channels are showing the same thing.

Normal Mother   So shut it off.

The **Normal Father** *shuts off the TV with a gesture to the blackboard.*

Normal Father   You knew it was him, didn't you?

Normal Mother   I knew it was someone who needed help, and that's always been enough for us. Or isn't it? Besides, he's a child . . .

Normal Father   A child who's killed people.

They look at each other for a moment.

Normal Mother   Call the kids, it's almost ready.

Normal Father   It's not right for them to be mixed up in this.

Normal Mother   They've always been mixed up in this, I don't see why now would be any different.

Normal Father   You call them.

Normal Mother (*towards the inside of the house*)   Kids! Time to eat!

The kids enter, played by **Riquelme** *and* **Maldonado**. **Normal Boy** *and* **Normal Girl**, *respectively.*

Normal Girl   What about the news? Aren't we going to watch?

Normal Father   Not today.

Normal Boy   What's up?

Normal Father   Nothing's up, we're going to eat without the TV. I don't suppose that's so strange.

Normal Girl   And him . . . is he going to eat with us?

Normal Mother   I'll go ask him.

Normal Girl   I'll go!

The **Normal Father** *and* **Mother** *look at each other.*

Normal Father (*stops her*)   No, I'll ask him.

The **Normal Father** *goes up to the grate of an air vent and knocks on it gently. From inside, we hear the voice of* **Alpha Centauro**.

Aged Youth   Yes . . .?

Normal Father   Food is ready. If you'd like, you can come, or if you prefer we can bring it to your room . . .

Alpha Centauro *comes in through the grate.*

Aged Youth   No, please . . . I prefer to eat with you all.

The **Normal Father** *and* **Alpha Centauro** *sit with the family. The* **Normal Mother** *serves him food. The kids look at each other. The situation is tense. After a long silence,* **Normal Mother** *speaks.*

Normal Mother   Have you been feeling all right?

Aged Youth   Better, thank you very much.

Normal Mother   If you'd like anything washed, tell me. Juan can lend you clothes in the meantime.

Aged Youth   Don't worry about it.

Normal Girl   Your head doesn't hurt anymore?

Aged Youth   Not as much.

Normal Boy   It's because of your eyes, isn't it?

Aged Youth   Yes, I have vision problems.

Normal Boy   What happened to you?

Alpha Centauro *looks at* **Normal Father** *and* **Mother**, *who look uncomfortable.*

Aged Youth (*lying*)   I got hit once, when I was little . . . and my retina got detached.

Normal Girl   You don't use glasses?

Normal Father   Don't ask questions, kids.

Normal Mother   Maybe we can get some glasses for you.

Aged Youth   It's not necessary, but thank you very much.

The family keeps eating in silence.

Normal Girl (*to* **Alpha**)   How long are you staying?

Alpha *looks at* **Normal Mother** *and* **Father**.

Normal Father   We don't know, sweetie. And don't ask any more questions, I told you already.

Alpha *finishes eating.*

Aged Youth   Thank you so much, that was delicious. Would it bother you if I went back to my room? I'm still feeling a bit dizzy.

Normal Mother   Go, don't worry, rest.

Alpha *stands and returns to his room.*

Normal Girl   He's nice, I like him.

Normal Boy   You have a crush on him.

Normal Girl   Don't be an idiot!

Normal Father (*annoyed*)   Kids, stop talking bullshit please.

Normal Mother (*to Father*)   Relax.

The family keeps eating in silence. Suddenly a phone rings. **Riquelme** *is the one who makes the sound. The phone could be represented by the clean blackboard or any object in the laboratory. The* **Normal Girl** *gets up to answer it.*

Normal Boy   I'll go!

Normal Father (*stopping her*)   No, I'll go.

The **Normal Father** *answers the phone.*

Normal Father   Hello? (. . .) Yes, it's me. (. . .) Now? (. . .) It's just, my kids are here. (. . .) All right . . .

The **Normal Father** *hangs up. The family looks at him.*

Normal Boy   Who was it?

The **Normal Father** *speaks quietly, so that* **Alpha** *won't hear from his room.*

Normal Father   Go to your room.

Normal Girl (*unsettled*)   Why?

Normal Father   Because I'm your father and I'm asking you to.

Normal Girl   But why do you want us to go to our room?

Normal Father   Go and hide yourselves under the bed.

The **Normal Mother** *peers through the window to outside. She seems frightened by what she sees.*

Normal Mother (*alarmed*)   Juan, what did you do . . . ? We were going to hide him.

Normal Father   And we have.

Normal Mother   He's a child . . . we're responsible for what happens to him.

Normal Father   Your kids are also children. And we're also responsible for what happens to them. Get them out of here.

The **Normal Mother** *looks at her husband, stunned. Then she takes her children away. The* **Normal Father** *is left alone. He looks out the window. Then he approaches the grate through which* **Alpha** *emerged and knocks on it as if it were a door.* **Alpha** *looks through.*

Aged Youth   Yes?

Normal Father   . . . they're asking for you outside.

Aged Youth (*very surprised*)   Who?

Normal Father   I assume they're your comrades, no one else knows you're here.

Aged Youth   That wasn't the plan we agreed on. Did they give you a contact name?

Normal Father   No.

Aged Youth   Then it isn't them.

Normal Father   Son, they know you're here. They just told me so. If you don't go out that door, they could come storming into my house. Neither you nor I want that, do we?

The **Aged Youth** *looks at the* **Normal Father** *for a moment. He tries to get back through the grate he came out of, but the* **Normal Father** *stops him.*

Then, resigned, the **Aged Youth** *moves toward the front door. He puts his hand on the doorknob. He opens the door to the street.*

Normal Father   Son . . .

The **Aged Youth** *looks at the* **Normal Father**.

Normal Father   Forgive me . . .

The Aged Youth looks toward the street. He raises his arms as a sign of surrender. A perfectly aimed bullet to the forehead drops him to the ground.

The bell rings, marking the end of the play.

Notes

1. The Lautaro Youth Movement, an armed organization and youth guerrilla movement during Chile's military dictatorship, named after Lautaro, the leader of the indigenous resistance against the Spanish, was founded in 1982.
2. This is a Chilean term of endearment between women and is pronounced cheek-EE-yahs.
3. The Telethon is a yearly charity event broadcast on Chilean television during the first week of December.
4. During her second term (2014-2018), President Michelle Bachelet attempted to address a diverse array of student protests.
5. This short play by the character Fuenzalida is to be performed as a conclusion to *School for Girls*.

The City of Fruit:

Sexual Violence, Witness, and Transformation

Coca Duarte

English Translation
Constanza Brieba

Leyla Selman's *The City of Fruit* explores the sexual abuse the playwright suffered as a child at the hands of her grandfather and three of her uncles. The play unfolds through two main situations: on the one hand, it portrays the present with Her, the victim, who, together with her therapist Marcela, confronts the consequences of the abuse; on the other, we see the perpetrators—Superman, Maradona, Grandpa, and Pillow—gathering, seemingly to align their version of events in response to Her's accusations. Alongside these two planes, the abuse itself is recounted. As the play unfolds, it reveals a structure that interweaves all these dimensions through a single dramatic motor: Her's potential healing through narration and confrontation.

The City of Fruit premiered in Santiago, Chile, in May 2019 at Teatro de la Memoria, directed by Rodrigo Pérez. The roles were performed by Catalina Saavedra, Marcela Millie, Francisco Ossa, Jaime Leiva, Marco Rebolledo, and Guillermo Ugalde. In the years leading up to its debut, gender-related issues gained unprecedented visibility in Chilean society, especially with the massive feminist mobilizations of 2017 and 2018. These protests, which originated in student movements, denounced gender violence—whose most extreme expression is femicide—harassment and abuse within educational settings, and the symbolic erasure of women across all areas of culture. The emergence of *The City of Fruit* within that context can be understood as yet another testimony regarding the sexual violence endured by women.

Selman's play also draws on elements of documentary theatre, though in a refracted way. Since 2006, Chile has seen a resurgence of documentary theatre, which according to theatre scholar Ivan Insunza[1] may be attributed to the 2004 publication of the Valech Report—the first official document addressing human rights violations committed during the dictatorship. Theatre scholar Mauricio Barría[2] links this resurgence to the reactivation of social movements, particularly with the 2006 student uprising. Between that year and the premiere of *The City of Fruit*, numerous plays emerged that incorporated archival elements and employed devices from global documentary theatre: performances by non-professional actors, the display of real documents and real-life materials (videos, photographs, objects), testimonial accounts, and so on. However, some plays—while based on true events—moved away from strict documentary frameworks by introducing fictional strategies, avoiding raw exposure of reality. In this latter vein, *The City of Fruit* offers a theatrical reconstruction of the real: the situations are fictionalized and the characters are portrayed by actors.

According to the playwright, the Santiago production emerged from an earlier version of the play in which the protagonist was imagined as a child living in a state-run children's home under Chile's National Child Services. That version premiered in 2015 in Concepción and was directed by the author herself. Later, prompted by director Rodrigo Pérez, who had previously collaborated with Selman, a new version was developed. This second version emphasized the autobiographical nature of the material and introduced the character of Marcela, the therapist, as a kind of mediator between Her and the audience. One of the most compelling aspects of the final version of *The City of Fruit* is the confluence of three representational planes: Her's account of the abuse; Marcela's mediation; and the gathering of the perpetrators in a space that does not construct a fictional world but instead occupies an intermediate realm—the theatrical space in which we, the audience, encounter the play.

In the opening scene, Marcela enters the space and washes her feet, an action that carries ritual overtones. Played by Marcela Millie, the character establishes the representational code of the play, blending fiction and reality. Marcela introduces Her through her current diagnosis—Borderline Personality Disorder—and addresses us directly, outlining the character's psychological profile.

> **Marcela** Okay, let's see, for every one hundred people, two suffer from BPD, or borderline personality disorder, meaning that proportionally she and someone else here in this room have it. The disorder has this name because these people are easily inclined to depression and also a great deal of anxiety, a lot of emotional dependency. They depend a lot on others, as a child would; they don't want to be alone but in the manner of a child. They're very impulsive. It's a very complicated cocktail of traits, there are very well-known cases of patients who self-harm and cut themselves, on their arms or on their thighs.[3]

We are then introduced to the abusers through a brief scene that reveals a male camaraderie charged with discomfort.

> **Maradona** I'm not going to be able to sleep. I haven't been able to sleep since that kid opened her trap.
>
> **Superman** It must be for a reason.
>
> **Pillow** That's all that I need.
>
> **Grandpa** Have you slept?
>
> **Superman** Of course, like a baby.
>
> **Pillow** It's better to keep quiet until everything is cleared up.
>
> **Superman** It's true. Everything seems so suspicious–your shoes, your laugh, your hands, that watermelon, everything . . .[4]

To close this initial section, Marcela urges Her to step onto the stage and recount her past.

> **Her** *has to get up onstage.* **Her** *does not.*
>
> **Her** I can't
>
> **Marcela** Yes, yes, you can.[5]

Although Her reveals her initial inability to step onto the stage, once she manages to do so, she declares:

4 Her (Catalina Saavedra) attempts to confront Maradona (Guillermo Ugalde), Grandpa (Francisco Ossa), and Pillow (Jaime Leiva), in *The City of Fruit* by Leyla Selman, directed by Rodrigo Pérez, Teatro de la Memoria, Santiago, Chile, 2019. (Photo: © Paula Campos)

Today I came to heal myself from four people who have harmed me: Superman, Grandpa, Maradona, and Pillow. I came to heal myself through theatre. They told me that you could do that through reenacting. They told me that you could heal your soul, your mind, and your voice . . .

So, thank you for joining me.[6]

With this declaration, which concludes the first unit where the play's three representational layers are established, Her addresses us directly, making the audience participants in an experience. On the one hand, she assigns us a role as spectators: that of accompanying her character in the reconstruction of the events she is about to recount. On the other hand, she establishes the purpose of the performance we are about to witness: to contribute to Her's healing from the harm she endured—as the character represents the author herself.

In the narrative dimension of the play, the account of the first two instances of abuse follows a similar structure: it begins by stating the year and Her's age, then introduces the perpetrator and explains the origin of his nickname: "my uncle José . . . we call him Superman because he lifts weights and because a small pile of his hair sticks out and, gathered toward his forehead, makes him look more like the superhero."[7] "My uncle Jorge . . . he has very black, very curly hair and he lets it grow like Maradona's (according to him)."⁸ Once this background is established, Her, with a certain degree of detachment, recounts the events in detail. She stands before the audience and directly involves them in the narration. None of the abuses are reenacted; Marcela investigates, reinterprets, and fills in what remains unsaid: "Her heart beat strongly/the sun followed her/she stayed silent/she doesn't remember what happens next/but immediately she felt the weight of keeping something. Things remained, as I said, between the sun and her."⁹ The third account, concerning Grandpa, is recounted briefly and ironically through a reference to the song "Abuelito, dime tú"¹⁰ from the 1970s children's television series *Heidi*.

At the end of each account, we return to the scene with the men, who arrive one by one to the meeting, gradually revealing what has brought them together.

Grandpa   I'm innocent.

Superman   Innocent?

Grandpa   Yes.

Superman   Then I'm innocent, too.

Maradona   We have to prepare ourselves.

Superman   A terrible winter is coming, they say it's the worst one ever. Are you sure that you're innocent?

Grandpa   If I'm sure of anything it's my innocence. That girl is crazy, she made everything up and I don't know why.

Maradona   It's true, that girl went totally crazy.

Superman   That's right, she even walks like a weirdo.

Maradona   I haven't noticed that

Grandpa   Me neither

Superman   Yeah, and always wearing so many layers—one hundred degrees and she looks like we were in the worst winter ever and it's the middle of summer.

Grandpa   No one will believe her.

Superman   No one.

Maradona   All of this is bullshit.

Superman   That's true.¹¹

Up to this point, we have followed the narrative of the abuses through the interplay of the three representational realms. However, when Pillow arrives at the meeting, we reach the most severe abuse—the only one that is not recounted. "**Her**: Pillow. This one I won't name because he took everything from me. I should give him a piece of white paper but not as a truce."¹² Here, the resistance to represent resurfaces, signaling that representation falls short—words are not enough to convey the magnitude of the harm. Ultimately, the most traumatic episode remains outside the staging, existing only as a possibility in the audience's imagination.

Leyla Selman's play goes beyond addressing the abuse itself; it also explores its relationship with the society in which it took place and the consequences for the survivors. At several points in the play, the historical context of the abuse is underscored: the civil and military dictatorship of Augusto Pinochet.

> **Her** 1983. I'm seven years old, we're living under dictatorship. People are being fractured, divided, violated, as if in parallel to my life, at the same moment that they're eating me, but I have no idea because I'm seven years old and my mother's family, who I grew up with, deeply believes in the legitimacy of the dictator. So I'm seven years old and I don't understand anything that's happening in the long country where my house and its door are [. . .] the monsters were inside and also outside.[13]

Although Her confesses that, at the time of the abuse, she was unaware of the torture taking place during the dictatorship, from the present perspective, drawing that parallel becomes significant.

> **Her** Shit runs down all the walls. Shit runs down the middle of that dictatorship, in between the corpses that were separated from Chilean life but remain around here, in the hidden depths of Chile. Run, shit, run, how pretty, ooze through the tragic hallways where anything was possible, where anything was possible, rats in vaginas, broken fingers, water dripping on brains.[14]

Selman seems to reaffirm that, during the historical period in question, silence and the coexistence of the sinister and the unspoken under a guise of normality were possible—and that, when framed within the gender-based violence historically endured under the dictatorship, the experience of sexual abuse portrayed in the play transcends the private realm.

As for the men's scenes, beyond illustrating their response to Her's accusations, they expose their toxic masculinities, machismo, childish behaviors, and inefficacy. The men talk about their relationships with women from an objectifying perspective—seeing them either as beings meant to admire them or as subjects of domination fantasies. They minimize the accusations by blaming Her for being strange or asserting that no one will believe her. They bicker over debts and borrowed clothes and ultimately fail in their goal. Despite the tone, the characters do not descend into complete ridicule and retain the danger inherent in their narrow worldview, thereby reinforcing the patriarchal ideology that sustains abuse.

The question of consequences for survivors is deeply tied to the possibility of healing through theatrical representation. The undefined space where the men meet, along with the loosened sense of time, creates a sense of lingering suspense that pulses throughout the play. It is as if this scene is what keeps Her tied to the past—and it is the one she must face. As the play nears its end, the abusers realize they don't know who summoned them.

> **Grandpa** Each one of us will decide what to do, but she is accusing all of us.
>
> **Superman** I never touched her.

Pillow I'm done worrying, she can't prove anything because it's impossible to do, it's impossible to do, and no matter how early you wake up, the day won't come any sooner.

Maradona It's true.

Superman So, this meeting . . .

Maradona Stick it up your ass!

Superman Stick it up yours, you organized it!

Maradona What? No, it was Pillow.

Pillow Me? No.

Grandpa How?

Superman I don't understand.

Grandpa It wasn't you.

Maradona No.

Superman It wasn't me, either.

Grandpa Everyone calm down. Raise your hand if you organized this meeting.

Maradona . . .

Superman . . .

Pillow . . .

Grandpa No one.

Superman This is a trap.

Pillow Really?

Maradona Shit.[15]

In addition to the fact that the play ends by repeating the opening scene of the meeting, Selman shows that the men's relationship is a projection of Her—a kind of reenactment of the dynamics she imagines in a state of confinement to which the male characters must respond. The meeting is nothing more than a theatrical encounter orchestrated by the author. And here we return to what we have been called to witness: Her must confront her abusers in order to heal. In a way, she has already done so by staging them, yet she must still complete the final scene of her healing, as Marcela states in one of the closing scenes of the play.

Marcela She has decided to heal herself. When her psychiatrist told her that she was deformed, that emotional stunting was preventing her from maturing, and that a personality disorder and severe, chronic bipolar disorder didn't allow her to develop in a balanced way, she decided to use theatrical representation to confront those who caused her pain. Even though it seemed to be too late, she decided to ask for help, and here we are.[16]

Her must step into the meeting space, and once again we are faced with the possibility that representation—this time the staged encounter between Her and her abusers—might fulfill the goal of healing. However, when confronted with those who caused her such profound harm, Her finds it difficult to face them and confesses, "I forgot my lines,"[17] as if stepping out of the representation. An actor, breaking character, replies, "Say it however you want." Her finally reveals:

> **Her** So much work to get to this moment . . . And I don't know what to say, I didn't write anything for this moment . . . I'm the same seven-year-old girl sitting under the eaves of the door, getting some fresh afternoon air, giving shape to this question that's grown over time and that no longer needs a response: Why?[18]

On the surface, Her remains trapped in the past and haunted by ghosts, holding onto the question that drives her—"Why?"—and revealing the incomprehensibility of the pain inflicted by others, the banality of the abusers, and their reasons for having caused such disproportionate harm to her as a child. Once again, representation fails: it cannot construct a viable dialogue between a survivor and her abusers, nor provide a definitive answer to the "why," nor offer a resolution to the dramatic situation presented.

However, the act of narrating and representing the abuse is not without consequence. Even though the encounter could not be fully staged and Her was unable to speak eloquently before her abusers, the power of theatrical representation lies in the transformation it has afforded the playwright. Leyla Selman affirms that bringing *The City of Fruit* to the stage healed her, and that this act of unveiling, of courageous exposure carried out "with fear," is reinforced by her belief that "what matters is that it stops happening."[19] Those of us who attend the play are invited to complete the process with our presence and our listening. We accompany the author and witness a tremendous act of generosity, and we leave speechless and changed. We know that, beyond watching a play, we have been part of a transformative experience of pain, exposure, and revelation that sheds light on a reality that must be confronted because hiding abuse allows it to continue.

Notes

1. Insunza, Iván. "¿Qué decimos cuando decimos Teatro Documental?" *Revista Hiedra*, 2017. http://revistahiedra.cl/opinion/decimos-cuando-decimos-teatro-documental/
2. Barría, Mauricio. "Emergencias documentales. Retorno de la historicidad y de un nuevo teatro político" In *Actores, demandas, intersecciones: debates críticos en el Cono Sur*, edited by Fernando Blanco and Cristián Opazo. Santiago de Chile: Cuarto Propio, pp. 267-81.
3. Selman, Leyla. *The City of Fruit*, Dramaturgas Chilenas: Plays by Chilean Female Writers in the Early 21st Century, edited by Coca Duarte, Anne García-Romero and Inés Stranger, Methuen Drama, 2025, p. 165.
4. Ibid.
5. Ibid., 166.

6 Ibid.
7 Ibid., 169.
8 Ibid., 170.
9 Ibid.
10 *Abuelito, dime tu* (*Grandpa Tell Me*, 1975) music and lyrics by Takeo Watanabe, originally a Japanese animated television series, was later broadcast in Spain and Latin America, with Spanish lyrics by Carlos Murciano.
11 Selman. *The City of Fruit*, p. 172.
12 Ibid., 178.
13 Ibid., 169.
14 Ibid., 180–1.
15 Ibid., 183–4.
16 Ibid., 184.
17 Ibid., 191.
18 Ibid.
19 Selman, Leyla. Personal Interview. 19 October 2023.

Further Reading

Barría, Mauricio. "Emergencias documentales: Retorno de la historicidad y de un nuevo teatro politico." In, *Actores, demandas, intersecciones: debates críticos en el Cono Sur*, edited by Fernando Blanco and Cristián Opazo. Santiago de Chile: Cuarto Propio, pp. 267–81.

Duarte, Coca. "La ciudad de la fruta de Leyla Selman: representar el trauma." *Talía: Revista de estudios teatrales* vol. 4, 2022, pp. 23–29.

Ponce Lara, Camila. "El movimiento feminista estudiantil chileno de 2018: Continuidades y rupturas entre feminismos y olas globales." *Izquierdas*, vol. 49, no. 80, 24 Mar. 2021. https://dx.doi.org/10.4067/s0718-50492020000100280

Thompson, Jennifer Joan, "An Explosion of Feminism: Dramaturgies of Excess and Revolution in Chile's New Feminist Vanguard," in *Bodies on the Front Lines: Performance, Gender, and Sexuality in Latin America and the Caribbean*, edited by Brenda Werth and Katherine Zien, University of Michigan Press, 2024. pp. 39–58.

The City of Fruit

Leyla Selman

Developed with Rodrigo Pérez, Teatro la Provincia

English translation
Alexandra Ripp

Leyla Selman is an actor, poet, playwright, director, and novelist, born in 1976 in Concepción, Chile, who is a member of Colectivo Frío (Cold Collective). She has produced more than fifty works in Santiago and Concepción, as well as publishing many of them with LAR, a publisher founded by the Chilean poet Omar Lara. Her works include *El pájaro de Chile* (*The Bird of Chile*, 2014), *La Ciudad de la Fruta* (*The City of Fruit*, 2019), *No Es Mi Nombre* (*That's Not My Name*, 2020), *Ivanov* (2020), *Ifigenia* (2021), *Mas Allá de Ellas (Farther Away from Them, 2021)*, *Umbra* (2022), *Otra Muerte Anunciada* (*Another Death Announced*, 2022), and *Trilogia Final* (*Final Trilogy*, 2023): *Edipo Stand Up Tragedy*, *Hablan* (*They Talk*), and *Los Ojos de Lena* (*Lena's Eyes*). Her awards include the 2003 National Playwriting Award, 2003 Playwriting Award of the South, 2014 City of Santiago Literature Award, Ceres Award 2012, 2014, 2020, 2022 Tennyson Ferrada Regional Playwriting Award, and 2024 Art Critics Circle Best Playwright Award. Since 2010, she has led playwriting and creative writing workshops. Since 2002, she has written and directed more than thirty productions for Colectivo Frío. In 2024, she published her first science fiction novel, *La Columna Oscura* (*The Dark Column*, Mocha Editorial).

The City of Fruit received its world premiere by Teatro la Provincia, at Teatro de la Memoria, 2019, Santiago, Chile, directed by Rodrigo Pérez, with the following cast:

Her	Catalina Saavedra
Marcela	Marcela Millie
Grandpa	Francisco Ossa
Maradona	Guillermo Ugalde
Superman	Marco Rebolledo
Pillow	Jaime Leiva

Subsequently, the play was produced as part of the Santiago A Mil Festival, at Teatro de la Memoria, Santiago, Chile, 2019.

The play was published in Chile by Ediciones Oxímoron (2024).

Characters

Her, *30s, the author of the story, who tries to confront her ghosts by using theatre and do more than just survive life.*

Marcela, *30s, a psychologist who accompanies this fiction of therapy.*

Grandpa, *70s, Her's Grandpa. Clean, very clean, appearance of what is clean, good, and fair. A strict father with apparently high morals.*

Maradona, *50s, Grandpa's son, Her's uncle. Ruder than corresponds to his social and cultural membership. Likes very young women. Can't control his language.*

Superman, *50s, Grandpa's son, Her's uncle. Seems like a good person, almost exemplary. No one would think anything bad about him.*

Pillow, *50s, Grandpa's son, Her's uncle. The most intelligent, the most silent, the most scathing.*

Setting

2010s. Chile.

Very possibly a secret place, like a room that you rent in order to carry out all of your crimes.

And a place from my memory. I imagine it like a locked drawer—with no key, but locked—from which memories still escape. Almost all of them are blocked; these are the ones I can recall.

And a place in the memory of my country, too, because my childhood took place under full military dictatorship, in the shadow of a terrible cry that still breathes beneath the earth.

And a theater, a magical place for representation, poetic justice, and healing.

Life. (How many times has one said and written that?)

Playwright's Note

I wrote this episode from my childhood as a simple fun exercise, and out of ambition—I wanted to be able to tell my story with all the technical elements that a well-told story requires. For example, to defend each character who comes on stage until the end of their part.

This version of the play was developed with Rodrigo Pérez, director of Teatro La Provincia, to whom I thank and send hugs.

Scene One

My place in the world, it is in the storm of the world . . .

Lights rise on Marcela.

Marcela What I like the most about it here is the poplar grove (it's actually just three trees) and the ocean (which is a pool where you can get your feet wet), where I rest a bit every day; this helps me enter her world with more kindness. Okay, let's see, for every one hundred people, two suffer from BPD, or borderline personality disorder, meaning that proportionally she and someone else here in this room have it. The disorder has this name because these people are easily inclined to depression and also a great deal of anxiety, a lot of emotional dependency. They depend a lot on others, as a child would; they don't want to be alone but in the manner of a child. They're very impulsive. It's a very complicated cocktail of traits, there are very well-known cases of patients who self-harm and cut themselves, on their arms or on their thighs. In short, people with this disorder (which, of course, is chronic) have very poor emotional regulation, because we are all neurotic. Everyone is, but they more, she is more—we're all a little dependent, but she more so. We can all be anxious, but she is much, much more so. That's all.

Scene Two

Lights rise on **Superman**, **Grandpa**, **Maradona**, *and* **Pillow**.

Pillow I need a plane in order to fly.

Maradona I'm not going to be able to sleep. I haven't been able to sleep since that kid opened her trap.

Superman It must be for a reason.

Pillow That's all that I need.

Grandpa Have you slept?

Superman Of course, like a baby.

Pillow It's better to keep quiet until everything is cleared up.

Superman It's true. Everything seems so suspicious—your shoes, your laugh, your hands, that watermelon, everything . . .

Maradona My eleventh daughter asked me about it today.

Superman No one has asked me anything.

Grandpa This is the first time I've gone out since she spoke up.

Pillow Really?

Superman Does anyone have a cigarette?

Maradona Yeah, does anyone have a cigarette?

Scene Three

Lights rise on **Her** *and* **Marcela**. **Her** *has to get up onstage.* **Her** *does not.*

Her   I can't.

Marcela   Yes, yes, you can.

Scene Four

The Play

Lights rise on **Her** *on stage.*

Her   Today I came to heal myself from four people who have harmed me: Superman, Grandpa, Maradona, and Pillow.

Today I came to heal myself from four people who have harmed me: Superman, Grandpa, Maradona, and Pillow. I came to heal myself through theatre. They told me that you could do that through reenacting. They told me that you could heal your soul, your mind, and your voice . . .

So, thank you for joining me.

Scene Five

The City of Fruit

Lights rise on **Grandpa** *and* **Superman**.

Grandpa   It seems that we got here a little late.

Superman   Or a little early.

Grandpa   Or we're the first to arrive.

Superman   Or the last.

Grandpa   Are you sure it was here?

Superman   I'm sure that you were sure that it was here—I just followed you.

Grandpa   How convenient, right?

Superman   Definitely, but this doesn't seem like a party.

Grandpa   Party?

Superman   Yes, if you notice, there's nothing here to indicate that this is a party, like party balloons . . .

Grandpa   Because it's not a party.

Superman   Ah, how boring, I came thinking it was a party. And so what is it?

Grandpa   A meeting.

Superman   And that's not the same thing.

Grandpa   No.

Superman   So why did I spend so much time getting ready?

Scene Six

Memory (Chaotic Writing for Forgetting)

Lights rise on **Her** *and* **Marcela**.

Her   In the City of Fruit I would spend summers

   with so much sun

   with lots of sun

   in full sun, full . . .

Marcela   Yes, and what you remember is dark, right?/and small/cut/recorded/ stamped with your pressure/repeated a thousand times in the international news. She writes from what was black/burned by that sun, the same that lightens her keyboard today. Sometimes she thought the sun was God and that was why it stained her—because it saw her, even in the shade and it knew what she knew. So she hid from it.

Her   With little success.

Marcela   But she would hide. The words curdle if you tighten them too much. They go bad like milk goes bad. They get disfigured, like political types disfigure us when they promise us heaven in order to take the earth from us.

Darkness.

Scene Seven

Lights rise on **Grandpa** *and* **Superman**.

Grandpa   That jacket is too big for you.

Superman   I think it fits me well.

Grandpa   It's obvious that it's too big for you.

Superman   It's obvious that you're jealous.

Grandpa   Not at all, I just want to help you.

Superman   To do what?

Grandpa   To look good.

Superman I think you're the one who doesn't look good, because this jacket, I saw myself a little while ago, and it looked amazing. A girl even whistled at me in the street and cat-called me.

Grandpa What did she say?

Superman "I just found the father of my children!"

Grandpa I don't believe you.

Superman I don't care. Okay, we got here either too late or too early.

Grandpa I don't know.

Superman So what do we do?

Grandpa Wait a little.

Superman How long?

Grandpa A while.

Superman Okay . . . but how long is a while?

Grandpa I don't know, why? You have to go? What do you have to do?

Superman What?

Grandpa I'm asking you.

Superman If I'm in a hurry?

Grandpa I'm asking you.

Superman I don't know, do you believe it?

Grandpa How could I know?

Superman I thought you knew what I had to do.

Grandpa What you have to do?

Superman Yeah, I had forgotten something a while ago.

Grandpa No, I don't know what you have to do.

Superman Me neither.

Grandpa So we'll wait.

Superman How many minutes do we have to wait?

Grandpa Ten minutes.

Superman Ten minutes?

Grandpa Yes

Superman Why not fifteen?

Grandpa Fine, fifteen.

Superman   Easy as that?

Grandpa   Simple as that.

Silence.

Scene Eight

Sucking Fingers

Lights rise on **Her** *and* **Marcela**.

Her   Sucking fingers is my first memory in the City of Fruit, so that's why my first scene is called that.

Marcela   The monsters were inside and also outside.

Her   1983. I'm seven years old, we're living under dictatorship.[1] People are being fractured, divided, violated, as if in parallel to my life, at the same moment that they're eating me, but I have no idea because I'm seven years old and my mother's family, who I grew up with, deeply believes in the legitimacy of the dictator. So I'm seven years old and I don't understand anything that's happening in the long country where my house and its door are. My ignorance, which I still can't forgive . . . I should have/could have/how I wish/I should have picked up a stone and thrown it with all my might until it hit a star and woke it up, one of those stars, so many of which had stopped shining in my country . . . the monsters were inside and also outside.

Marcela   Darkness and shame.

Scene Nine

Superman

Her   It happens in my uncle José's room—wood, a window, scattered things, breath, him. He is the most beloved of all my uncles, joyful, the youngest of my grandma's five sons, the spoiled brother of my mother, everyone does what he says. He knows how to speak well, and to laugh. He is all of the kids' favorite uncle, because in the backyard, he takes our hands, picks us up, and turns us around until we're dizzy. It's great, he makes us fly . . . we call him Superman because he lifts weights and because a small pile of his hair sticks out and, gathered toward his forehead, makes him look more like the superhero. Summers in this city are incredibly hot. While the fruit grows, my uncle is on the bed and I'm standing in front of him, he calls to me. I don't remember how but I feel lucky, the superhero likes me. I get on the bed, it's not made. I sit like a girl and he asks me to close my eyes and we play, he makes me suck his fingers one by one without opening my eyes until I get to the final thumb. Then what he puts in my mouth is not a finger but something thicker, more serious–his penis. I know because I saw it, I'm looking at it because I opened my eyes while I was waiting to suck the last thumb. His enormous, intimidating intimacy. I know because I was there in that image that I kept like a photo, my first. It stayed intact in my brain, the unerasable.

Marcela   Her heart beat strongly/the sun followed her/she stayed silent/she doesn't remember what happens next/but immediately she felt the weight of keeping something. Things remained, as I said, between the sun and her.

Scene Ten

Lights rise on **Superman** *and* **Grandpa**.

Superman   Let's talk, please.

Grandpa   I don't want to.

Superman   But I don't like silence.

Grandpa   Why?

Superman   I don't know, it makes me scared . . . let's talk.

Grandpa   Okay, okay.

Superman   What are we going to talk about?

Grandpa   I don't know, suggest something.

Superman   . . .

Grandpa   . . .

Scene Eleven

The Girlfriend

Lights rise on **Her**.

Her   1986, now I'm ten years old and already deformed, all of my summers are in the City of Fruit, always stained. My fear grows and nightmares now consume my sleep. Meanwhile, the dictator doesn't die—in the attack planned on him, he doesn't die . . . how sad. All of Chile, long as it is, is all sad, all cracked, all sad, cracked, distressed. If I'd been there, at age ten, I would have blown up everything, exploded everyone. But I wasn't there, I was at home.

My uncle Jorge is not the black sheep of the family but he is the rudest one of all, including of all the men I've met in my life. He has very black, very curly hair and he lets it grow like Maradona's[2] (according to him). His goals live in the bellies of a list of women that my aunt Sonia keeps so she can throw it in his face when she's annoyed. Second floor—I'm hiding in the small closet, with the smell of cologne or men's deodorant, and then my uncle comes in wearing just a towel around his waist, very wet, with his hair wet too, dripping. He opens the door and there I am. He says to me . . .

Marcela What does he say to you?

Her "Do you want to see?" I don't respond . . . he takes off the towel, he holds my hand against his penis. "Take off your pants," he tells me/I take off my pants very obediently/ he asks me to rest my hands on the dresser and he starts to rub against me, without entering me, he's holding my waist with one hand, with the other he presses my back, he asks me to press my legs together / he ends up completely soiling me and then he cleans me with a paper towel, I pull up my pants but I don't remember it – what I remember is that he gives me a 100-peso coin. I go down the stairs—everyone's downstairs, we have a large family—and I go into a corner. I have the coin in my hand, I'm only thinking about that. I find my sister and tell her I found a 100 peso coin, come with me to the store. We go out and walk happily to the store, and we buy chocolates and multi-colored candies. I don't remember the chocolates but I remember the candies, delicious and so many colors. Even today I'm amazed when I remember them.

Scene Twelve

Maradona *enters to join* **Superman** *and* **Grandpa**.

Maradona Did you two just get here?

Superman No.

Maradona How did you get in?

Superman Through the door.

Maradona And Pillow?

Grandpa He hasn't arrived.

Superman Or he already left.

Maradona (*to* **Superman**) That jacket's too big for you.

Grandpa I told you.

Superman Can we start?

Maradona We have to wait for the plan.

Grandpa And who's bringing it?

Maradona Pillow.

Superman He's not coming.

Grandpa And why isn't he coming?

Superman I figured.

Maradona   For some reason?

Superman   None.

Grandpa (*to* **Superman**)   So why don't you shut up?

Superman (*to* **Grandpa**)   Yeah, why don't you shut up?

Grandpa (*to* **Superman**)   That's what I told *you*.

Superman (*to* **Grandpa**)   Right, why don't I shut up?

Grandpa   We have to be in agreement about all the details.

Maradona   Our voices have to be one . . .

Superman   . . . out in the open.

Grandpa   There's something I don't get: why do we have to agree on all the details?

Maradona   What?

Grandpa   I'm innocent.

Superman   Innocent?

Grandpa   Yes.

Superman   Then I'm innocent, too.

Maradona   We have to prepare ourselves.

Superman   Yes, a terrible winter is coming, they say it's the worst one ever. Are you sure that you're innocent?

Grandpa   If I'm sure of anything it's my innocence. That girl is crazy, she made everything up and I don't know why.

Maradona   It's true, that girl went totally crazy.

Superman   That's right, she even walks like a weirdo.

Maradona   I haven't noticed that.

Grandpa   Me neither.

Superman   Yeah, and always wearing so many layers—one hundred degrees and she looks like we were in the worst winter ever and here it's the middle of summer.

Grandpa   No one will believe her.

Superman   No one.

Maradona   All of this is bullshit.

Superman   That's true

Maradona   . . .

Grandpa   . . .

Superman We have to agree.

Maradona Shit, we need Pillow here for that.

Superman Here we go with the cursing again. Can I tell you something, brother? No one is going to believe that you're innocent when you curse that much. I'm telling you, I listen to you and I go, "Well, this guy is full of shit." You get me?

Grandpa It's true, it looks suspicious.

Maradona It doesn't matter because no one is going to believe her at all.

Superman But it will raise doubts.

Grandpa That's true.

Maradona We need a plan . . . let's go over exactly what that kid said . . .

Superman I don't know what she said exactly.

Grandpa Yesterday you said you knew exactly what that kid had said.

Superman That was yesterday, today's another matter.

Maradona Then we can't continue.

Grandpa Then we can't.

Superman That seems suspicious to me.

Grandpa What does?

Maradona Let's continue, please.

Superman Where do you want to go?

Maradona Dammit, let's continue.

Superman That's what I mean, where?

Maradona With the topic.

Grandpa Let's start from the beginning: the girl said that we had abused her when she was a child.

Maradona I don't even remember her.

Superman I do.

Grandpa That's what she said.

Superman No one will believe this abuse thing.

Maradona Because it's not true.

Grandpa She could give details.

Maradona . . .

Superman . . .

Scene Thirteen

The Scene Just as It Happened

Lights rise on **Her**.

Her Through the window I see my uncle Jorge with a woman and I feel really bad, really complicated, with a heaviness in my stomach. I'm going to the place where you do laundry, it's my favorite place because it's cool and dark, the sun never hits there—I don't like heat and in the City of Fruit everything is heat and more heat.

Light shift. Lights rise on **Maradona** *and* **Her** *as a girl.*

Maradona What are you doing here?

Girl (Her) I saw you with that girl outside.

Maradona So what?

Girl (Her) She's your girlfriend?

Maradona Not yet.

Girl (Her) And us/ he kisses me, he makes me take his penis.

Maradona . . .

Girl (Her) I'm not your girlfriend?

Maradona You're my fiancée.

Lights shift.

Her That is the saddest scene of my life—out of the million sad scenes that make up my life, that is the saddest. Afterwards, I went out to buy multi-colored candies. They looked like a bunch of flowers, green, yellow, red, orange, pink, fuchsia, purple, light blue . . . I didn't think that as the years passed I'd replace them with these white pills.

Scene Fourteen

Lights rise on **Superman**, **Maradona**, *and* **Grandpa**.

Superman Okay, why invent something like that? We're all family.

Maradona It happens even in the best families.

Grandpa Wait, what does?

Superman Yeah, what happens even in the best families? Let's be very clear what we're talking about—we can't get confused, we can't!

Maradona We need the plan.

Grandpa   And what time is he coming?

Superman   And what if he doesn't come?! And what if he doesn't come?! What do we do if he doesn't arrive?

Maradona   Calm down, he'll come.

Grandpa   We have to wait.

Scene Fifteen

Lights rise on **Marcela** *and* **Her**.

Marcela   Thank you! Why do they use the word "borderline" for this disorder? I really don't like this label, but it means they're true neurotics, right, but on the borderline of psychosis—thus the name. She is clearly neurotic—I mean, we all are, but she more so, and you could say, "Well, these people are acting crazy," but we've all acted crazy sometimes, she's just crazier.

When you lack strong emotional regulation when you're young, then everything gets complicated. You grow up in a vacuum, growing without direction, and then you react immaturely. We can all change and grow until we become mature people, and using reason we keep growing more mature, but in her case, she doesn't have the tools that normally permit growth when she is faced with setbacks. For example, if she loses her partner, then she devolves practically to suicide. If a normal person does one day of therapy to solve a problem, she has to do three or more.

Her   More.

Scene Sixteen

Lights rise on **Superman**, **Maradona**, *and* **Grandpa**.

Superman   Okay now, why did you bring a watermelon?

Maradona   I found it thrown out in the street. It made me sad and I picked it up. It looks good.

Superman   I thought it had to do with our plan.

Maradona   What would a watermelon have to do with it?

Grandpa   Let's see, how could a watermelon explain . . .

Superman   Like Columbus explained with an egg.

Maradona   You're right but I don't see how to explain with a watermelon.

Grandpa   It doesn't matter—that's why we have our plan that's coming, right?

Superman   In any case, I wouldn't abandon the possibility of the watermelon.

Grandpa It doesn't matter. If something occurs to you let us know.

Superman What's that?

Grandpa What's what?

Maradona What?

Grandpa What you have there.

Maradona What?

Grandpa There.

Maradona Nothing.

Superman A flower?

Maradona No.

Grandpa No, of course it's a flower.

Superman And who is the flower for?

Maradona I'm getting married

Superman In love again.

Grandpa To who?

Maradona I'm not telling you.

Grandpa And why not?

Superman Now you're ashamed of us.

Maradona I'm not going to tell you who it is.

Grandpa So we know her.

Maradona No, and I don't want you to know her.

Superman Meaning you're not inviting us to the wedding.

Maradona No.

Grandpa All for the best, so we can wash our hands.

Maradona Of what?

Superman Of what? That she would be your fifth fiancée, that's what.

Grandpa For example.

Superman Yes, among other things.

Maradona I'm not inviting you.

Superman It doesn't matter, sooner or later we'll meet her.

Scene Seventeen

Grandpa, Tell Me[3]

Lights rise on **Her**.

Her Grandpa, tell me, why do I have to kiss your stinking mouth? And so many times, tell me! Why do I have to touch your sleeping, flaccid, soft, flabby, limp, slack, sad, gelatinous penis? Where is my grandma? Grandpa, tell me, I should have been your Heidi, not porn, not sexy, a Heidi because I liked flowers and was always red from the sun that burned me over and over. You tell me, weren't you supposed to be the grandpa, the one on the TV, the one from my cartoon days, or not? Or do grandpas always do those things? I would ask myself this every time I saw an old man walk by.

Silence! Be quiet! Don't let anyone know!

Scene Eighteen

Lights rise on **Grandpa**, **Maradona**, *and* **Superman**.

Superman I just remembered, the girl said that she was going to make all the details public and I, planning on shopping tomorrow, made a great business deal. I sold a piece of land, and the commission—wow, wow, wow!

Grandpa So you should pay me what you owe me.

Superman I don't have enough to pay back debts.

Grandpa So not that "wow, wow, wow?!"

Superman Not so much, not so much, that was an exaggeration on my part.

Maradona You owe me, too.

Superman I don't owe you anything.

Maradona What do you mean, of course you owe me, and quite a lot, so why did you ask me for money in the morning?

Superman Well, I didn't have change.

Maradona Doesn't that embarrass you?

Grandpa She said that we had abused her when she was seven.

Superman Yes, she said that.

Maradona No one's going to believe that we all . . . did things to her that young. No one's going to believe it because it can't be.

Pillow *enters.*

Lights shift. Lights rise on **Her**.

Her Pillow. This one I won't name because he took everything from me. I should give him a piece of white paper but not as a truce.

Lights shift. Lights rise on the men.

Pillow It looks like I got to the party late.

Superman See, I'm not the only one who thought it was a party.

Grandpa It's a good thing you got here.

Pillow It was rough out there, a lot of traffic. I almost died, I almost didn't make it.

Maradona You have the plan?

Pillow They were super expensive.

Grandpa You went to buy the plan?

Pillow And you, what are you doing with my jacket?

Superman Me?

Pillow I was looking for it everywhere, give it back to me.

Superman I got paid what you owed me.

Pillow Me? You owe me.

Superman Me? No, you owe me.

Maradona Why don't you pay what you owe us?

Superman I don't owe anyone anything. Now that I made a deal, you come here inventing debts.

Pillow You made a deal?!

Grandpa Yeah, a deal that's wow, wow, wow!

Pillow Wow, wow, wow! Pay me, I need to get money together.

Maradona You want to get away.

Pillow From what?

Superman Be quiet. Now that we're all here I want to say something before we deal with this situation that brought us all together, okay?

Grandpa This is terrifying.

Pillow What?

Maradona Everything.

Superman Yesterday I waited for you all but you didn't come.

. . .

Superman None of you are going to say anything?

Pillow We'd love to . . .

Superman Really?

Pillow . . . to pull out your tongue!

Superman Can I continue?

Grandpa I don't understand.

Superman We decided to go to the cemetery and leave flowers for Mamá and no one came.

Pillow When did we decide that?

Superman When she died.

Pillow Yes! You're right.

Maradona I forgot.

Grandpa I have her here in my heart, I don't have to go to that ugly place.

Superman It's the least we can do. Plus she must be rolling over in her grave with all of this, the least we can do is leave her a few flowers.

Grandpa I have her here in my heart, I don't have to go to that ugly place.

Superman Exactly, Mamá's neighbors—all well-tended, with flowers, pretty flowers—and Mamá's grave—forgotten, ugly, full of dirt.

Pillow Okay, okay, okay, tomorrow we'll go and bring some flowers, a big bouquet of different kinds. Which did she like? Roses?

Superman Poppies.

Pillow Poppies, right, poppies—make a note, poppies . . . tomorrow we'll go.

Grandpa All right, let's continue please.

Maradona Please.

Grandpa And the plan?

Pillow Like I said, they were super expensive.

Maradona I don't understand, you'd think there would have been a big sale on plans.

Pillow I'll explain it to you . . . can you give me back my jacket?

Grandpa Once again, the plan, the plan.

Pillow First thing's first: my jacket, and then each of you owes me 30,000 pesos.

Maradona 30,000 pesos!

Superman 30,000 pesos!

Grandpa That's robbery.

Pillow   If you don't want it, I'll take it.

Grandpa   Fine.

Maradona   And who the hell did you buy the plan from?

Grandpa   For the price it must have been amazing.

Superman   It must have been from the Joker, Bane, that type of person.

Pillow   It was the cheapest plan I could find.

Grandpa   And where is it?

Pillow   Here.

Superman   In that envelope?

Pillow   In this envelope, yes.

Grandpa   Well, all we have to do is pay.

Pillow   If I wasn't getting together all the money I could, I wouldn't charge you anything.

Superman   You always tell us the same thing.

Pillow   Really?

Superman   Yes, you're always getting money together.

Pillow   Really?

Grandpa   And we never know why.

Pillow   Give me back my jacket now.

Grandpa   Give him the jacket.

Superman   But I'm cold.

Maradona   I'm hot.

Pillow   The jacket.

Superman   Please, I'm dying of cold!

Pillow   Fine but as soon as we're done here, you give it to me.

Superman   Thank you, brother.

Scene Nineteen

Lights rise on **Her** *and* **Marcela**.

Her   Shit runs down all the walls. Shit runs down the middle of that dictatorship, in between the corpses that were separated from Chilean life but remain around here, in the hidden depths of Chile. Run, shit, run, how pretty, ooze through the tragic hallways where anything was possible, where anything was possible, rats in vaginas, broken fingers, water dripping on brains, what else! We're too civilized to keep being animals or too animal-like to pretend to be civilized.

Marcela   In terms of self-harm, it's strange. It's strange because it's not what one would imagine. She hurts herself but not to get attention (although some people do that, to warn others that something is happening to them). She does it to release her anguish and it works for her, so it's not a negative action. When you don't go to therapy and use that as a way of calming yourself, alleviating yourself, getting through anxiety, it's a good thing, because imagine if you don't do it and it explodes. But it bothers us, it bothers us, because our society sees it as a very negative action. But the truth is that physical pain dulls some emotional pain, that's all, and if you're not getting help, what more can you do?

Scene Twenty

Lights rise on the men.

Grandpa   What's this?

Pillow   The plan.

Maradona   I don't understand.

Superman   These are numbers. A plan written in numbers? That's what you bought? A plan written in numbers?

Pillow   What? Let me see it. You're right, it's written in numbers.

Maradona   But we don't know anything about numbers.

Pillow   Let me see it again. Yes, these are definitely numbers.

Grandpa   Who did you buy it from?

Maradona   Yes, who?

Pillow   From a young lady

Superman   I don't want to hear any more.

Maradona   I told you that we shouldn't send him.

Pillow   You didn't send me anywhere, I offered.

Superman   What kind of plan, what kind of plan is this?

Grandpa   One that doesn't help us.

. . .

Pillow   Don't worry, nobody's going to believe her.

Superman   That we abused her—nobody, how? In what kind of mind? No, nobody.

Grandpa   Seven years old, that's abnormal.

Maradona   So young, no, things weren't like that.

Superman   Exactly, she didn't know how to receive affection, she doesn't know because, because . . .

Pillow   She's weird.

Grandpa   Her papá is to blame, yes, her alcoholic dad.

Superman   We're fine, now with the watermelon.

Pillow   With the watermelon what?

Superman   We'll explain it with the watermelon.

Pillow   Really?

Maradona   How Columbus explained with an egg.

. . .

Pillow   A better world.

Music.

Maradona   I liked that.

Pillow   I'd like a better world.

Superman   And that exists?

Pillow   A better world to live in. One day I'm going to buy myself a plane, a small one that's red, bright red, and I'm going to leave, I'm going to fly far away.

Superman   To the moon?

Pillow   No, to Africa and I'll stay there a few days, picking.

Maradona   Picking what?

Pillow   A Black woman, obviously, they're the best. And when I pick the one I like the most, the darkest of all, then I'll propose a trip to her.

Superman   If she doesn't want it?

Maradona   Kidnap her, of course.

Pillow   And I'll take her in my red plane, I'll take her to an island, where we'll be the first ones and no one else, just us, her and me. That will be for a short time, for as long as our love lasts, and then ten years for ten kids, that's what life's about. And then, then, I return to my red plane, my Black woman will cry black tears of hate and love because I'm going to leave her to raise the kids, and I'm going to fly higher, the highest I can, singing a song.

Superman   And then?

Pillow   Nothing, I fall.

. . .

Maradona Silence.

Grandpa What's happening now?

Maradona What exactly did this deformed girl say?

Grandpa That we abused her when she was a child, starting when she was seven.

Maradona What else?

Pillow What do you mean, what else?

Maradona She didn't say in a premeditated way.

Superman What?

Maradona That we had done it together.

Grandpa Together, no, she didn't say that. How? All together, no, no, it wasn't like that.

Pillow Really?

Maradona Okay, then how?

Grandpa . . .

Pillow . . .

Superman . . .

Maradona Shit.

Superman I don't understand.

Pillow Me neither.

Grandpa All right, we don't need the same version, each of us should defend himself alone . . . it's more that, maybe one of you did do it.

Pillow Really? And so the plan I bought . . .

Maradona Stick it up your ass.

Grandpa Each one of us will decide what to do, but she is accusing all of us.

Superman I never touched her.

Pillow I'm done worrying, she can't prove anything because it's impossible to do, it's impossible to do, and no matter how early you wake up, the day won't come any sooner.

Maradona It's true.

Superman So, this meeting . . .

Maradona Stick it up your ass!

Superman Stick it up yours, you organized it.

Maradona   What? No, it was Pillow.

Pillow   Me? No.

Grandpa   How?

Superman   I don't understand.

Grandpa   It wasn't you?

Maradona   No.

Superman   It wasn't me, either.

Grandpa   Everyone calm down. Raise your hand if you organized this meeting.

Maradona   . . .

Superman   . . .

Pillow   . . .

Grandpa   No one.

Superman   This is a trap.

Pillow   Really?

Maradona   Shit.

Grandpa, Superman, Maradona, *and* **Pillow** *sing a verse from Cucurrucucú Paloma.*[4]

Scene Twenty-One

Therapy Post Dictatorship

Lights rise on **Marcela**.

Marcela   She has decided to heal herself. When her psychiatrist told her that she was deformed, that emotional stunting was preventing her from maturing, and that a personality disorder and severe, chronic bipolar disorder didn't allow her to develop in a balanced way, she decided to use theatrical representation to confront those who caused her pain. Even though it seemed to be too late, she decided to ask for help, and here we are.

Scene Twenty-Two

Lights rise on the men.

Pillow   . . .

Grandpa   . . .

Superman . . .

Pillow The good thing is we haven't said anything.

Maradona No?

Grandpa No.

Pillow Nothing that could implicate us.

Superman Nothing.

Pillow Find her.

Superman Who?

Grandpa Her.

Superman Ohhh.

Maradona Find her.

Superman Where do I find her?

Grandpa Over here.

Pillow Over there.

Superman She's not there.

Maradona How do you know she's not?

Pillow Look hard for her.

Superman I am.

Pillow No, you're not.

Superman How do you know? Of course I am.

Grandpa You look for her.

Pillow Why me? You do it.

Maradona Why me? No.

Superman Because you have a fiancée.

Maradona And what does that have to do with it?

Superman You don't want things to go badly with your fiancée.

Pillow He has another fiancée?

Maradona And what do you care?

Pillow Ahhhh! I know the . . .

Grandpa Quiet!

Superman This is the end of my political career.

Grandpa What career?

Superman The one I was thinking of starting with the far right–revolutionary thought, mayor of . . .

Pillow She's not here.

Superman Unless she's invisible . . . because she's so strange, that little girl . . . that it wouldn't be weird . . . we haven't even seen a boyfriend or anything . . . a girlfriend, whatever . . . nothing . . . God is with everyone, they say.

Grandpa Don't involve God here.

Superman And why not, if God is everywhere, as they say, right?

Pillow . . .

Maradona . . .

Superman . . .

Grandpa She could be recording us.

Superman But we haven't said anything.

Pillow Nothing.

Maradona At all.

Grandpa We haven't done anything, we don't have anything to be afraid of.

Superman It's true, we're acting as if we're guilty.

Pillow Exactly, and we're innocent.

Superman So why are we here?

Maradona Because we feel guilty.

Pillow To be or not to be, therein lies the dilemma.

Grandpa Everything rotted away when my cat Claudio died . . . my cat, that day, everything got dark for me.

Superman That was a hundred years ago.

Grandpa Twenty years ago, my cat, my friend and companion, died. My life ended and I was alone . . . with these guys and his shadow and I'll never forget him, his little eyes, and how we used to play, as if nothing else in the world existed. He was with me through my whole illness, when I broke my hip. While you all went off and left me alone, my cat Claudio was with me, he was with me through the desperation of not being able to get up from that bed, he was with me. He loved me and he died and everything ended for me.

Superman And if you loved him so much then why did you kill him?
. . .

Grandpa I don't know.

Superman   Why are you eating the watermelon?

Pillow   Why do you care, what's wrong with that?

Grandpa   Is it good?

Pillow   Yeah.

Maradona   Let me try it.

Pillow   Refreshing.

Maradona   Refreshing and sweet.

Pillow   Tasty.

Grandpa   It's good, really good.

Maradona   Juicy.

Pillow   Yeah.

Maradona   I'd eat it all.

Grandpa   Really very tasty.

Pillow   I haven't tasted one this fresh in a long time.

Grandpa   They're the best, the ones that are green on the outside.

Maradona   How delicious.

Superman   Enough!

Scene Twenty-Three

Lights rise on **Marcela** *and* **Her**.

Marcela   Thank you.

Her   Yes, the dictatorship ended, no, my uncles never touched me again, they stopped touching me, but I keep feeling bad, bad, bad, deformed.

Marcela   The main issue for these patients is their problem with attachment, with a dependency on the feeling of danger regarding losing another person. They make rapid judgments when they might lose relationships. They don't have it, because they don't have it, the capacity to maturely understand loss, and they react to facts with subjective interpretations. They have the tendency to feel like they're being abandoned.

Frequently, though not always, these people report trauma, mistreatment, or child abuse. This is what inhibits the normal strengthening of their personality, so there emerges an insecure early childhood attachment that doesn't allow the child to mentally develop in the proper way and generates this insecure attachment that explains the universe of a BPD patient. Although not all of these patients are victims of mistreatment or abuse, in this case, yes, her, yes.

Scene Twenty-Four

Lights rise on the men.

Grandpa One of us here is screwing us all over.

Pillow Really? Don't make things up.

Superman It's a problem of old age.

Grandpa What is?

Superman The zipper on my pants.

Maradona I want to tell you that I'm not going to put my hands in the fire for anyone.

Pillow Good of you to tell us. Later, don't complain.

Grandpa I don't know, but I'm clean.

Pillow I think this meeting is already over.

Maradona You all want to blame me.

Pillow This meeting is already over.

Maradona And why do you want to end it?

Superman Yeah, why?

Pillow Because it's already over, what don't you understand? It's not that I want it, it already happened.

Maradona I'm not afraid.

Superman He who doesn't stink casts the first stone.

Grandpa Doesn't sin.

Superman What?

Grandpa He who doesn't sin, not stink.

Superman It's the same thing, why are you always correcting me?

Maradona We're definitely done.

Pillow That's what I said.

Superman But why? I only just started to understand, and now you want to end everything.

Maradona This meeting is over.

Pillow And why do you get to decide? Plus it happened a while ago!

Superman What did?

Pillow The end of the meeting.

Maradona You're a motherfucker.

Grandpa Don't bring your mother into this.

Scene Twenty-Five

Lights rise on **Marcela** *and* **Her**.

Marcela This is what I like the least: this moment, when we're face to face during this brief silence, and she takes the pills and sips the water . . . this tiny moment is so intense, it's the most concrete thing we've experienced. It's so concrete, so firm, but so brief that many times I think I've taken the pills and returned the glass to her after drinking the water.

Her Be quiet silence peace/a woman breastfeeding/peace/ me in the last car/ peace/ she could nurse us all/ I want to be there, between her breasts and asleep/ the city watches me/a woman breastfeeding/ in the middle of a war/life/and me in the last car waiting for my turn to find the end/peace

Scene Twenty-Six

Lights rise on the men.

Pillow I need a plane that I can fly.

Maradona I won't be able to sleep, I haven't been able to sleep ever since she opened her piehole.

Superman There must be a reason.

Pillow That's all I need.

Grandpa Maybe you've slept.

Superman Of course, like a baby.

Pillow It's better to stay quiet until everything's been cleared up.

Superman It's true. Everything seems so suspicious—your shoes, your laugh, your hands, that watermelon.

Maradona My eleventh daughter asked me about all of this today.

Superman No one has asked me anything.

Grandpa This is the first time that I've gone out since she spoke up.

Pillow Really?

Superman Does anyone have a cigarette?

Maradona Yeah, does anyone have a cigarette?

Lights shift.

. . .

Scene Twenty-Seven

Lights rise on **Her** *and* **Marcela**. **Her** *has to get up on stage.* **Her** *doesn't do it.*

Her   I can't.

Marcela   Yes, you can.

Scene Twenty-Eight

(Fear) The Scene She Imagines

Marcela   I toss the cigarettes. We don't talk, but they babble and I pee myself. There they are, the four of them, like an encyclopedia, and I can't speak, I just pee and feel the heat and then the cold on my legs, a lump in my throat. They deny everything but they don't look at me. They are about to leave, I tremble and they—it seems like they are afraid. I uncover myself, I'm wearing my favorite vest and on it are hundreds, thousands of explosives. They stand there with mouths hanging open. I'm trying to play the redeemer. This scene is elusive, indescribable . . . they run away, first one and then another and another and the last. I am terrified. I stand there deformed, pathetic, pissed-on, and with life passing me by, a scary nightmare that they denied in front of me, they confuse me, they make me doubt myself, I feel guilty, I think I invented everything, that I'm crazy, the ceiling flies away, and there it is. The sun reminds me, stains me. I can't avoid it, cover it up, darken it. I think, now's the time, stuck in the last car in order to find the end.

Her   In front of me, a mother nursing her son—I want to be there, sleeping, but the end has come, and the finality.

Scene Twenty-Nine

The actors abandon their characters. It's the moment of the question, it's the moment in which **Her** *confronts them, it's the moment for which she wrote the entire play, it's the moment that will never exist in reality.* **Her** *has to ask, but not the audience, nor* **Marcela**; *she has to ask them directly. This is the heart of the play; that's why it's essential to arrive here.*

Actor 1   Let's take it a little bit before.

Actor 2   Let's go.

Actor 3 (as Maradona)   My eleventh daughter asked me about all of this today.

Actor 4 (as Superman)   No one has asked me anything.

Actor 1 (as Grandpa)   This is the first time that I've gone out since she spoke up.

Actor 2 (as Pillow)   Really?

Actor 3 (as Superman)   Does anyone have a cigarette?

Actor 4 (as Maradona)   Yeah, does anyone have a cigarette?

Her   I have cigarettes but I forgot my lines.

Actor 1   Say it however you want.

Her   So much work to get to this moment . . . And I don't know what to say, I didn't write anything for this moment . . . I'm the same seven-year-old girl sitting under the eaves of the door, getting some fresh afternoon air, giving shape to this question that's grown over time and that no longer needs a response: Why?

. . .

Thank you for joining me . . . thank you so much!

The actors exit.

Scene Thirty

The Corner

Lights rise on **Her**.

Her   I'm with my 100-peso coin

it says 1980

1980, *nothing about revolution*

on one side 100

on the other a face

despite its age the coin shines

although the time that has passed is not shiny,

the coin has continued shining

the dictatorship ended

but without justice until today

I close my hand in a fist with the coin inside

until I stop feeling it

now it could be anything

a sadness/a chill/a war/an earthquake/a tsunami/an act of torture/a kick/a violent word/ a lost body/a hungry child/a country that forces us to forget

but it could also be something else

a flower/a hope/a big open street where you walk with your kids/a bit of peace/the voice of a friend/a sincere smile/a true love

. . . now I'm no longer in my corner

I don't know what will come tomorrow

but I'm no longer hiding from the sun

> . . . *my place in the storm is in the greatest quietude of its chaos.*

End of play.

Notes

1. "On 11 September 1973, the first socialist president ever to be elected by the people, Salvador Allende, was overthrown by the Chilean military forces supported by the country's right wing. During the Dictatorship that followed (1973–90), thousands of politically active citizens went into exile, and many of those who remained in the country to fight for the recovery of democracy were victims of torture and disappearance." For further information, please see Grass, Kalawski and Nicholls.
2. Diego Armando Maradona (1960-2020), Argentine professional soccer player and manager widely considered to be one of the greatest players in the sport.
3. *Grandpa, Tell Me* (*Abuelito Dime Tu*) refers to a well-known song written by Takeo Watanabe from the children's television series, *Heidi*.
4. The men sing a verse from *Cucurrucucú Paloma* (1954), a well-known Mexican song by Tomás Méndez (1926-1995). The translation is as follows: cucurrucucu/they say that at night he would just cry, they say that he wouldn't eat, he would just drink, they swear that heaven itself would tremble upon hearing him crying, how he suffered for her that even in her death he kept calling out for her . . .

Sentiments:

Gendered Cruelty, Dark Comedy, and the Ethics of Spectatorship

Anne García-Romero

In *Sentiments*—this volume's only dark comedy—Carla Zúñiga M. provides early twenty-first-century audiences with a cautionary tale about a Chilean teenage girl who attempts to pursue sexual and personal freedom while confronting an oppressive internet environment as well as the conservative adults in her life. The protagonist Antofagasta, a student at a private, parochial high school, challenges heteronormative, patriarchal society as she tries to navigate her relationship with her girlfriend and a group of boys at her school. Zúñiga examines the dire consequences that arise as Antofagasta experiences diminished agency when confronted by online bullying that crescendos to in-person violence. At the play's conclusion, the protagonist tragically chooses to end her life. Zúñiga shows Antofagasta's plight by creating a theatrical world that is heightened, non-naturalistic, darkly comedic, and absurd in order to dramatize gendered cruelty and examine the ethics of spectatorship. Zúñiga employs various strategies to do so, including creating darkly humorous and excessive play and performance texts, exploring the female body as a site for violence, highlighting dangerous and unreliable characters, and engaging a viral video news story.

In *Sentiments*, Antofagasta exists in a sector of society that has no tolerance for female desire, female sexual expression, and same sex love. Set in 2013 Chile, the play opens as Antofagasta arrives home at midnight. Nelly María, a single mother, is very upset and wants to know why her only daughter arrived so late. Antofagasta lies that she was studying for a biology exam. Her mother believes her until she later finds her daughter's cellphone with *"997 missed phone calls from MAMÁ."*[1] In scene two, Zúñiga reveals that Antofagasta returned home late after enjoying a sexual encounter with her male schoolmates. Antofagasta expresses female desire that is full of curiosity and pleasure. She is also in love with her girlfriend, Pato Piñata. However, her sexual exploration is met by her parent's ignorance and her teacher Miss Francisca's misogyny and homophobia. Soon, Antofagasta learns that the boy who filmed their sexual encounter with her consent has uploaded the video to YouTube, against her wishes. As the online scandal grows, with the video of her sexual encounter broadcast on television, people on the street accost Antofagasta and inflict bodily harm. Antofagasta's desire and passion are met with rejection, physical and psychological violence, and death.

Zúñiga creates darkly comedic and excessive stage directions and dialogue to underscore the cruelty that her female characters endure. While the play follows a traditional, linear structure, her narrative grows in excess as more and more extreme events occur with clarity, absurdity, and tragedy through the stage directions and dialogue. Scene one's subtitle, "The night the daughter never arrived and the mother agonized like crazy in the living room,"[2] highlights Nelly María's aggravation as her daughter arrives at midnight. Before the first line of dialogue, Zúñiga describes Nelly María's mental state: "Atrocious images run through her mind, images filled with the most horrific rapes and murders."[3] Zúñiga provides the reader and the theatre artists who will interpret this role with a narrative view of the violent world that surrounds these characters and how precarious and dangerous life could be for a teenage girl in 2013 Chile. Scene five's subtitle, "The day the house exploded and glass from one of the windows fell on the poor mother and punctured her sad soul,"[4] foreshadows Nelly María's devastation after watching the video of her daughter's sexual encounter broadcast on national television. Additionally, Zúñiga provides the reader and actor with a poignant backstory about Nelly María's relationship with her daughter when she was a child. As she stands, immobile, after viewing the video, "A tear falls from the mother's cheek, the last time she had seen her daughter completely naked was when she was nine years old, Nelly María had bathed her after Antofagasta had drawn animals all over her body"[5] Here Zúñiga recounts a tender memory of a mother as she washes the transgression off her child's body. However, at this moment, Nelly María cannot remove her daughter's transgression. In the dialogue, characters make sudden pronouncements that advance their extreme conditions: Nelly María calls her daughter garbage while accusing her of lying, Miss Francisca offers a graphic sex education lesson, Antofagasta announces her pregnancy to her girlfriend, and Pato Piñata reveals Antofagasta was violently attacked by people in an outdoor market. This dramaturgical strategy on the page provides the readers and potential collaborators with moving and shocking insights into how these women are trying to survive.

In her performance text, Zúñiga fuels this examination of gender cruelty through employing an absurdist theatricality, first developed with director Javier Casanga in their company, The Horrible Girl (La Niña Horrible). Cofounded in 2012, The Horrible Girl was a multidisciplinary company whose work was "oriented to the creation of a new dramatic and stage language, which inquires into a mixture between expressionism and the grotesque, encouraging a reflection about the different social constructs with regard to gender roles."[6] The company, which disbanded in 2020 after six successful play collaborations, utilized a heightened theatrical vocabulary to illuminate themes of gender and sexuality in Zúñiga's plays, including gender violence, female empowerment, and LGBTQ+ rights. She reflects, "For me, [these themes] are important because I'm a woman and I've experienced discrimination firsthand, at the beginning writing from that place wasn't so premeditated, but in writing more plays I've become more conscious of this gender discourse."[7] In 2013, Zúñiga was a theatrical pioneer by exploring these themes in *Sentiments*, several years before Chile's "Ni Una Más" movement (translation: Not One More). As Coca Duarte mentions in her essay on *The City of Fruit*, " . . . gender-related issues gained unprecedented visibility in Chilean society, especially with the massive feminist mobilizations of 2017 and 2018. These protests, which originated in student movements, denounced gender violence—whose most extreme expression is femicide—harassment and abuse within educational settings, and the symbolic erasure of women across all areas of culture."[8] *Sentiments* is the first of many subsequent works in which Zúñiga explores gender violence as a means to combat erasure. Theatre scholar Jennifer Joan Thompson describes The Horrible Girl's aesthetic in the 2013 world premiere production of *Sentiments*:

> The feminist excess is accompanied by an aesthetic excess, and the play combines kitsch, absurdism (entrances and exits are made through a refrigerator), expressionism, and dark humor as it interrogates the roles

women are relegated to and critiques the restrictions placed on individual liberties, in particular efforts to control desiring adolescent female bodies.[9]

Thompson's description highlights the excessive production strategies Zúñiga and Casanga utilized. The absurdist acting style included an elongated vocal delivery, a complex physical gestural vocabulary, and a balletic physicality that generated a pervasively dark comedic tone throughout. Elizabeth Pérez's costume design included characters wearing brightly colored wigs (Antofagasta in long, auburn tresses, Nelly María with an almost nineteenth century, auburn updo, and Miss Francisca in a jet-black pompadour), as well as her monochromatic, aqua blue colored one room set, with a large, asymmetrical, antique-style black sofa centerstage. Above the stage, Pérez designed a screen where the scene titles and stage directions were projected, allowing audiences to respond with laughter to Zúñiga's narrative descriptions. Thus, the seemingly domestic, realistic setting was distorted and refracted to underscore the precarity of female existence in an oppressive, heteronormative, patriarchal society. The resulting dark humor allowed the audience to respond to the characters' violent circumstances with both somber, emotional silence and subversive, uproarious laughter.

The 2024 revival of *Sentiments*, also directed by Casanga, employed their advanced, experimental aesthetic, developed over a decade of collaboration. The actors engaged in stylized vocal delivery, amplified by lavalier microphones, presenting their dialogue as direct address to the audience, using elongated articulations, highly choreographed gestures, and with each actor's face painted the same color as their bright, monochromatic costumes, designed by Pérez (aqua, pink, yellow, purple, red and blue). On a spare monochromatic set, designed by Sebastián Escalona, with only a long white sofa and an excessively tall yellow door that never opens, the scene titles and stage directions were projected on the upstage wall in ticker tape fashion, announcing the inner and outer turmoil of the characters. The distancing and alienating effects of the production and performance aesthetic during this revival created an even greater sense of urgency regarding the gender cruelty that Antofagasta experiences.[10]

In her play, Zúñiga presents the female body as a site for violence with a teenage female protagonist who is victimized by the other women in the play, as well as societal forces outside the play. The levels of violence in *Sentiments* includes physical, psychological, and suicidal. Antofagasta experiences physical violence by being hit by a ball thrown through a window, being attacked by a market crowd, and being hit by her girlfriend. She experiences psychological violence through her teacher's violent and homophobic bullying and the online bullying from the boys in her school and others. Miss Francisca recommends that Antofagasta's only escape from this online torment is death, and the play concludes as she ends her own life. Antofagasta is also the name of a mining city in northern Chile in the Atacama Desert and the capital of the Antofagasta region. By creating a teenage girl with this name, Zúñiga presents the female body as geography, and land that is being mined. With this name, Zúñiga offers a reflection on the violent relationship between the state and the body, where the young female body is ultimately devalued and relegated to death.

Zúñiga creates dangerous, adult, female characters who reinforce the oppressive structures in post-dictatorship, democratic Chile. While the teenage characters seek sexual freedom, the adult authority figures (mother and teacher) relate to Antofagasta and Pato Piñata in ways that are ignorant and antagonistic. Nelly María, a widow and the teenager's single mother, remains largely ignorant of her daughter's sexual exploration. She is more concerned with providing hospitality for her guests than truly connecting with her daughter's reality. Zúñiga shows how Nelly María is also seemingly unaware of Pato Piñata's female gender and assumes that her daughter would only be romantically involved with a boy, not a girl. In Miss Francisca, Zúñiga creates a darkly comedic antagonist who represents the misogyny and homophobia in the educational authority structure. Miss Francisca is also grotesque and absurd, with pronouncements that are so cruel as to appear farcical. She reveals her own hysterectomy to Antofagasta with glee, as she never wanted to be a mother. And yet, she cannot tolerate female desire, teenage female sexuality, or queer sexuality. Miss Francisca states that women should only have sex after the age of twenty, should only be heterosexual, and should die if they transgress heteronormative values. However, Miss Francisca also shows desire for Antofagasta, commenting on her attractive body in the viral video, thus presenting another layer of antagonism for this teenage girl. This cruelty also extends to the other female characters who operate as bystanders to Antofagasta's plight.

Zúñiga's supporting, adult female characters try and fail to rebel against their patriarchal and misogynist society and remain unreliable for Antofagasta. The neighbor, María Teresa, engages in a passionate affair with her son's male therapist while she is petrified of the murderous rage of her distant husband Horacio. As María Teresa confesses her infidelity, Miss Francisca recommends María Teresa's death. Meanwhile,

5 Miss Francisca (Coca Miranda) lectures Antofagasta (Carla Gaete) and her mother Nelly María (Viviana Basoalto) in *Sentiments* by Carla Zúñiga, directed by Javier Casanga, Teatro Sidarte, 2017. (Photo: © Nicolás Calderón)

Pato Piñata suggests that this neighbor leave her husband and explore her newfound sexual freedom. With that encouragement from this teenage student, whom she also thinks is male, María Teresa begins to flirt. Yet María Teresa remains anguished and trapped in her loveless marriage. The Cosmetics Lady, a type of everywoman, arrives at the door to sell makeup. She soon reveals she's in an abusive relationship with a boyfriend who beats her. She covers up her bruised eye with makeup and later reveals she killed her abusive boyfriend. While she is the only adult character who truly tries to assist the teenager, her help is provisional as she abandons Antofagasta in the end.

With Pato Piñata, Zúñiga presents a lesbian character, with a deep voice, who loves Antofagasta, but still adheres to certain patriarchal values and ultimately proves equally unreliable. Pato behaves respectfully to Antofagasta's mother and does not correct Nelly María's gender misidentification. At one point, Nelly Maria states, "Ugh! These men! They're such a necessary evil. We can't live with them or without them ... Patricio, what's your opinion about all of this? You're a man."[11] Zúñiga humorously underscores that Antofagasta's mother can only envision her with a man. However, Miss Francisca knows Pato's gender and reveals her homophobia when she sees Pato and Antofagasta kissing. Pato defends her relationship with her girlfriend and challenges her homophobic teacher. However, Zúñiga also complicates this lesbian relationship with violence as they both hit each other after Pato is angered by Antofagasta's admission that she enjoyed her sexual encounter with the boys. Yet, they reconcile in the subsequent scene, and Pato continues to defend her against the school bullies. Though she does have violent tendencies, Pato ultimately envisions a hopeful future with her girlfriend and their child and becomes the only acceptable "male" character in this world. However, even though Pato offers freedom, she, too, exists within this patriarchal view of gender by suggesting that Antofagasta stay home, taking care of their child, while Pato works in the countryside. At the conclusion of the play's sixth and final scene, Pato Piñata reveals her chest and her birth name to Nelly María, suggesting that exposing her truth may lead Pato/Lucía to eventually be able to live freely and escape the oppressive gender roles that plague the women in this play.

In *Sentiments*, Zúñiga highlights how teenage girls are placed in dangerous and violent circumstances by unethical spectatorship of the female body. Her play is inspired by a local news story about one of Chile's first viral videos, but departs from the actual events to delve into a broader consideration of the ethics of spectatorship in the internet age. The viral video began after a teenage girl had a consensual sexual encounter with boys at her school who, unbeknownst to her, filmed it and shared it on the internet. Then the girl was expelled from school, and later she attempted suicide. The girl and her family filed a lawsuit against the boy who recorded the video and his family. In 2015, the civil court in Santiago ordered the boy and his family to pay 35 million pesos in damages (approximately USD 35,700).[12] When she first heard of the story, Zúñiga was angered by the fact that the school principal showed the sexually explicit video to the girl's parents after it had gone viral.[13] She was angered by the adult's lack of ethics and the resulting violence the girl suffered. Though she doesn't describe the video in detail in her play, Zúñiga's characters react to the video with contradictions of horror, pleasure, and violence.

A further twist on this ethical dilemma of spectatorship and justice is that the young woman from the viral video filed another lawsuit in 2014, attempting to prohibit the

Santiago A Mil International Theater Festival from presenting *Sentiments*. The festival responded to the lawsuit, saying that it would continue to present Zúñiga's play: "Teatro a Mil Foundation, in its year-round work, unrelentingly supports freedom of expression in artistic creation and is against prior censorship, so it will keep the production running. Especially considering that no court in the Republic has ordered otherwise."[14] Director Javier Casanga responded to the lawsuit directly, "[The play] is fiction and does not have anything to do with the life of the young girl in the video. It is not based on her life, it is a play that was inspired by a 2007 news story, and we used this to speak about feminine themes, violence against women, lesbianism, single mothers, etc."[15] Casanga underscores the importance of artistic freedom and how Zúñiga creates a fictional world in order to generate a broader consideration of gendered cruelty.

At the end of her darkly comedic play, Zúñiga provides no catharsis for the characters or the audience. Even her play's title, *Sentiments*, evokes the irony and cruelty of the society in which these Chilean women struggle to exist. The word "*sentimientos*" in literal translation means "feelings." However, Zúñiga's play demonstrates the cruelty that awaits women who explore their feelings, and especially their sexual feelings. Emotion and desire are seen as dangerous if they do not conform to a heteronormative, ultra-conservative reality. Bowen and Prizant translate the title as "Sentiments," which is defined as "What one feels with regard to something; mental attitude (of approval or disapproval, etc.); an opinion or view as to what is right or agreeable."[16] This term emphasizes a relation to external evaluation. In this play's world, sentiments and feelings are viewed as volatile by society. Characters and audiences are allowed to be alienated by those feelings and by the play itself. Zúñiga's humorous, absurdist, and heightened theatrical alienation, in the true Brechtian sense, may lead her audiences to take action and reject the notion that feelings, especially as they relate to sexuality, must remain conformist in order for women to survive.

Notes

1. Zúñiga M., Carla. *Sentiments*, in *Dramaturgas Chilenas: Plays by Chilean Female Writers in the Early 21st Century*, edited by Coca Duarte, Anne García-Romero and Inés Stranger, Methuen Drama, 2025, p. 209.
2. Ibid., 207.
3. Ibid.
4. Ibid., 229.
5. Ibid., 233.
6. For more information on La Niña Horrible, please consult https://yourszene.com/companies/teatro-la-nina-horrible, accessed April 7, 2025.
7. Zúñiga, Carla. "Me cuesta mucho pensar la dramaturgia desde el poder." Interview by Constanza Rifo. Fundación Teatroamil, November 15, 2018. https://teatroamil.cl/noticias-2019/carla-z%C3%BA%C3%B1iga-me-cuesta-mucho-pensar-la-dramaturgia-desde-el-poder/. Accessed April 7, 2025.
8. Duarte, Coca. "*Hilda Peña*: Unconventional Motherhood, Grief and Subjectivity," *Dramaturgas Chilenas: Plays by Chilean Female Writers in the Early 21st Century*, edited by Coca Duarte, Anne García-Romero and Inés Stranger, Methuen Drama, 2025, p. 153.
9. Thompson, Jennifer Joan, "An Explosion of Feminism: Dramaturgies of Excess and Revolution in Chile's New Feminist Vanguard," in *Bodies on the Front Lines:*

Performance, Gender, and Sexuality in Latin America and the Caribbean, edited by Brenda Werth and Katherine Zien, University of Michigan Press, 2024, p. 46.
10 Casanga, Javier. *Sentimientos*, 30 March 2024. Vimeo. Accessed 15 May 2025.
11 Zúñiga. *Sentiments*, p. 223.
12 https://www.ucsh.cl/actualidad/pornovenganza-el-popular-delito-que-se-extiende-y-busca-ser-tipificado-en-chile/ Accessed 9 April 2025
13 Zúñiga, Carla. Personal Interview. 7 May 2025.
14 https://www.theclinic.cl/2014/01/13/fundacion-santiago-a-mil-no-retirara-de-cartelera-obra-inspirada-en-wena-naty/ Accessed 10 April 2025
15 https://www.theclinic.cl/2014/01/15/director-de-obra-basada-en-wena-naty-encuentro-que-su-accion-fue-super-arrebatada/ Accessed 10 April 2025
16 "Sentiment, N." Oxford English Dictionary, Oxford University Press, June 2024, https://doi.org/10.1093/OED/2049162803.

Further Reading

Capona, Daniela. "Women Don't Exist. The Deconstruction of Gender in the Work of Carla Zúñiga" Recherches (Strasbourg), no. 31, 2023, pp. 77–90, https://doi.org/10.4000/cher.15838

García-Romero, Anne. "La Dramaturgia Grotesca/Grotesque Dramaturgy and Gender Critique in the Postdictatorship Southern Conc," in *Bodies on the Front Lines: Performance, Gender, and Sexuality in Latin America and the Caribbean*, edited by Brenda Werth and Katherine Zien, University of Michigan Press, 2024, pp. 288–304.

García-Romero, Anne. "Un nuevo amanecer: la justicia transicional de género en El amarillo sol de tus cabellos largos de Carla Zúñiga." *Apuntes De Teatro*, no. 146, 2021, pp. 94–102. https://doi.org/10.7764/apuntesdeteatro.146.49283.2021

Thompson, Jennifer Joan. "An Explosion of Feminism: Dramaturgies of Excess and Revolution in Chile's New Feminist Vanguard," in *Bodies on the Front Lines: Performance, Gender, and Sexuality in Latin America and the Caribbean*, edited by Brenda Werth and Katherine Zien, University of Michigan Press, 2024, pp. 39–58.

Sentiments

Carla Zúñiga M.

English translation
Susan E. Bowen and Yael Prizant

Carla Zúñiga M. is an actor, playwright, and educator born in Santiago, Chile, in 1986. She received her degree in acting from Universidad Arcis. She co-founded La Niña Horrible (The Horrible Girl, 2013–2020) with director Javier Casanga. She's written and produced more than thirty plays. Her plays include *Sentimientos* (*Sentiments*, 2013), *Historias de amputación a la hora de té* (*Histories of Amputation at Tea Time*, 2014), *La trágica agonía de un pájaro azul* (*The Tragic Irony of the Blue Bird*, 2016), *Los tristísimos veranos de la princesa Diana* (*The Sad Summers of Princess Diana*, 2017), *Prefiero que me coman los perros* (*I Prefer to be Eaten by Dogs*, 2017), *El amarillo sol de tus cabellos largo*s (*The Yellow Sun of your Long Locks*, 2018), *Yo también quiero ser un hombre blanco heterosexual* (*I also want to be a white heterosexual man*, 2018), *Cosas que suceden en el pasillo de los animales* (*Things that happen in the hallway of animals*, 2019), *Malas madres conversando en una plaza una tarde de verano* (*Bad mothers talking in the plaza on a summer afternoon*, 2020), *Hace poco salió el sol y ya está escondiendo otra vez* (*The sun came out a while ago and now it's hiding again*, 2021), *Retrato de una mujer que un día miró la luna y le pareció que era falsa* (*Portrait of a woman who looked at the moon one day and thought it was fake*, 2022), *Lloremos juntas cuando descubramos que todas las estrellas ya están muertas* (*We cry together when we discover that all the stars are already dead*, 2023), and *En la oscuridad de la noche* (*In the darkness of the night*, 2024). Her work has also been produced in Argentina, Uruguay, Mexico, Spain, and Portugal. Her awards include the 2017 and 2021 Best Play from the Chile Drama Critics Circle and the Cultural Council's 2019 Best Literary Work. She was invited by the British Council to participate in the Royal Court playwriting workshop in Chile. She has taught at the Universidad Mayor, Universidad de las américas, AIEP and ARCOS. From 2022 to 2023, she served as co-artistic director, with Bosco Cayo, of the 20th National Playwriting Festival in Chile.

Sentiments received its world premiere by La Niña Horrible at Teatro El Ladrón de Bicicletas, Santiago, Chile, in July 2013. It was directed by Javier Casanga with the following cast:

Antofagasta	Carla Gaete
Nelly María	Viviana Basoalto
María Teresa	Carla González y Loreto Araya
Miss Francisca	Coca Miranda
Pato Piñata	Fiorella Schiaffino
Cosmetics Sales Lady	Elisa Vallejos

After its world premiere, *Sentiments* was produced at the 2014 Santiago A Mil International Theatre Festival, Teatro del Puente (2014), Teatro Sidarte (2017), Matucana 100 (2023), and Centro Cultural Ceina (2024).

The play was published in Chile by Ediciones Oxímoron (2019).

For Rae del cerro and for all the butches of the world.

Characters

Antofagasta, *a teenage girl*
Nelly María, *her mother*
María Teresa, *her neighbor*
Miss Francisca, *her teacher*
Pato Piñata, *her teenage girlfriend*
Cosmetics Sales Lady, *a stranger*

Setting

2013. Santiago, Chile.

Scene One

"The night the daughter never arrived and the mother agonized like crazy in the living room."

Twelve midnight on the dot. A woman named **Nelly María** *is sitting in her living room having a coffee and her last cigarette. She is waiting for her daughter,* **Antofagasta**, *to get home from school. Atrocious images run through her mind, images filled with the most horrific rapes and murders. She fantasizes for a while about what she will say when the coroner arrives and she has to go identify the squalid and broken body of her only child, who doesn't have a father. Suddenly the door opens. It's her, the sweet and trustworthy teenager, named* **Antofagasta**.

Nelly María Where were you, Antofagasta? Where the hell were you? Don't tell me you were at school because I know that's a lie! Don't tell me you were at school because you weren't! My god, where were you? Where were you?

Antofagasta At school.

Nelly María That's a lie! You left at exactly four in the afternoon. Where were you for the last eight hours?

Antofagasta At school.

Nelly María Liar! Trash! You are trash!

Antofagasta Mamá, I'm telling you . . .

Nelly María Garbage!

Antofagasta . . . the truth.

Nelly María Oh, really?

Antofagasta Yes.

Nelly María It's the truth?

Antofagasta Yes.

Nelly María You're not lying to me?

Antofagasta No.

Nelly María No, what?

Antofagasta No, I'm not lying to you, Mamá.

Nelly María And what were you doing all this time at school?

Antofagasta Studying.

Nelly María For what class?

Antofagasta Biology.

Nelly María What did you study?

Antofagasta The Krebs cycle, cellular respiration, endoplasmic reticular function.

Nelly María Do you have a test?

Antofagasta Yes.

Nelly María When?

Antofagasta Day after tomorrow.

Nelly María Who was tutoring you?

Antofagasta Julieta.

Nelly María And why didn't you answer your phone?

Antofagasta I left it at home.

Nelly María Where?

Antofagasta It's upstairs, in my room.

Nelly María That's strange, I didn't hear it ring, I called more than a thousand times.

Antofagasta It was on silent.

Nelly María Why?

Antofagasta Because . . . because I always keep it on silent now, I don't like when people interrupt me while I'm talking to you, we never see each other and it bothers me when the phone interrupts us, cuts our conversations short, you feel like I prefer the people who are calling me and that's not right, you're my mother and you gave me life.

Nelly María Why didn't you tell me you'd be home so late?

Antofagasta I did. I told you last night.

Nelly María I don't remember. I would never forget something like that, you didn't let me know, don't lie to me.

Antofagasta I told you last night, but you'd already taken your sleeping pill, I came to talk to you in your room while you were watching the variety show, remember?

Nelly María I did watch the variety show last night . . . that's true. So you came to talk to me?

Antofagasta Yes! I went up to your room, I was wearing my fleece pajamas, and I turned off the light. Remember? Before turning your light off I told you: Tomorrow I'll be home later than usual, maybe around ten o'clock, I don't want you to get scared and that's why I'm letting you know, to reassure you, Mamita, and then I turned off your light, you blew me a kiss with your hand.

Nelly María I blew you a kiss with my hand?

Antofagasta Remember?

Nelly María A little, the whole night's a bit fuzzy.

Antofagasta Because of your sleeping pill.

Nelly María And why didn't you remind me this morning at breakfast?

Antofagasta I left before you today, remember? I went to remind you when I said bye, but you were in the bathroom, you probably couldn't hear me over the sound of the shower.

Nelly María Antofagasta, I thought you were dead.

Antofagasta No, don't think things like that. I'm fine, I was studying with Cristina, that's all.

Nelly María With Cristina?

Antofagasta I made a mistake . . . I meant to say Julieta.

Nelly María You really scared me. Let's go to bed, sleep with me please, I don't wanna sleep alone.

Antofagasta I can't.

Nelly María Why not?

Antofagasta I've got my period. I don't wanna stain your sheets.

Nelly María Don't be stupid. You're supposed to get your period on the seventeenth and it's only the fourth.

Antofagasta It came early.

Nelly María Why did that happen?

Antofagasta It's probably stress over school.

Nelly María How strange, we'll have to take you to the doctor.

Antofagasta Good night, Mamá.

Nelly María Good night, my daughter. Antofagasta?

Antofagasta Yes?

Nelly María No, nothing. Nothing. Sleep well. Antofagasta?

Antofagasta What, Mamá?

Nelly María School was open until midnight?

Antofagasta Yes, they extended the study hours for exam week. Call my teacher and ask her, she can confirm it for you.

Nelly María That's okay, daughter. I believe you.

Antofagasta *walks upstairs to her room. Her mother quietly approaches her daughter's backpack and takes* **Antofagasta***'s cell phone from one of the pockets. On the phone she reads a message that clearly says "997 missed phone calls from MAMÁ."* **Nelly María** *is surprised, she could swear on her life that she had actually called more than 1000 times that day.*

Scene Two

"The day after the day when everything bad, but something delectable happened."

Nelly María *talks to her lifelong friend,* **María Teresa**. *The latter cries, inconsolably and intensely, as if one of the thorns from Christ's crown had been forever encrusted in the center of her own poor heart.*

María Teresa   I don't know what's wrong with me, this isn't me . . . I don't recognize myself when I go to sleep, I wake up with a jolt in the middle of the night, I have horrible nightmares where I stare at myself in the mirror, I have an enormous dog's head and a very long nose, an empty, impenetrable gaze and when I try to speak. . . . .my bark sounds exactly like the poodle doggie I had when I was little. You know what that doggie's name was? "Nobody Knows," which gave us such a laugh. "What's the dog's name?" "Nobody Knows." "But give her a name." And we'd just keep laughing and laughing. The adults thought the doggie didn't have a name, but she did, she was called "Nobody Knows." As a child, one has an infinitely dumb sense of humor. But life was much easier then . . . .

Nelly María   What are you gonna do?

María Teresa   I don't know.

Nelly María   How could such a dreadful thing happen?

María Teresa   I don't know. He looked at me, I looked back at him, we looked at each other, then we lowered our gaze, then looked up again and stayed there, taking each other in with an all-consuming lust.

Nelly María   But he's your son's therapist!

María Teresa   Don't judge me! From the start I begged you not to judge me and you swore on your daughter's life that you wouldn't.

Nelly María   It's alright, love. Don't be upset . . . these things are normal.

María Teresa   Has it ever happened to you? Oh . . . right, you don't have a husband.

Nelly María   You and your husband haven't made love for years, it's obvious you still have your needs.

María Teresa   I do.

Nelly María   Are you planning to cheat on him?

María Teresa   No! How can you think such a thing? If Horacio found out he would kill me in an instant. He's a very proud man, or at least he was when we were closer, when we confided in each other, when we would laugh really hard, when we would walk barefoot on the beach.

Nelly María   Then there's no reason to worry. This is a little crush, nothing more.

María Teresa   It's true, I would never hurt Horacio, because I know he's been faithful to me . . . at least that's how it seemed before, when we were closer.

Nelly María   You have to stay away from this man.

María Teresa   It'll be very difficult for me, he's a very . . . sensual man.

Nelly María   So ask someone else to take your son to therapy. You have to stay on the sidelines, these things are very dangerous.

María Teresa   It's true, I don't know what happened to me. I'm not like this. There are a lot of women who give in to their most base instincts, prostitutes . . . and I'm a decent woman not a slut.

Antofagasta *enters.*

Antofagasta   A slut? I'm not a slut!

María Teresa   Antofagastita!

Nelly María   We weren't talking about you, child! Why do you think we were talking about you?

Antofagasta   I don't know. I thought I heard my name. Did one of you mention my name?

María Teresa   Not that I remember.

Nelly María   Never.

Antofagasta   I must be imagining things. What were you talking about?

Nelly María   Grown-up things.

María Teresa   Things that don't concern you. You thank God for your youth, because in fifteen minutes you're gonna be old, wrinkled like a raisin and with your boobs hanging down like two testicles. And soon after that is death, because when you get old the only thing left is to sit and wait to die.

Nelly María   I think you'd better go, María Teresa. I'll call you tonight.

María Teresa   Okay. Thanks for listening to me, Nelly María. You're my most loyal friend.

María Teresa *leaves.*

Nelly María   How was school?

Antofagasta   Fine.

Nelly María   Why are you back so early?

Antofagasta   They let us out early.

Nelly María   Why?

Antofagasta   They beat up a girl.

Nelly María   Why?

Antofagasta   For being fat.

Nelly María   What?

Antofagasta   In P.E.[1] they made her go climb up a rope. The poor thing trained all last week and today she was finally able to do it. But once she got up there, she realized she had vertigo and she couldn't get down. She started to shout for them to come get her and the teacher burst out laughing. She laughed and laughed. In the end the teacher laughed so hard that her hands were weak. Sister Malva had to go up and get the girl. When they got down, the fat girl was crying, and she had this giant green booger hanging from her nose. Everyone started to yell at her, shouting: disgusting little red head, fish head, piss head on her period, all redheads are sexy but you're as ugly as sin. And they started to throw basketballs at her, and Crazy Juan got carried away and threw a heavy exercise ball at her. And now the fat girl is in the ICU.[2]

Nelly María   And you didn't feel sorry for her?

Antofagasta   Yes. That's why I didn't laugh.

Nelly María   And you didn't do anything?

Antofagasta   And what was I gonna do?

Nelly María   I don't know . . . something.

A knock at the door. It's **Miss Francisca**, **Antofagasta**'s *teacher.*

Miss Francisca   Antofa!

Nelly María   Miss Francisca! How are you doing?

Miss Francisca   I'm doing great. And you all? How are you doing, you gorgeous pair of ladies?

Antofagasta   We're doing fine. What brings you around here?

Miss Francisca   That's what I like about Antofa! She always likes to get right to the point.

Antofagasta   What do you mean by that?

Miss Francisca   Exactly what the sentence says, nothing more. There's nothing hidden, there's no subtext.

Nelly María   Would you like a little coffee?

Miss Francisca   Actually, I'm only stopping by.

Nelly María   Did something happen?

Miss Francisca   I don't know if Antofa told you anything about what happened today at school, a regrettable event with a student who's overweight.

Nelly María   She was mentioning something about that just now.

Miss Francisca   We're extremely worried at school, the girl is now in a coma. And you know what's a millimeter away from being in a coma.

Nelly María   What?

Miss Francisca   Death.

Nelly María   My God!

Miss Francisca   We teachers feel very guilty . . . the level of violence at school is escalating at the speed of light. That's why I'm talking to every guardian so they can keep an eye on their children's behavior. It's very important that you know everything your pupil is doing. Are you aware of your child's activities and thoughts?

Nelly María   I would say yes.

Miss Francisca   In times like these, one can never be too careful. You know? Now I'd love that coffee you offered me a few minutes ago. You think that would be possible?

Nelly María   I'll go make it right away, Miss Francisca.

Nelly María *exits. Silence.*

Miss Francisca   Your house is so lovely, Antofagasta.

Antofagasta   Thank you.

Miss Francisca   Do you own it?

Antofagasta   We rent.

Miss Francisca   How many bedrooms does it have?

Antofagasta   Three.

Miss Francisca   And how much is the rent?

Antofagasta   What's the real reason you came, Miss Francisca?

Miss Francisca   Because I know what you were doing last night in the plaza next to school.

Antofagasta   Who told you?

Miss Francisca   Who do you think?

Antofagasta   I'm gonna ask you to please leave.

Miss Francisca   I see you haven't told your mother.

Antofagasta   Would you tell your mother, Miss Francisca?

Miss Francisca   I would never have behaved that way, let alone while living under the same roof as my mother.

Antofagasta   Go.

Miss Francisca   Make no mistake, I'm on your side. That's why I came, to protect you. Don't tell me that when you saw that poor little fatso writhing in pain on the floor, with her t-shirt hiked up and her rolls of flesh exposed in front of the entire school, that you weren't thinking of the number of objects they'd stick up your vagina once everyone found about what you did. If someone found out they would tell someone else and that someone would tell another person and then it would reach your mother's ears, sooner or later that poor woman would be doing housework and hear a knock at the door, you know, one of the neighborhood gossips, and she would blab the disgusting rumor, salivating with every word, and your mother would drop the broom and the dustpan, and pass out on the table she'd just set, imagine if she made some chicken soup that day, she'd burn her face on that hot soup and be left with a horrendous scar on her innocent cheek, a mark of the incandescent shame her own daughter heaped on her.

Antofagasta What do you want, Miss Francisca?

Miss Francisca To protect you from all that. My life's work is education and to show you I take it seriously, I'll stay here with you, I'll teach you right here so that you don't have to go to school for a bit, while things calm down.

Antofagasta Here at home?

Miss Francisca Yes!

Antofagasta But how?

Miss Francisca The rumor is starting to spread, Antofagasta, nobody has proof but imagine if someone shows up with that proof. Do you know what the fourth bathroom stall, from right to left in the women's bathroom, said? Antofagasta likes it . . .

Antofagasta Stay here! Stay! But please don't tell Mamá.

Miss Francisca My little chickadee, I would never make your mother go through something so horrific. I wouldn't wish an experience like this on my worst enemy. And know that every night before I go to sleep, I wish the enemies on my list would die.

Scene Three

"When the person who knew firsthand told someone who went running to tell the principal of the school."

The same living room. One of the windows is broken, a heavy exercise ball has just soared through the window and hit **Antofagasta** *in the face, leaving one eye violently bruised.* **Pato Piñata**, *her only friend from school, comforts* **Antofagasta** *as she sits in the armchair.* **Pato Piñata** *has short hair and a seductive, raspy voice. She secretly reminds* **Antofagasta** *of the leading man from "Twilight."*

Pato Piñata   Do you think it was Crazy Juan?

Antofagasta   I don't know.

Pato Piñata   You didn't see anything?

Antofagasta   Only when the ball came at my face.

Pato Piñata   Does it hurt?

Antofagasta   A lot.

Pato Piñata   I'm gonna kill that idiot.

Antofagasta   Don't talk like that. We don't even know who it was.

Pato Piñata   I'm sure it was him.

Antofagasta   Why?

Pato Piñata   Because he was walking around school talking shit about you.

Antofagasta   What'd he say?

Pato Piñata   You don't wanna know.

Antofagasta   Yes, I do.

Pato Piñata   It's nothing more than a web of lies.

Antofagasta   Tell me!

Pato Piñata   He said you . . .

Antofagasta   What?

Pato Piñata   I can't even say it, you know how people are . . .

Antofagasta   Say it!

Pato Piñata   He said last Tuesday you were in the plaza next to school, for hours, doing things with Raúl, Jaime, Casimiro, Johnny, Ítalo, Rodolfo, Jano, and Héctor.

Antofagasta   What kind of things?

Pato Piñata   Terrible things.

Antofagasta   Disgusting things?

Pato Piñata   Disgusting things.

Antofagasta   And where'd he get that from?

Pato Piñata   He said the principal had told him, that she had a video Héctor recorded.

Antofagasta   That's impossible!

Pato Piñata   I know. But he says it's true and that's why you've been missing school, because you wanna hide . . .

Antofagasta   That's not true!

Pato Piñata   I figured it wasn't true. If that were true, I think you'd be very scared, locked in your bedroom, with insomnia, with nausea, and above all, really, really, really wanting to die.

Antofagasta   I swear to you it's a lie!

Pato Piñata   I know, don't worry . . . Know what? Even if it were true, I couldn't let anything bad happen to you.

Antofagasta   Thank you, but I'm telling you it's not true.

Pato Piñata   I would never judge you, I know you and I'm gonna be with you forever. Do you know what I'm gonna do to Crazy Juan? I'm gonna steal a pool ball from my sister and I'm gonna throw it right at that idiot's mouth, I'm gonna take out a couple of his teeth.

Antofagasta   They'll throw you in jail!

Pato Piñata   Yes, but I'll get out immediately because I'm under eighteen.

Antofagasta   You would really do that for me?

Pato Piñata   Without a doubt.

Antofagasta   You're my best friend, Pato Piñata, I love you so much.

Pato Piñata   And I love you. I can't stand them talking shit about you, they don't know you, you're . . .

Pato Piñata *approaches* **Antofagasta** *slowly, takes her by the waist and kisses her tenderly, in a way that* **Antofagasta** *has never been kissed by anyone.* **Antofagasta** *trembles and begins to feel her cheeks flush. She imagines that not even the delicate leading man from "Twilight" could have excited her this much. Suddenly* **Nelly María** *and* **Miss Francisca** *enter. The latter drops a full teacup of green tea that she made.*

Nelly María   Antofagasta! What's happening?

Antofagasta   Nothing, Mamá, it's not what you're thinking, we were talking . . . .

Miss Francisca   They weren't talking!

Pato Piñata   Señora, your daughter and I . . .

Nelly María You be quiet! Who is this man, Antofagasta?

Antofagasta What?

Nelly María Who is this man?

Pato Piñata Who?

Nelly María Well, you mister. Who are you? Where did you come from?

Pato Piñata Well . . . from . . . from

Antofagasta From Youth Group![3] We met at Youth Group! He was my prayer leader.

Nelly María Is that true?

Antofagasta Yes.

Nelly María Is he religious?

Antofagasta Very much so.

Nelly María And why is he here?

Antofagasta He came to take care of me because I hit myself in the eye . . . with the door.

Nelly María This man did this to you?

Antofagasta No! He only came to take care of me . . .

Nelly María And why haven't you introduced him before?

Antofagasta Because he's very shy.

Nelly María Are you shy? What's your name?

Pato Piñata Pato Piñata.

Nelly María Pato Piñata! What a cheerful name, that's exactly what we need in this house.

Pato Piñata A pleasure meeting you, Señora.

Nelly María You're leaving already?

Antofagasta Yes, Mamá, he was leaving. Say goodbye, Pato Piñata.

Pato Piñata See you soon.

Nelly María No! I was just going to buy bread. I'll drop you at the bus on the way.

Pato Piñata Don't go to any trouble. I've got my bike.

Nelly María Let's go! I'll walk you to the bus! The bakery is next to the bus stop.

Pato Piñata See you soon, Antofagasta, I'll call you later.

Antofagasta See you soon.

Pato Piñata *and* **Nelly María** *exit.*

Miss Francisca Your "boyfriend" left his exercise ball.

Antofagasta Yes, you're right . . .

Miss Francisca Don't take me for an idiot. I know very well that Pato Piñata is a woman, you're not fooling me, that tomboy is in the class below yours . . .

Antofagasta Miss Francisca, I think we don't need you in this house anymore.

Miss Francisca You need me more than ever! You can't control yourself. First you had that orgy with your classmates on Tuesday and now this, you're sick . . . you know? I just looked online and noticed that someone uploaded your video to YouTube. It's four and a half hours long. I saw the whole thing, up close. Who do you think uploaded it? Héctor? Manuel? Ignacio? Or perhaps your lady friend Pato Piñata? You're very thin. That isn't noticeable in your uniform, you have a beautiful body and a wide rib cage . . . you're lovely. Be careful . . . I called the police and I told them to please help me get the video taken down as soon as possible. Anyone who sees this video would fall in love with you. Imagine if some relative of yours sees it, an uncle, it would be a disaster.

Antofagasta I feel sick . . .

She exits, running to the bathroom to vomit.

Miss Francisca Why are you vomiting? Don't tell me you're pregnant now!

Scene Four

"All of the women together."

The same place. **Antofagasta** *is seated in one of the armchairs.* **Miss Francisca** *has put some posters on the wall, with annotations and diagrams.*

Miss Francisca Look, in my grandmother's day, women got married and on their wedding night men and women had intercourse. She would cry in pain, because she felt like he was sticking a hot iron into her feminine cavities. Back then my grandmother told my mother to be careful, that love was one thing, but the sexual act was something totally different. That men only wanted that.

Antofagasta What?

Miss Francisca To penetrate the woman with the hot iron. My mother, on the other hand, met my father at the movies. They went every Sunday, and they started to smile at each other. Then they sat together. One day their hands brushed against each other and everything changed. My mother, a woman who one would never characterize as terribly intelligent, lost her virginity on the third of September in the year 1977,[4] in the movie theater bathroom. And do you know what happened?

Antofagasta She got pregnant?

Miss Francisca She got pregnant! With me! At eighteen years old! My grandmother wanted to die, she couldn't understand why women were willing to suffer that pain in exchange for nothing, without having the obligation that comes with holy matrimony. They immediately married my mother off to my father. My parents didn't even know each other when this happened, but it didn't matter, one does things in life and those things have consequences. Do you understand, Antofagasta? One can't succumb to horrifying filth and expect that the world will keep spinning the same way afterward. My parents hated each other, they didn't know each other, they didn't get along well, my father hit my mother, and I believed that my mother deserved it. My mother was a hummingbird, she didn't have a clue. My father, however, was a strict man who taught me everything I know with respect to discipline. If it weren't for him, I would be pregnant with my sixth child, unmarried, and huffing Neoprene under some bridge.

Antofagasta You don't plan to have children, Miss Francisca?

Miss Francisca I'm going to tell you a secret. I had barely turned eighteen when my father took me to a doctor and asked him to remove my uterus. And he did it. It was a clean and easy operation. And now I am safe.

Antofagasta You didn't get angry at your father?

Miss Francisca I will be infinitely grateful to him until the day I die. I can't be a mother, I'm a teacher and my life's work is education, all of you are my children. That's why I worry so much. Girls your age are beginning to have relations at thirteen years old. Thirteen! I was pissing and pooping in my bed at that age. Imagine how the world will progress in three or four more years. Girls will start sucking dick at eight!

Antofagasta Miss Francisca!

Miss Francisca Forgive me; this is not easy for me. But what I want to tell you, Antofagastita, is that you must be careful. There are horrendous things on the internet, women who make love with twenty guys, little girls who lie down in flowery fields and let men spray semen into their mouths, girls who sleep with girls, men penetrated by men . . . if you get seduced by all of this, imagine all of the atrocities the baby you're carrying will commit one day . . .

Pato Piñata *enters.*

Pato Piñata Hey!

Miss Francisca Just what I needed.

Antofagasta Hey Pato Piñata, how are you?

Pato Piñata I'm good and you? How's your eye?

Antofagasta Much better.

Pato Piñata I brought you these flowers.

Antofagasta Thank you so much, they're beautiful.

They kiss.

Miss Francisca I cannot stand this repugnant spectacle! Stop kissing right this moment! I'm going to vomit . . . I swear to you both I'm going to vomit.

Pato Piñata But why?

Miss Francisca Don't come at me with that question, tomboy. You may have fooled that naïve Nelly María, but I'm a lot sharper. Besides, I taught you, my beloved Pato. I taught you math when you were in fourth grade. You were only a little girl, but I knew right away you'd be a gentleman when you got older.

Pato Piñata I'm not a gentleman!

Miss Francisca Yes, you are.

Antofagasta We are in love!

Miss Francisca My dear, I've fallen in love with thousands of people who weren't for me, all my life. Because of an age difference, or because we were the same sex, or second cousins, et cetera. But every time I stepped up and did what was right.

Pato Piñata What was right?

Miss Francisca Normal relations.

Antofagasta What is normal?

Miss Francisca What everybody does.

Pato Piñata Having sexual relations is normal?

Miss Francisca It's normal after twenty.

Pato Piñata After twenty?

Antofagasta But your mother got pregnant at eighteen.

Miss Francisca My mother was abnormal, and she paid the consequences, my father hit her and she got uterine cancer when she got old.

Pato Piñata And how old were you when you lost your virginity?

Miss Francisca Twenty-five, with a man I loved very much and under perfect conditions because he was my spouse.

Pato Piñata I didn't know you were married, Miss Francisca.

Miss Francisca We separated.

Antofagasta Why?

Miss Francisca Because of different circumstances that don't concern you.

Pato Piñata And women never interested you, Miss Francisca?

Miss Francisca Why would you ask me that?

Pato Piñata There was a rumor when I was in eighth grade, they said that you and Miss Marina would meet up in the school chapel and kiss.

Miss Francisca They were kisses of friendship. People always distort every act of love.

Antofagasta Pato Piñata and I kiss each other out of love.

Miss Francisca That's different.

Pato Piñata Why?

Miss Francisca Because it's a very big sin called lesbianism.

Antofagasta And why is it a sin?

Miss Francisca Because it's unnatural and everything that is unnatural is part of hell. God is very disappointed in you both. Not so much in you, Antofagasta. I am sure that Pato Piñata dragged you into committing these atrocities. He's . . . very masculine and sensual, he has that masculine force that one seeks out, just looking at him makes me want to surrender my body over to him. But God will punish you for your aberration, Pato Piñata . . .

Pato Piñata Do you believe in God, Miss Francisca?

Miss Francisca Eh, well, you got me. I don't believe in God. Still, I think you should kill yourself, Pato Piñata. Think about it, I don't believe in God, but I do believe in reincarnation. Maybe if you're reincarnated, you'll come back as a man and make love to all the women you want.

Antofagasta You believe that if somebody commits suicide they're immediately reincarnated as another person?

Miss Francisca   I'm sure of it.

Pato Piñata   But suicide is also unnatural.

Miss Francisca   God can pardon a suicide, but he will never pardon a lesbian . . .

Pato Piñata   But God doesn't exist, right? You're an idiot, Miss Francisca.

Someone bangs on the door. **Miss Francisca** *gets up and answers it. A beautiful young woman, dressed entirely in purple and pink, enters the house. She is the* **Cosmetics Sales Lady**. *Her right eye is completely bruised, as if a man had hit her for flirting with his best friend.*

Miss Francisca   How may I help you, young lady?

Cosmetics Sales Lady   Good morning, I'm selling all kinds of cosmetics. Lipsticks, creams, bases, mascara, shadows.

Miss Francisca   Shadows?

Cosmetics Sales Lady   Yes, shadows!

Miss Francisca   Wearing makeup is for prostitutes, I'd suggest you go to the house next door, they might be interested over there.

Miss Francisca *closes the door in the* **Cosmetic Sales Lady**'s *face.* **Nelly María** *and* **María Teresa** *enter through the kitchen door.* **María Teresa** *is crying.*

Nelly María   Patricio! Give your seat to María Teresa, she's very fragile.

Pato Piñata   Of course.

Antofagasta   Mamá, the name is Pato.

Miss Francisca   What happened, María Teresa?

Nelly María   I don't think María Teresa wants to talk about it.

María Teresa   I'm in love!

Miss Francisca   But that's wonderful!

Nelly María   But the thing is, she's married . . .

Miss Francisca   Even better! Keeping the fire alive after such a long time together.

María Teresa   I'm in love with a man who's not my husband.

Miss Francisca   Jesus Christ!

María Teresa   He's my son's therapist . . . last night I spent the night at his house. I lied to my husband, I told him that my mother was sick and I had to take care of her. This man drives me crazy, I adore him, he's precious, he's like chocolate that I wanna devour naked in a hot bath. When he smiles I wanna die, to faint in his muscular arms. I love him. I adore him. We kiss each other . . .

Nelly María   My god!

María Teresa His kisses were delicious. I had three orgasms while we were kissing, and he wasn't even touching me. But I'd been fantasizing about that moment for so long that I'd barely felt the warmth of his mouth and I thought I'd die from the excitement, I thought I was about to have a heart attack . . .

Miss Francisca Another one who should kill herself and come back as someone decent.

Antofagasta Miss Francisca . . .

María Teresa Don't think that I feel good about this, I feel terrible.

Miss Francisca You deserve it.

Antofagasta Miss Francisca! You have to stop judging people!

Nelly María Antofagasta! Don't speak to your teacher like that!

Pato Piñata And what else happened?

María Teresa Everything. He took me to his house and we did it on every piece of his furniture. I wanted him so much that I bit him and his shoulder bled. We didn't care and we kept doing it all night long.

Miss Francisca That's disgusting.

María Teresa We slept intertwined in an embrace. I had never slept so well, so deeply. When we said goodbye this morning I told him we should do it again tonight . . .

Nelly María But María Teresa!

María Teresa I couldn't help myself, I felt so happy. But he told me it would be better if we didn't. That it wouldn't happen again, that he was free and didn't want anything serious. What am I gonna do now? I can't stop thinking about him . . . .

Miss Francisca What you should do is go to your house and make your husband a delicious pot roast and be his slave for the rest of your life.

María Teresa You don't understand, Miss Francisca. My husband is a very distant man, we haven't spoken in years . . .

Nelly María Ugh! These men! They're such a necessary evil. We can't live with them or without them . . . Patricio, what's your opinion about all this? You're a man.

Miss Francisca A very handsome man.

Pato Piñata I think you, María Teresa . . . should get divorced . . .

Nelly María But Patricio!

Pato Piñata Please, let me finish. I believe you should separate from your husband and start a life of freedom. How old were you when you got married?

María Teresa Nineteen.

Pato Piñata All the more reason. You couldn't enjoy your youth in all its glory.

María Teresa It's true.

Pato Piñata You should get separated and meet other men.

María Teresa But the man I love doesn't want me anymore . . .

Pato Piñata You'll find other men . . .

Miss Francisca Don't pay attention to this degenerate.

María Teresa But would a man like you be interested in going out with a woman like me, for instance?

Antofagasta What?

Nelly María María Teresa, Patricio is my son-in-law . . .

María Teresa It's only in theory . . .

A knock at the door. **Nelly María** *goes to open it. It's the* **Cosmetics Sales Lady** *again.*

Nelly María Yes?

Cosmetics Sales Lady Good morning, I'm selling all kinds of cosmetics. Lipsticks, creams, bases, mascara, shadows . . .

Nelly María Shadows?

Cosmetics Sales Lady Yes, shadows!

Miss Francisca You already came by here, stupid.

Cosmetics Sales Lady Really? I don't remember, I'm not right in the head.

María Teresa I'm interested in cosmetics!

Miss Francisca I told you prostitutes might be interested.

Nelly María Miss Francisca!

Pato Piñata You could also use a little help, Miss Francisca.

Miss Francisca Do you think so?

Cosmetics Sales Lady It's such a pleasure to go out and sell! I just stopped by a house around here, a really ugly woman opened the door. But she threw me out right away.

Antofagasta Ugly people don't know what they're doing.

Cosmetics Sales Lady Ugly people don't exist!

Nelly María What?

Cosmetics Sales Lady Ugly people don't exist! That's what Nuribell Cosmetics are for. They wipe out everything that's wrong, the imperfections on your face, and highlight its own beauty.

María Teresa Fabulous!

Cosmetics Sales Lady Who would like a free demonstration?

Miss Francisca Pato Piñata!

Pato Piñata But I'm a man . . .

Nelly María Don't be ridiculous, Miss Francisca, he'd look like a drag queen.

Cosmetics Sales Lady (*to* **Antofagasta**) Do we know each other from somewhere?

Antofagasta I don't think so.

Cosmetics Sales Lady Your face looks familiar.

María Teresa I want to try the makeup!

Cosmetics Sales Lady No, it's better if I put it on myself. Let's get started. First, you apply the base, then the mascara, and then the shadow. And the finishing touch, the lip color. That's it. How do I look?

Pato Piñata Beautiful!

Antofagasta What do you mean "beautiful"?

Miss Francisca You put too much black shadow on your right eye.

Nelly María Miss Francisca, don't speak to this poor woman like that.

Cosmetics Sales Lady Why this poor woman?

Nelly María Because it's clear someone hit you.

Cosmetics Sales Lady I ran into a door.

All Ah.

Awkward silence.

Cosmetics Sales Lady Okay. My boyfriend hit me.

María Teresa He's not even your husband?

Pato Piñata Men shouldn't hit women.

Cosmetics Sales Lady I hit him first though.

Nelly María Even so.

Cosmetics Sales Lady I think that was the last time he'll hit me. He asked for forgiveness with flowers, he was crying . . . I think it really scared him.

Pato Piñata You shouldn't let anyone touch you, least of all a man. Let me tell you that your boyfriend is a piece of shit.

Antofagasta And why do you care so much?

María Teresa Nelly María, will you come with me to the kitchen to make me a cup of tea?

Nelly María Of course.

Cosmetics Sales Lady Now I know where I know you from!

Antofagasta Where?

Nelly María *and* **María Teresa** *exit.*

Cosmetics Sales Lady You're Antofagasta!

Antofagasta Yes . . . .

Cosmetics Sales Lady You're the girl that slept with your classmates in the plaza next to the school!

Nelly María *and* **María Teresa** *enter from the kitchen.*

Nelly María Anyone want a little tea?

Antofagasta No thank you, Mamá.

Miss Francisca I'd like a green tea, please.

Nelly María *exits.*

Cosmetics Sales Lady I saw your video on YouTube. My boyfriend and I watched the whole thing. I really wanted to meet you. People have written terrible things online, they say you're a prostitute, easy, whore, bitch, that you're the worst, that you should charge money, that you should kill yourself . . .

Nelly María *reenters.*

Nelly María How do you take your tea, Miss Francisca?

Miss Francisca With sugar.

Nelly María *exits again.*

Antofagasta Please don't tell my mother!

Cosmetics Sales Lady Your mother doesn't know?

Nelly María *appears.*

Nelly María Would you like an ice cube in your tea, Miss Francisca?

Miss Francisca No, thank you. I like it hot, like others I know.

Nelly María *leaves.*

Cosmetics Sales Lady Don't worry! My lips are sealed, I won't tell your Mamá. Let me just say that the video was really good. Did you have fun?

Antofagasta What?

Cosmetics Sales Lady Did you have fun? Was it good?

Antofagasta Yes . . .

Nelly María *and* **María Teresa** *enter from the kitchen.*

Nelly María Here's your tea, Miss Francisca. It's hot, just like you asked.

Miss Francisca Do you like it hot, María Teresa?

Pato Piñata (*to* **Antofagasta**) So it was good, eh?

Antofagasta What?

Pato Piñata Was it better than with me?

Antofagasta Pato Piñata!

Nelly María What are you talking about?

Pato Piñata I should've listened to Crazy Juan.

Antofagasta Don't talk to me like that.

Pato Piñata Everything they say about you is true. I thought they'd forced you to do those things.

Antofagasta Why should I regret it?

Pato Piñata What you did was disgusting.

Miss Francisca Well said, Pato Piñata!

Antofagasta You're just like the rest of them.

Pato Piñata And you're a whore.

Antofagasta *slaps* **Pato Piñata**. **Pato Piñata** *slaps* **Antofagasta**. **Nelly María** *goes up to* **Pato Piñata** *and gives her a slap that knocks her to the floor.*

Nelly María You're not gonna come to this house to hit my daughter right in front of my eyes.

Pato Piñata Forgive me, Señora.

Pato Piñata *runs out of the room.*

Cosmetics Sales Lady See? That's what always happens. You get angry and hit your boyfriend and then he slaps you back, only a little harder. That doesn't mean you're a battered woman, battered women get hit for no reason. Those women are sitting watching TV and bam! They get kicked in the face.

Nelly María Child, you cannot let your boyfriend hit you . . .

Antofagasta But he's not a man . . .

Nelly María He may seem like an angel to you, but he's not.

María Teresa Come, Nelly María let's go put your hand in some ice.

María Teresa, **Nelly María**, *and* **Miss Francisca** *exit.*

Cosmetics Sales Lady Don't worry. Your boyfriend'll get over it.

Antofagasta Not boyfriend, girlfriend, she's a woman.

Cosmetics Sales Lady Really? That explains why she has such great skin.

Antofagasta My mother can't know about that either.

Cosmetics Sales Lady Don't worry, honey. My mother doesn't know my boyfriend hits me either.

Scene Five

"The day the house exploded and glass from one of the windows fell on the poor mother and punctured her sad soul."

Antofagasta *is asleep in one of the armchairs. She's half naked, covered in scratches and has a broken leg.* **Pato Piñata** *is seated next to her. They kiss.*

Pato Piñata   I love you, I love you a lot.

Antofagasta   Never say those things you said to me yesterday again.

Pato Piñata   No, I won't, I swear. I'm stupid.

Antofagasta   Stupid.

Pato Piñata   I don't want them to do any more bad things to you, people don't know what you're like.

Antofagasta   Do you think those things Miss Francisca says are true?

Pato Piñata   What things?

Antofagasta   Do you think someone can really be reincarnated and come back to start over?

Pato Piñata   Miss Francisca is an imbecile.

Antofagasta   How can she be an imbecile if she has a degree?

Pato Piñata   A lot of stupid people have degrees.

Antofagasta   I'm tired. You should have seen how people were . . . it was like they hated me. They said the most terrible things to me. What do they care what I did? I was so stupid, I shouldn't have let them record me . . .

Pato Piñata   Those sons of bitches posted it online. But don't you worry, today I hit Héctor, I broke his nose. I can protect you. Come with me.

Antofagasta   Where?

Pato Piñata   Far away. Let's go to Mexico or to Calama,[5] I don't know. Let's get out of this city.

Antofagasta   But how?

Pato Piñata   I have savings that would cover our tickets. It would be marvelous, I can do whatever for work, I'm very strong and I'm patient with farm animals. You can stay and take care of the house or you could also work and little by little we'll get by.

Antofagasta   It's just . . . Pato . . .

Pato Piñata   What's wrong?

Antofagasta   I'm pregnant.

Pato Piñata Seriously?

Antofagasta Yes . . .

Pato Piñata But that's really good news!

Antofagasta How is that good?

Pato Piñata It's a miracle!

Antofagasta I don't even know whose it is!

Pato Piñata It's mine!

Antofagasta No . . .

Pato Piñata I believe it's mine, I feel like it's mine. I love you and I'm never gonna be able to give you a child. But now we can pretend that I can. That a miracle has occurred and that I got you pregnant.

Antofagasta But I don't want this child. What if the father is the exact same idiot who uploaded the video to YouTube?

Pato Piñata No need to think about that if we're going to live out in the country.

Antofagasta I like the country.

Pato Piñata We could be happy, have a normal family, picture it.

Antofagasta It would be nice.

Miss Francisca *runs in. She is crying, very upset. She gives* **Antofagasta** *a big hug.*

Miss Francisca Antofagasta! Something horrible has happened!

Antofagasta What is it?

Miss Francisca She died.

Antofagasta Who?

Miss Francisca Her!

Antofagasta Who?

Miss Francisca The fat girl, the fat girl passed away.

Pato Piñata And?

Antofagasta We all knew that was gonna happen . . .

Miss Francisca Why are young people so insensitive? The poor fat girl died, she died alone, and nobody cared. The students were making jokes, they were saying a crane would have to carry her to the funeral . . . those damn sons of bitches were joking about another person's death. They don't have any heart, they only think about themselves. And you two are just like them.

Pato Piñata Miss Francisca, there was nothing to be done . . .

Miss Francisca Did you two go donate blood for the potbellied girl?

Antofagasta No . . .

Miss Francisca You're going to hell!

Pato Piñata Miss Francisca, you haven't seen how they beat Antofagasta, they broke her leg . . .

Miss Francisca They beat you?

Antofagasta Yes.

Miss Francisca And where were you to protect her, big man?

Pato Piñata We'd broken up . . .

Antofagasta I went to shop at the street market, people recognized me and started to throw rotten tomatoes at my head. Then they came up to me and hit me really hard.

Miss Francisca Where is the little girl who sells cosmetics?

Pato Piñata She's upstairs.

Miss Francisca Cosmetics Sales Lady!

The **Cosmetics Sales Lady** *comes running down the stairs.*

Cosmetics Sales Lady What's going on?

Miss Francisca This little girl urgently needs someone to make up her face, she looks like one of those apples that falls on the ground and ends up all bruised.

Cosmetics Sales Lady Antofagasta, no matter what, you can't let your mother turn on the television, they're broadcasting your video on every channel, your face is covered by a cloud, but you can still see a titty and your butt.

Antofagasta On television?

Cosmetics Sales Lady Yes, right now there are some models and politicians sharing their opinions about your case.

Miss Francisca I knew this was gonna happen, I told the officers to remove the video from YouTube, but those fools are all illiterate. They didn't even know how to turn on the computer. And there was one of them, the oldest, who was quite lascivious, and I think he talked to the television station.

Antofagasta What am I gonna do now? My mother cannot find out about this, for any reason.

Pato Piñata Let's go to the country!

Cosmetics Sales Lady Perhaps we should drug her and keep her unconscious until all this news dies down.

Miss Francisca Believe me when I say that this news will last forever. Nobody will be named Antofagasta anymore because the name will be associated with orgies and disgusting acts.

Nelly Maria *and* **María Teresa** *enter.*

María Teresa Hello! We're late to watch our telenovela.

Nelly Maria Hello! (*To* **Pato Piñata**) And you, faggot? What are you doing here?

Antofagasta Mamá, we made up, he's a good person . . . .

Nelly Maria Did he do this to you? Did you hit my daughter again?

Pato Piñata No, Señora. I swear.

Nelly Maria Then what happened to you?

Antofagasta I fell down the stairs . . .

María Teresa Okay then, Nelly María we have to turn on the TV.

All except Nelly Maria No!

Nelly Maria And why can't we turn on the TV?

Pato Piñata Because the president is giving a speech.

Miss Francisca The president, my delicious boy.

Pato Piñata He's on all the channels and he's really boring, we were watching a while ago and we almost fell asleep.

Nelly Maria I'd like to see the president.

Nelly María *walks toward the television, but the other women stop her.*

María Teresa How can the president be speaking? If my telenovela is on right now.

Cosmetics Sales Lady Well, the president isn't interested in a telenovela, he's not very romantic.

Nelly Maria What's going on? Why won't you all let me turn on the television?

Antofagasta They already told you!

Nelly Maria I want to see the president!

Miss Francisca Let her see, she'll get bored right away.

Pato Piñata No!

María Teresa Let me see the telenovela! The main actor is so good looking.

Pato Piñata I think we can watch TV later.

Nelly Maria Okay. You all win. We won't watch the telenovela.

María Teresa Mother of God.

Nelly Maria A mouse! There's a mouse!

They all begin to scream and to run away from the mouse. They get on top of the table. When this happens, **Nelly Maria** *runs to the television and turns it on. She* *stands watching with her mouth open. On the screen there is an image of her daughter having sexual relations with nine classmates. The girl's full name and the name of her school appear on screen. They all stop searching for the rodent and also stand watching.*

Nelly Maria   What does this mean? Is this a joke? Is this on every channel . . .? Antofagasta? Why did you do that? Antofagasta?

Without anyone explaining how, **Antofagasta** *and the* **Cosmetics Sales Lady** *disappear from the room. A tear falls from the mother's cheek, the last time she had seen her daughter completely naked was when she was nine years old,* **Nelly María** *had bathed her after* **Antofagasta** *had drawn animals all over her body. That time she had looked at her daughter and lamented that she had grown so quickly. She thought the same thing again this time, only with many more thoughts in her head, thoughts that had to do with fear and with everything that didn't make sense.*

Scene Six

"The queen's preparation."

Antofagasta's *room. Lots of stuffed animals and a large mirror.* **Antofagasta** *sits in front of the mirror and the* **Cosmetics Sales Lady** *stands behind her. They chat while the* **Cosmetic Sales Lady** *makes up* **Antofagasta**'s *face.*

Cosmetics Sales Lady   My father died last year. Do you have a father?

Antofagasta   No.

Cosmetics Sales Lady   Where is he?

Antofagasta   He died when I was a kid.

Cosmetics Sales Lady   From what? How?

Antofagasta   Cancer.

Cosmetics Sales Lady   What was he like?

Antofagasta   I don't remember much. I only know that he was kind. He had a really beautiful smile. Right before he died, he took me to see the ocean. I don't recall exactly what we did or what we talked about, I only know that the sun was shimmering on the water and that I have never again been as happy as I was on that day. In that moment I thought we would live forever, him and me.

Cosmetics Sales Lady   But everyone dies.

Antofagasta   Yes.

Cosmetics Sales Lady   You think the dead can see us?

Antofagasta   No.

Cosmetics Sales Lady   I do. That millions and millions of dead people are watching us at this very moment.

Antofagasta   Then my Papá saw the video?

Cosmetics Sales Lady   I think he closed his eyes.

Antofagasta   I don't think so. People don't do bad things because they're afraid that someone will punish them. When my father died I felt a really sad sense of freedom. I thought about that while I was naked in the park, there would be a punishment I was never gonna receive. And I was fine, I wasn't doing anything wrong.

Cosmetics Sales Lady   And how was it?

Antofagasta   It was good. I'm the one who proposed it to my classmates as a joke. Suddenly we were walking toward the park. We'd barely arrived when I lay on the grass, the day was beautiful, there were a lot of birds in the trees. They started to touch me a little, I closed my eyes, and I started to get really turned on. I felt like leaving, like being at home in bed with my mom. But another part of me felt like I had to do it. I could do it, I had the freedom and nobody was gonna take it from me.

Cosmetics Sales Lady And Pato Piñata?

Antofagasta Pato Piñata is something else. I fell in love with her. I am hers and she is mine.

Cosmetics Sales Lady You're ready. You look beautiful.

Antofagasta Thank you so much. What's your name?

Cosmetics Sales Lady Yohanna.

Antofagasta Yohanna, what a lovely name.

Cosmetics Sales Lady Thank you very much. I'm gonna leave you alone now.

Antofagasta Yohanna, I hope everything works out for you.

Cosmetics Sales Lady It's gonna work out well for me. Yesterday I killed my boyfriend. He hit me again and I shoved a screwdriver in his neck. I'm gonna be happy now. If I have a daughter one day, I'll name her Antofagasta.

The **Cosmetic Sales Lady** *leaves the bedroom.* **Antofagasta** *gets on a chair and hangs a rope from the ceiling. She thinks one last time about the freedom she felt when she covered her body with the animal drawings. She had drawn an ugly horse on her heart. She finally has the courage to kick the chair away and die with her face covered in makeup. Moments later* **Pato Piñata** *enters the room. She came to tell* **Antofagasta** *that they should pack to move far away to live in the country, that she had the suitcase. Afterward,* **Nelly María** *enters and stands frozen. She thinks about how one day a long time ago she had had a family, but now she is alone.*

Nelly María Patricio . . .

Pato Piñata My name isn't Patricio.

Nelly María What?

Pato Piñata *removes her shirt and shows her torso to* **Nelly María**, *who starts to cry.*

Nelly María You're a woman.

Pato Piñata Yes.

Nelly María What's your name?

Pato Piñata My name is Lucía.

End of play.

Notes

1 Abbreviation for Physical Education class
2 Abbreviation for Intensive Care Unit in a hospital

3 In the original Spanish, Antofagasta lies and says that she met Pato Piñata in EJE (Encuentro de Jovenes en el Espíritu or Youth Encounter in the Spirit), which is a youth group for Catholic spiritual formation.
4 September 3, 1977, is almost four years after the start of the Chilean dictatorship on September 11, 1973.
5 Calama is a desert city in Northern Chile, 1535 km or 954 miles from Santiago.

Appendix

Contemporary Chilean Female Playwrights

This list includes the names and works of many contemporary Chilean female playwrights. Each playwright has written more plays than those mentioned here. The titles below are intended to provide an entry point into the body of work of these playwrights as well as to illustrate the abundance of plays by female writers in the Chilean theatre community.

Aguilera, Gabriela. *Casandra la Sandra* (2019)

Aros, Paula. *Correo* (2016)

Bauer, Karen. *Maleza* (2006)

Baez, Tania. *La niña descubierta* (1995)

Campusano, Sally. *Hambre* (2006)

Carrera, Ximena. *Medusa* (2010)

Césped, Marcia. *La historia de una mujer que regaba su planta con una cuchara* (2023)

Colomba, Amarilis. *Chajnantor, mirar hacia atrás* (2011)

Contreras Bocic, Daniela. *Lo que se perdió. Superhéroes en tu jardín* (2015)

Corbalan, Ana. *Tarde de verano* (2016)

De la Maza, Lucía. *Asesinato en la calle Illinois* (1997)

Droully, Mónica. *Querido John, take a chance on me* (2018)

Duarte, Coca. *Plaga* (2015)

Fernández, Nona. *Liceo de Niñas* (2015)

Fierro, Ingrid. *Ausencia* (2023)

Franco, Andrea. *Mutilados* (2015)

Fuentes, Carla. *Animales binarios* (2018)

Garcia Castro, Antonia. *Escribe de nuevo antes de volver* (2017)

Giadach, Andrea. *Mi mundo patria* (2009)

Gonzalez, Josefina. *Cómo cuidar de un pato* (2015)

Gonzalez, Trinidad. *Memoria* (2023)

Harcha, Ana. *Lulu* (2003)

Hidalgo, Claudia. *Hijos de . . .* (2015)

Infante, Manuela. *Estado vegetal* (2018)

Lagos, Soledad. *¿Quién es Chile?* (2014)

Le-Bert, Camila. *Chan!* (2018)

Lopez-Montaner, Ana. *El Thriller de Antígona y Hnos. S.A., La maldición de la sangre Labdácida.* (2006)

Martínez, Florencia. *Tiempos mejores* (2013)
Moro Winslow, Andrea. *No soy la novia* (2002)
Noguera, Emilia. *Un niño* (2019)
Oyarzun, Manuela. *Alba y los 100 pasos* (2018)
Pérez, Mónica. *Voces en el barro* (2000)
Pinto, Malucha. *Carta para Tomás* (1996)
Piriz, Trinidad. *Coro* (2019)
Pizarro, María José. *Desdémona* (2015)
Radrigán, Flavia. *Acabar con todo* (2011)
Romero, Carla. *La Compañera* (2020)
Ronderos, Pilar. *Hija de tigre* (With Ítalo Gallardo, 2017)
Selman, Leyla. *La Ciudad de la Fruta* (2018)
Sparza, Gisel. *Zapata en Chile* (2010)
Stevenson Bordeu, Isidora. *Hilda Peña* (2014)
Stranger, Inés. *Cariño Malo* (1990)
Ugalde, Begoña. *La causa del siniestro* (2011)
Valles, Carla. *Chilean factory* (2005)
Zulueta, Elisa. *Gladys* (2011)
Zúñiga, Carla. *Sentimientos* (2013)

Resource

González Fajardo, Gabriela. *Creando Escena: Dramaturgas Chilenas Contemporáneas*. Primera edición, Editorial Cuarto propio, 2023.
https://www.dramaturgaschilenas.cl/

Works Cited

Barría Jara, Mauricio Adrián, and Iván Insunza Fernández. *Escenas Políticas: Teatro Entre Revueltas 2006–2019*. Ediciones Oxímoron, 2020.

Boyle, Catherine M. *Chilean Theater, 1973–1985: Marginality, Power, Selfhood*. Fairleigh Dickinson University Press; Associated University Presses, 1992.

Boyle, Catherine M. "Text, Time, Process and History in Contemporary Chilean Theatre." *Theatre Research International*, vol. 26, no. 2, 2001, pp. 181–89. https://doi.org/10.1017/S0307883301000190

Bulman, Gail. *Feeling the Gaze: Image and Affect in Contemporary Argentine and Chilean Performance*. 1st ed., The University of North Carolina Press, 2022.

Carrera, Ximena (*Medusa*), Fernandez, Nona (*El Taller*), Leonart Marcelo (*Grita*). *Bestiario: Freakshow Temporada 1973/1990*. Ceibo Ediciones 2013.

Cornejo, Marcela, et al. "Representaciones de La Dictadura Chilena a 50 Años: Dramaturgias y Trauma Psicosocial." *Latin American Theatre Review*, vol. 58, no. 2, 2025, pp. 29–50, https://doi.org/10.1353/ltr.2025.a957398.

Duarte Loveluck, Coca. *Escribir La Escena, Trazar El Presente: Estrategias Dramatúrgicas Del Teatro Chileno 2007–2017*. 1st ed., Editorial Cuartopropio, 2023.

Duarte Loveluck, Coca. "*La Ciudad De La Fruta* by Leyla Selman: Representing Trauma." *Talía. Revista De Estudios Teatrales*, vol. 4, 2022: 23–29.

Fernández, Nona. *El Liceo de Niñas*. Ediciones Oxímoron, 2016.

García-Romero, Anne. "Grotesque Dramaturgy and Gender Critique in the Post-Dictatorship Southern Cone," in *Bodies on the Front Lines: Gender, Sexuality and Performance in Latin America and the Caribbean*, edited by Brenda Werth and Katherine Zien, University of Michigan Press, 2024, pp. 288–304.

García-Romero, Anne. "A New Dawn: Transitional Gender Justice in *The Yellow Sun of Your Long Locks* by Carla Zúñiga." *Apuntes Theater Journal, Pontificia Universidad Católica de Chile School of Theatre*, no. 145, March 2022, pp. 94–102.

González Fajardo, Gabriela. *Creando Escena: Dramaturgas Chilenas Contemporáneas*. 1st ed., Editorial Cuarto propio, 2023.

Grass, Milena, Andrés Kalawski, and Nancy Nicholls. "Torture and Disappearance in Chilean Theatre from Dictatorship to Transitional Justice" *Theatre Research International*, vol. 1, no. 3, 2015, pp. 303–13.

Hernández, Paola S., and Analola Santana. *Fifty Key Figures in Latinx and Latin American Theatre*. 1st ed., Routledge, 2022.

Hurtado, María de la Luz, "Teatro chileno: historicidad y autorreflexión" *Revista Nuestra América* no. 7, Aug.-Dec. 2009, pp. 143–58.

Lagos, M. Soledad. "Poéticas Del Encierro En Una Sociedad Re-Democratizada: Nuevas Miradas Sobre Viejas Heridas." *Latin American Theatre Review*, vol. 46, no. 1, 2012, pp. 13–20. https://doi.org/10.1353/ltr.2012.0047.

Núcleo de investigación y creación escénica (Chile). *Evidencias: Las Otras Dramaturgias: Un Siglo de Escrituras de Mujeres Chilenas*. Edited by Lorena Saavedra González et al., Ediciones Oximoron, 2020.

Opazo, Cristián. "Época 60: Dramaturgias universitarias, reformas del paisaje (Chile, 1941–1973)." *Latin American Theatre Review*, vol. 58, no. 2, 2025, p. 139–62. https://dx.doi.org/10.1353/ltr.2025.a957404

Ripp, Alexandra. "Remembering the Coup: Chilean Theatre Now." *PAJ: A Journal of Performance and Art*, 2014, pp. 87–101.

Ripp, Alexandra. "Don't Feed the Animals: Manuela Infante and Teatro De Chile's Zoo." *Theater*, 2017, pp. 61–66.

Rocco Núñez, Bernardo and Zurita Hecht, Federico. "Representación de La Historia Del Fracaso Nacional En El Taller y Liceo de Niñas de Nona Fernández." *Latin American Theatre Review*, vol. 53, no. 1, 2019, pp. 101–20. https://doi.org/10.1353/ltr.2019.0024

Selman, Leyla, *La Ciudad de la Fruta*, Ediciones Oxímoron, 2024.

Stevenson Bordeu, Isidora. *Hilda Peña*. Ediciones Oxímoron, 2024.

Stranger, Inés Margarita. *Cuaderno De Dramaturgia: Teoría Técnica y Ejercicios*. Frontera Sur 2011.

Stranger, Inés Margarita. *Cariño Malo; Malinche; Tálamo*. 1st ed., Editorial Cuarto Propio, 2007.

Thompson, Jennifer Joan. *Performing Citizenship in Postdictatorship Chile: Cultural Policy and the Making of Political Dramaturgies*. Northwestern University Press, 2025.

Werth, Brenda, and Katherine Zien, eds. *Bodies on the Front Lines: Performance, Gender, and Sexuality in Latin America and the Caribbean*. University of Michigan Press, 2024.

Villegas, Juan. "El teatro chileno de la postdictadura." *INTI*, no. 69/70, 2009, pp. 189–205. http://www.jstor.org/stable/23288703

Villegas, Juan. "La internacionalización del teatro chileno de la postdictadura." *Gestos*, vol. 29, no. 57, 2014, pp. 174–85.

Zúñiga M., Carla. *Sentimientos*. Ediciones Oxímoron, 2019.